KEEPERS
of the
SPIRITS

Recent Titles in
Contributions in American History

The Journalist as Reformer: Henry Demarest Lloyd and *Wealth Against Commonwealth*
Richard Digby-Junger

Reconciliation and Revival: James R. Mann and the House Republicans in the Wilson Era
Herbert F. Margulies

Varieties of Southern History: New Essays on a Region and Its People
Bruce Clayton and John Salmond, editors

A Utopian Experiment in Kentucky: Integration and Social Equality at Berea, 1866–1904
Richard Sears

A Mythic Land Apart: Reassessing Southerners and Their History
John David Smith and Thomas H. Appleton, Jr., editors

The Corporate City: The American City as a Political Entity, 1800–1850
Leonard P. Curry

Democracy Reformed: Richard Spencer Childs and His Fight for Better Government
Bernard Hirschhorn

French Newspaper Opinion on the American Civil War
George M. Blackburn

Andrew Jackson and His Tennessee Lieutenants: A Study in Political Culture
Lorman A. Ratner

Utopianism and Radicalism in a Reforming America: 1888–1918
Francis Robert Shor

The Senate Munitions Inquiry of the 1930s: Beyond the Merchants of Death
Matthew Ware Coulter

The Frontier in the Colonial South: South Carolina Backcountry, 1736–1800
George Lloyd Johnson, Jr.

KEEPERS *of the* SPIRITS

The Judicial Response to Prohibition Enforcement in Florida, 1885–1935

JOHN J. GUTHRIE, JR.

Contributions in American History, Number 179

GREENWOOD PRESS
Westport, Connecticut • London

Library of Congress Cataloging-in-Publication Data

Guthrie, John J.
Keepers of the spirits : the judicial response to prohibition enforcement in Florida, 1885–1935 / John J. Guthrie, Jr.
p. cm.—(Contributions in American history, ISSN 0084–9219 ; no. 179)
Includes bibliographical references and index.
ISBN 0–313–30190–5 (alk. paper)
1. Prohibition—Florida—History. 2. Civil rights—Florida—History. 3. Criminal justice, Administration of—Florida—History. I. Title. II. Series.
KFF375.G88 1998
344.759'0541—DC21 97–22810

British Library Cataloguing in Publication Data is available.

Library of Congress Catalog Card Number: 97–22810
ISBN: 0–313–30190–5
ISSN: 0084–9219

First published in 1998

Greenwood Press, 88 Post Road West, Westport, CT 06881
An imprint of Greenwood Publishing Group, Inc.

Printed in the United States of America

The paper used in this book complies with the Permanent Paper Standard issued by the National Information Standards Organization (Z39.48–1984).

10 9 8 7 6 5 4 3 2 1

To the memory of my father

Contents

Preface

As the title suggests, this book explores the judicial response to state and federal liquor laws in Florida between 1885 and 1935. The interpretation rests heavily on an array of previously unexamined source material, including court records, newspaper stories, and other public documents. It is a case study in law enforcement and the consequences of trying to make people do what they often had refused to do. The narrative, moreover, assumes a variety of viewpoints to provide the fullest dimension possible. The perspective, then, will occasionally shift from the bench, to the violators, to the enforcement officers. In doing so, this account underscores the significant role that judges played in mediating the inevitable tension that exists between individual rights and governmental authority. In other words, the implementation of Florida's anti-liquor laws coupled with national prohibition restricted individual property rights in alcohol while expanding the police powers. Enforcement of these laws set in motion a host of constitutional problems for the courts to unravel. As it happened, judges generally relied on common law jurisprudence to strike a balance between personal liberty and notions that the commonwealth stood paramount to individual interest. With that, the judicial rulings in Florida liquor cases neither reflected vacillating public opinion nor issued from some outside catalyst. Instead, state and federal judges in Florida liquor litigation acted independently and grounded their opinions on the cornerstones of American justice: precedent and citation of authority.

Nearly a decade has passed since I first initiated my research on this book. During this time, I incurred numerous personal and professional debts that I can hardly credit with words. My mentors, colleagues, friends and family have enabled me to do a task that, at times, seemed beyond my reach. To these people I feel deeply obliged. I want to extend my utmost appreciation to Kermit L. Hall, who labored through early drafts of the manuscript, chapter by chapter, and made generous comments and perceptive criticisms. Several professors at the University of Florida also deserve recognition for the part they played in this project. William Frazer has encouraged my work on this endeavor since its inception. Bertram Wyatt-Brown, through his scholarship and through his sound advice, has influenced me in more ways than he probably realizes. I owe the late George E. Pozzetta for broadening my "conceptualizations" shortly after I embarked on this research. Thanks, too, to Julian M. Pleasants, who exemplifies the teacher-scholar. By complementing insightful analysis with good humor, he is both brilliant and captivating.

Several colleagues read earlier versions of chapters and made suggestions that significantly improved the text. Sally Flocks and Paul Finkelman read an early draft of Chapter 1. Jerrell Shofner and Mark Greenberg both carefully read renditions of Chapter 5 and shared their useful remarks with me. Kathy Schoettler, Casey Blanton, Kurt Cumiskey, Allison Saville, Mark Edwards, and Ron Edwards, however, went the proverbial "extra mile" and read the entire manuscript. Thanks to their sharp editorial eyes and keen dissections, the final product shines when compared to earlier drafts.

I am especially grateful for the efforts of several librarians and archivists who eased my research. Fred Harden at Daytona Beach Community College obtained material through inter-library loans, which saved me time, effort, and travel expense. Nancy Dobson of the Florida Supreme Court Historical Society provided valuable information pertaining to the state's high court. Mary Ann Hawkins deserves special praise for tolerating my naiveté about accessing archival records. On my visits to the Atlanta branch of the National Archives, I often burdened her with requests for numerous case files. All the while, Ms. Hawkins remained gracious, cheerful, and extremely helpful to me.

Two administrators at my college have earned high accolades. Norm Will, Vice President of Academic Affairs, and Frank Wetta, Dean of Arts and Sciences, have always urged their faculty to develop professionally. For that reason, they awarded me sabbatical leave for a semester. My time away from teaching allowed me to revise, polish, and prepare the manuscript for publication. In addition, the hiatus rejuvenated my spirits and made me eager to return to the classroom.

I also want to thank my friends, Jack Henderson, Dave Tegeder, Tim Huebner, Daniel Stowell, and Toni and Joe Thompson. They shared with me the rigors and rewards of becoming historians. Besides the occasional bed they provided for me to sleep in, I appreciate deeply their camaraderie, wit, and good humor. Except for Toni, in the next few years they each will publish a book that promises to contribute significantly to American history.

Finally, I thank my family for always encouraging me in my pursuits over the years.

Of course, should any errors of fact or interpretation appear in the text, I am solely responsible for their presence.

Portions of the following articles appear in various chapters of this book and are reprinted with permission: "The Florida Supreme Court and the Intoxicating Liquor Laws: From Local Option to National Prohibition, 1885–1920," *Journal of Southern Legal History* 2 (Spring/Summer 1993), 99–137; "Hard Times, Hard Liquor, and Hard Luck: Selective Enforcement of Prohibition in North Florida, 1928–1933," *Florida Historical Quarterly* 73 (April 1994), 435–452; "Rekindling the Spirits: From National Prohibition to Local Option in Florida, 1928–1935," *Florida Historical Quarterly* 74 (Summer 1995), 23–39.

Introduction: Historians and the Liquor Laws

Historians have paid much attention to the prohibition of alcohol in the United States. Their work has addressed a wide body of liquor-related issues, including the cultural significance of the saloon, the political aspects of the temperance campaign, as well as the motivation behind the efforts to ratify and then repeal the Eighteenth Amendment.[1] A more recent and expanding body of literature, however, deals specifically with the enforcement of federal liquor laws.[2] Indeed, only during the last decade have scholars begun to probe more fully such closely related activities as moonshining, vigilantism, and federal law enforcement. Focusing mainly on the post-Reconstruction mountain South, these historians have generally portrayed moonshiners as traditionalists who resisted federal liquor laws in order to "preserve a way of life that was being threatened by the centralizing forces then shaping America."[3]

In one encompassing study, for example, Wilbur R. Miller raised the question: "What are the conditions under which unpopular laws can be enforced, and what are the limits of their enforcement?" After investigating this matter, Miller found that the universal hostility of state officials to federal authority posed one of the most serious difficulties that federal revenuers confronted in the mountain South. One state judge in Greenville, South Carolina, for instance, ordered a grand jury to indict every federal agent who "had infringed the rights of a citizen and he would see that they were tried and punished." Yet such obstructionism, Miller concluded, failed to prevent the development and completion of "an administrative apparatus capable of penetrating all parts of the nation's territory."[4]

Following Miller's lead, Stephen Cresswell broadened the expanse of investigation once again by including the American West in his comparative study of federal law enforcement between 1870 and 1893. Besides highlighting the evolution of the American criminal justice system, his work illuminates the conflicts that arose among local, state, and federal government. Assuming the perspective of federal officials, Cresswell also claimed that local resistance emerged as the "greatest impediment to the efforts of attorneys and marshals to enforce the nation's laws." State and local authorities, he noted, often "locked horns" with the Justice Department over jurisdictional disputes that turned ultimately on the larger issue of federalism. "When marshals shot and killed moonshiners in the southern mountains, local officers initiated murder prosecutions, then grew infuriated as the cases were removed to federal courts." At other times, citizens' groups, like the "Georgia Distiller's Union," labored in unison to "harass federal officers and intimidate witnesses." Yet these efforts worked to no avail, for the Justice Department, Cresswell concluded, "often achieved a surprisingly strong record of enforcement of the nation's laws."[5]

Miller and Cresswell deserve much praise for blazing new trails into an emerging and "increasingly important historiographical frontier." However, because each of them limited the time frame of their investigation to the late nineteenth century, questions still linger. Also, they both focused solely on federal liquor law rather than on the various state liquor laws enacted before, and effective during, national prohibition.[6] Consequently, each of these historians failed to sufficiently examine the role that courts played in either upholding or overturning such laws.

An examination of the intoxicating liquor legislation and the judicial response to it in Florida promises to sharpen the existing historiographical debate. After all, the temperance movement culminated in the Eighteenth Amendment, engendering an alteration of some well-established but often paradoxical constitutional and legal doctrines. The affected tenets included four important doctrines. The first was the commonwealth idea that the general welfare stood paramount to particular interest. The notion that the police powers of the state could supersede individual rights to preserve and protect the commonwealth, ranked second. A third affected doctrine was the concept that individuals possess an inalienable right to enjoy property free from arbitrary governmental power. Finally, substantive due process (a separate idea, but closely related to the preceding principle) also experienced some change during national prohibition. According to this concept, rights to life, liberty, and property remain "beyond the legitimate reach of governmental power."[7]

With these doctrines in mind, this book draws on a variety of sources, including court records, statutes, constitutional convention proceedings, and newspaper accounts, to shed additional light on the enforcement of state and federal liquor laws in Florida. Chapter One covers the period from 1885 to 1920, when liquor law went from local option to national prohibition. It shows how the judicial and legal institutions in Florida accommodated the demand for sobriety with the fundamental right to property.[8] In so doing, it examines how the judiciary managed the formidable task of balancing the state's police power to regulate or restrict property for the sake of the commonweal with the vested rights of the individual that protected him or her against such arbitrary power.[9]

In addition to illuminating how the courts balanced property rights with governmental authority, the same sources contain clues to how American federalism has evolved over time.[10] To elaborate, in a major study of the American state, Morton Keller has argued that the industrial expansion of the United States in the late nineteenth century placed new demands on the polity. Although the public acknowledged the need for change, traditional notions of localism and laissez-faire capitalism limited the federal government's response to the altered set of social and economic conditions. Since the citizenry proved unwilling to accept an expansion of the federal administrative capacity, the states, and courts in particular, rose to the occasion and attempted to work out the multitude of social, constitutional, political, and economic problems that industrialism brought forth. Emphasizing continuity rather than change, Keller concluded that two themes, persistence and pluralism, have characterized America's political culture from the turn of the twentieth century to the 1930s.[11]

Those same forces, unleashed by industrialization in the late nineteenth century, ultimately transformed America's ideological and material landscape. They also helped spawn the modern prohibitionist crusade. The ratification of the Eighteenth Amendment in 1920, then, seems particularly germane to Keller's model, for the essence of the American federal system had changed. The police powers, traditionally the province of the states, had become national in scope. Section 2 of the Eighteenth Amendment, for example, stipulated that state and local authorities share the responsibility of enforcing prohibition with the central government.[12]

If Keller's paradigm proves applicable to the prohibition era, then the judiciary should have impeded the expansion of federal power by restraining the reach of the national liquor law. Prior historical research lends credence to this hypothesis. Historian Norman H. Clark, for one, has suggested that the amendment's framers designed the concurrent power clause as an appeasement to states' rights advocates to assuage their fear of the federal government. Clark implied that Section 2 represented an ad hoc compromise between states' rights traditionalists and progressive reformers, rather than a well-conceived revision of the existing federal system.[13]

Likewise, Richard F. Hamm, in *Shaping the Eighteenth Amendment: Temperance Reform, Legal Culture, and the Polity, 1880–1920* (1995), has detailed the interaction between the prohibition movement and the federal system. According to Hamm, until the late 1890s a Mosaic view of law dominated the dry crusade. Stemming from biblical injunctions, the Mosaic conception assumed that government should foster morality and never promote evil. Drys, therefore, opposed the federal liquor tax because they considered it a license that permitted immoral behavior rather than a restriction designed to prohibit and punish crime. However, with the rise of the Anti-Saloon League in the early 1900s, the movement adopted a more realistic outlook. Subsequently, pragmatic prohibitionists, Hamm argued, converted governmental bureaucracy to their advantage and turned the state and federal powers over commerce "into a temperance tool." With the Webb-Kenyon Act of 1913, for instance, Congress empowered states to regulate interstate liquor traffic. After the Supreme Court upheld this law, temperance reformers used its manner of joint state and federal action as a blueprint for shaping the Eighteenth Amendment. In view of this, the triumph over "ardent spirits" seemed certain to prohibitionists. And yet, blinded by their legislative success, few drys realized that concurrent state and federal power over liquor, Hamm concluded, would lead to lax enforcement and "contribute to the collapse of national prohibition."[14]

Besides highlighting how the American polity shaped reform, Hamm's account deepens our understanding of prohibition. Still, had he pressed forward in time to the 1920s, he might have discovered two things. First, Hamm could have learned how national prohibition modified the relationship between the state and federal governments. Additionally, and perhaps more significantly, he may have realized that the Eighteenth Amendment's concurrent power clause posed an immediate threat to the Fifth Amendment's safeguard against double jeopardy.

True, the constitutional protection against dual prosecutions was never absolute. In the years preceding national prohibition the courts often invoked a dual sovereignty exception to double jeopardy in cases involving crimes against separate jurisdictions. That is, a conviction for a crime in one court did not preclude a subsequent prosecution by a second court. The rule, as practiced in the nineteenth century, thus helped maintain state autonomy by recognizing the authority of a state to try persons for violating its laws despite previous prosecutions in other courts, state or federal.[15]

With the ratification of the Eighteenth Amendment, however, the courts learned that the rule cut both ways. It could foster national supremacy as easily as it had promoted state autonomy. Chapter Two explores how the judiciary reconciled this kind of constitutional and legal tension arising from concurrent enforcement of the liquor laws between 1905–1922. As it played out, the courts generally used the dual sovereignty exception when it served state interests but invoked the Fifth Amendment when necessary to check an expansion of federal power.

Even so, the concurrent power clause posed more of a potential than a real threat to the safeguards against dual prosecutions, for the inherent conflict between concurrent power and double jeopardy proved short-lived. Other issues, such as the notion that the Fourth Amendment guarantees the right to privacy by protecting individuals from arbitrary searches and seizures, had become far more pressing.

Although the federal Constitution does not expressly contain a right to privacy, individual liberty and autonomy from governmental intrusion, as John H. F. Shattuck has noted, "are values deeply rooted in American constitutional history."[16] This profound constitutional and cultural commitment to privacy confronted one of its greatest challenges during the 1920s when the national prohibition laws, coupled with the establishment of a federal police force, fostered the government's capacity to violate "the right to be left alone."[17]

Although historical scholarship has slighted the impact that the enforcement of prohibition has had on individual liberties, *Federal Criminal Law Doctrines: The Forgotten Influence of National Prohibition* (1994) by Kenneth M. Murchison provides a good start at bridging this gap. While underscoring the historical significance of prohibition, Murchison deepens "our understanding of the Supreme Court's history and illustrate[s] how law responds to changes in public attitudes." Toward that goal, he explored the important constitutional issues that resulted from prohibition enforcement, including property forfeiture, search and seizure, double jeopardy, and trial by jury.[18]

According to Murchison, the Supreme Court assumed three distinct positions during the "noble experiment" that closely mirrored the changing perspective of the public. In the early years, the Court firmly supported the federal liquor law. During the latter half of the 1920s, however, the Court equivocated. Majority decisions then, Murchison claimed, reflected "incipient doubts about some of the techniques of prohibition enforcement, but most [rulings] affirmed convictions of serious violators." In other and simpler words, as prohibition cases reached the Court, it strove to protect the rights of ordinary citizens, while remaining insensitive to overzealous enforcement against commercial violators. After 1930, in response to the public's increased odium toward prohibition, the Court shifted its position again and demonstrated even greater concern for constitutional safeguards. With such decisions the Court manifested more sensitivity to wavering social attitudes, Murchison argued, "than conventional wisdom would predict."[19]

By addressing a long-neglected aspect of the Supreme Court's history, Murchison has scored high marks for raising important questions and building a framework for academic debate. As Hamm has noted, "Murchison's book opens the door to further investigation of the topic of liquor prohibition and the legal system." New research in the federal courts' inventory and state supreme court records will reveal how the dual judicial system functioned and, Hamm claims, show how state judges influenced legal doctrine in response to the issues raised by prohibition.[20]

With respect to that, Chapter Three poses two central problems to show how Florida courts defined the scope of Fourth Amendment safeguards within the context of prohibition enforcement. The first problem considers the extent of constitutional protection against unreasonable searches. Did the courts limit the protection solely to the home? Or did the privacy right extend beyond the dwelling to include outlying fields or woods? For that matter, did a person possess a similar, if not equal, right to privacy when driving an automobile laden with liquor on a public road? What about private businesses, such as restaurants that catered to a public clientele: did these enterprises possess less security from governmental intrusion than a private dwelling?[21]

The second problem considered in Chapter Three is what constituted a reasonable search. Did the courts allow unwarranted searches for liquor? If so, under what conditions did judges sustain such intrusions? How did the courts determine the reasonableness of a search? Did the courts ever rule a warranted search to be unreasonable? If the answer to this is yes, then why did they? The evidence found in Florida prohibition cases suggests that judicial discretion determined the reasonableness of any search and seizure. Judges invoked the common law maxim "Every man's house is his castle" when necessary to check governmental intrusion on personal liberty. Generally, when conflict arose between privacy and prohibition enforcement, the courts stayed with tradition and sided with liberty.

Such a conclusion, however, requires qualification in that occasionally the same judges loosened the rule of reason and upheld searches where the suspect had clearly intended to violate the law. These rulings, nonetheless, did not necessarily close a case. Instead, they prompted further litigation because the accused often abandoned the Fourth Amendment as a foundation for their legal defense and countered that the seizure of their property had violated the due process clause of the Fifth Amendment. That is, the government lacked the power to deprive people of their natural right to property.

Again, prohibition litigation became a contest between governmental police powers and individual property rights. According to constitutional historian James W. Ely, Jr., individual property rights deserve greater scholarly investigation. Notwithstanding the existence of several narrowly focused studies, historians generally have not given full attention to what Ely has described as "the constitutional protection of economic liberty." The safeguards inherent in individual property rights have undoubtedly set the parameters for numerous constitutional battles, which pitted property-minded judges against regulatory legislation designed to restrict individual economic liberties. During the Progressive Era state and federal liquor laws, according to Ely, hastened possibly "the most sweeping destruction of property rights" in the nation's history. In addition to restricting individual possession, prohibition inflicted a double-barrelled hardship on the owners of distilleries and breweries. They suffered a sharp decline in the value of their productive assets and at the same time experienced a total loss when their stock of booze on hand became legally unmarketable. Ely ended his discussion of prohibition and property rights after only one paragraph, however, concluding that "one cannot understand the constitutional guarantee of property by looking solely at the decisions of the Supreme Court."[22] A study of property rights and prohibition, therefore, opens rich possibilities for understanding how courts reconciled conflicting sets of rights.

In Murchison's treatment of the judicial response to property forfeiture during national prohibition, he saw three separate trends in forfeiture decisions by assuming the vantage point of the Supreme Court.[23] From his perspective, Court decisions emanated from "some external stimuli" instead of from internal logic.[24] Although helpful, Murchison's portrait of the impact of property forfeiture on American legal culture lacks depth. To provide a more complete picture of property rights under the Constitution, Chapter Four probes the records of the Florida Supreme Court and the inventory of the federal court archives to examine the judicial response to property forfeitures that stemmed from the enforcement of liquor law in Florida. As noted, such sources are virtually untapped and their exploration promises to deliver valuable intellectual dividends. Chapter Four, moreover, ultimately attempts to remedy an imbalance in the literature by offering a more profound understanding of property's constitutional protections within the framework of prohibition enforcement.

To illustrate the point, Murchison's thesis that "changing attitudes toward prohibition guided the development of the forfeiture decisions" does not hold true for either the lower federal courts in Florida or the state supreme court. Unlike the U.S. Supreme Court, the Florida courts provided a generally consistent approach to property forfeitures for enforcing national prohibition. In the vast majority of cases, property-minded judges checked laws designed to curb individual economic liberties. This conclusion not only fills a gap in the literature but also provides a deeper understanding of the constitutional bulwarks for property within the context of forfeiture law. After all, the government's confiscation of property involved in liquor violations represented another manner in which national prohibition assailed economic liberty.

While one could argue that the property issue served as the primary catalyst for the rapid rise in the widespread call for repeal of the Eighteenth Amendment, no scholar has yet advanced this thesis. As one scholar has noted, historians have long overlooked the repeal of national prohibition "as a subject for serious research" for at least two major reasons.[25] First, the Great Depression and the coming of Franklin D. Roosevelt's New Deal overshadowed the ratification of the Twenty-First Amendment. Second, repeal as a research topic presents problems for historians because it raises questions in disparate fields, including constitutional law, public policy, pressure politics, popular attitudes, and federalism.[26]

Despite the complexity of the subject, Clement E. Vose provided an early scholarly analysis of repeal in 1972. Noting the multifarious composition of the anti-prohibition crusade, Vose refuted the notion of a simple rural-urban dichotomy. Instead, he argued that old-stock white Anglo-Saxon Protestant members of interest groups, such as the Voluntary Committee of Lawyers (VCL) and the Association Against the Prohibition Amendment (AAPA), formed an unlikely alliance with newly arrived Catholic urban dwellers and successfully collaborated to end prohibition.[27]

Soon thereafter, David E. Kyvig expanded upon Vose's conceptual foundation and examined repeal through the lens of the AAPA. In a work of scholarly revision, Kyvig gave the AAPA the preponderance of credit for the ultimate success of repeal. Kyvig's book refuted Fletcher Dobyns's earlier account that portrayed the AAPA as a powerful clique bent on saving themselves millions of dollars by substituting an essentially regressive liquor tax for a progressive income tax, which in turn placed the burden of government expenses upon the shoulders of the middle classes. Instead, Kyvig portrayed the AAPA as a collection of civic-minded individuals motivated by strong constitutional convictions. More concerned about a dangerous and undue concentration of power within the federal government than personal gain, the AAPA, according to Kyvig, provided vital leadership to the anti-prohibition movement and achieved in 1933 what most contemporary commentators had considered unattainable in 1920.[28]

Yet despite early acclaim and widespread recognition as a major contribution, critics from both the left and the right wasted little time before assaulting Kyvig's conservative thesis. Harry Gene Levine, for example, acknowledged that capitalistic fear of governmental intrusions into both society and the economy had motivated the AAPA's elites to seek repeal. But Levine countered that the AAPA's membership proved far more class conscious than Kyvig implied and at times "found government intervention useful when it served their interests." Since prohibition had failed to promote social order or impose discipline on the proletariat, the corporate elite, as Levine saw them, found it essential to repeal the Eighteenth Amendment to sustain their hegemonic control over the masses. Thus, in place of national prohibition, the elite instituted a system of "regulation far more pervasive and intrusive . . . than anything before established in the United States." Taking one step backward, the bourgeoisie had advanced several steps forward by exerting further control over a wider range of the proletariat's behavior.[29]

These studies, meaningful as they are, illustrate the inherent difficulty in evaluating the catalysts behind the repeal movement or the implications of its success. To historians, repeal as a social and political dynamic appears somewhat like an inkblot used in a Rorschach test. That is, students have defined the movement's form according to their perspective or attitude. Whereas older interpretations perceived repeal as an inevitable consequence of urbanization and its concomitant modernization, a newer interpretative school sees conscientious citizens motivated by civic duty overcoming formidable obstacles and winning a major victory by repealing national prohibition.[30] Still other scholars, more contemptuous of the status quo, view the same events as the "capitalist hegemon, rearing its ugly head again," and imposing social control on the masses. So with the exception of Vose's pluralistic coalition model, historians have too readily treated the politics of repeal much as they have treated the politics of prohibition. Briefly put, they have viewed it as a contest between two opposing monolithic forces without considering the serious divisions that sundered both sides of the liquor issue.

Chapter Five suggests that three of the four general interpretations of the wet crusade, the urban-rural dichotomy, the benevolent capitalist reform model, and the Marxian social control thesis, fail to explicate the dynamic process of repeal. The chapter also supports arguments made by Keller and Vose, by showing that a plurality of diverse interests collaborated successfully to turn back prohibition in Florida. There, the anti-prohibition movement picked up steam following the presidential election of 1928, as a wet constituency began to coalesce around the idea of repeal. This coalition included judges, newspaper editors, lawyers, brewers, retailers, workers, hoteliers, state legislators, and many ordinary people. And while each group did have specific motivations for embracing the wet crusade—ranging from pecuniary interest to constitutional ideals—in the end, material gain appeared most crucial in unleashing the forces necessary to ratify the Twenty-First Amendment.

That notwithstanding, historians still need to know what happened to pending federal cases once Congress repealed the Eighteenth Amendment. How did the judiciary respond to the new set of circumstances caused by shifting the control of liquor from federal to state governments? Did repeal force judges to "reconceptualize" constitutional and legal tenets, such as the police powers, vested property rights, or the equal protection clause, which courts had previously adjusted, to fit national prohibition?[31]

Chapter Five tackles these issues also and shows that by returning the liquor question to the states, the repeal of national prohibition hastened a minor conflict between Florida's executive, legislative, and judicial branches over which body would control state alcohol policy. In the end, the Florida Supreme Court emerged as the principal agent affecting public policy on the liquor question. As the post-prohibition drama unraveled, the judiciary dealt with a series of constitutional questions that echoed the pre-prohibition litigation that had pitted property against state liquor regulations. By 1935 the court had thus come full circle and responded to Florida's intoxicating liquor laws by broadening the scope of the police powers.

The Epilogue, then, echoes Melvin I. Urofsky's thesis that courts, through judicial interpretation and precedent, defined the police power of the state and ultimately determined the fate of protective legislation during the Progressive Era. Depending upon their philosophical composition, the courts either expanded or contracted the state's police power. As Urofsky put it, the judiciary at times served as a conservative impediment to social reform but, more often than not, functioned as an agency of change ushering in further progressive measures.[32]

In Florida between 1885 and 1935, the enforcement of the liquor laws set into motion a host of constitutional issues that played out in the courts. The fundamental question revolved around the inevitable tension that exists between individual liberty, public interest, and governmental authority. Responding to this conflict, judges in the Florida Supreme Court, and those presiding in the federal district courts, used the common law and skillfully struck a tenuous balance between the rights of individuals and the power of the state.

NOTES

1. For a deeper discussion of this literature, see Paul Johnson, "Bottoms Up: Drinking, Temperance, and the Social Historians," *Reviews in American History* 13 (March 1985), 45–53; Jedd Dannenbaum, "Crusade Against Drink," *Reviews in American History* 9 (December 1981), 498–500; Joseph Kett, "Temperance and Intemperance as Historical Problems," *Journal of American History* 67 (March 1981), 878–879; Charles W. Eagles, "Urban-Rural Conflict in the 1920s: A Historiographical Assessment," *Historian* 49 (November 1986), 26–48; Mark Edward Lender, "The Historian and Repeal: A Survey of the Literature and Research Opportunities," in David E. Kyvig, ed., *Law, Alcohol, and Order* (Westport, Conn.: Greenwood Press, 1985), 177–205. For specific literature on prohibition in the South, see Richard L. Watson, Jr., "From Populism through the New Deal: Southern Political History," in John B. Boles and Evelyn Thomas Nolen, eds., *Interpreting Southern History: Historiographical Essays in Honor of Sanford W. Higginbotham* (Baton Rouge: Louisiana State University Press, 1987), 308–389, esp. 347–350; Dewey W. Grantham, *Southern Progressivism: The Reconciliation of Progress and Tradition*, 2nd ed. (Knoxville: University of Tennessee Press, 1987), 160–177.

2. In addition to the works cited throughout the text, see also Rayman L. Solomon, "Regulating the Regulators: Prohibition Enforcement in the Seventh Circuit," in Kyvig, ed., *Law, Alcohol and Order*, 81–96; Harry G. Levine, "The Birth of American Alcohol Control: Prohibition, the Power Elite, and the Problem of Lawlessness," *Contemporary Drug Problems* (Spring 1985), 63–115; John F. Padgett, "Plea Bargaining and Prohibition in the Federal Courts, 1908–1934," *Law and Society Review* 24 (1990), 413–450.

3. William F. Holmes, "Moonshining and Collective Violence: Georgia, 1889–1895," *Journal of American History* 67 (December 1980), 589–611, 603, 610. See also Joel W. Williamson, ed., *An Appalachian Symposium* (Boone, N.C.: Appalachian Consortium Press, 1977); William Lynwood Montell, *Killings: Folk Justice in the Upper South* (Lexington: University Press of Kentucky, 1986).

4. Wilbur R. Miller, *Revenuers & Moonshiners: Enforcing Federal Law in the Mountain South, 1865–1900* (Chapel Hill: University of North Carolina Press, 1991), 4, 108–109; Idem, "The Revenue: Federal Law Enforcement in the Mountain South, 1870–1900," *Journal of Southern History* 55 (May 1989), 195–216.

5. Stephen Cresswell, *Mormons & Cowboys, Moonshiners & Klansmen: Federal Law Enforcement in the South and West, 1870–1893* (Tuscaloosa: University of Alabama Press, 1991), 16, 264.

6. The best state studies include Robert Smith Boder, *Prohibition in Kansas: A History* (Lawrence: University of Kansas Press, 1986); Jimmie Lewis Franklin, *Born Sober: Prohibition in Oklahoma, 1907–1959* (Norman: University of Oklahoma Press, 1971); Paul E. Isaac, *Prohibition and Politics: Turbulent Decades in Tennessee, 1885–1920* (Knoxville: University of Tennessee Press, 1965); Daniel J. Whitener, *Prohibition in North Carolina, 1717–1945* (Chapel Hill: University of North Carolina Press, 1945); James Benson Sellers, *The Prohibition Movement in Alabama, 1702–1943* (Chapel Hill: University of North Carolina Press, 1943); Edwin Hendricks, *Liquor and Anti-Liquor in Virginia, 1619–1919* (Durham, N.C.: Duke University Press, 1967).

7. These concepts are defined in Kermit L. Hall, *The Magic Mirror: Law in American History* (New York: Oxford University Press, 1989), 94, 114, 361; see also

Melvin I. Urofsky, "State Courts and Protective Legislation during the Progressive Era: A Reevaluation," *Journal of American History* 72 (June 1985), 63–91; Harry N. Scheiber, "Instrumentalism and Property Rights: A Reconsideration of American Styles of Judicial Reasoning in the 19th Century," *Wisconsin Law Review* (1975), 1–18.

8. As David R. Colburn and Richard K. Scher have noted, historians "have paid little attention to law enforcement . . . in Florida." *Florida's Gubernatorial Politics in the 20th Century* (Tallahassee: Florida State University Press, 1980), 329. For prohibition in Florida, see Frank Alduino, "The 'Noble Experiment' in Tampa: A Study of Prohibition in Urban America," (Ph.D. diss., Florida State University, 1989); Paul S. George, "Bootleggers, Prohibitionists, and Police: The Temperance Movement in Miami, 1896–1920," *Tequesta* 39 (1979), 3–41.

9. This approach not only helps redirect the focus of legal history from the North to the South, but also explains the dynamics of continuity and change that characterize regional legal culture. For a probing analysis of this issue, see Paul Finkelman, "Exploring Southern Legal History," *North Carolina Law Review* 64 (1985), 77–86. For a recent work that contributes significantly to southern legal history, see Kermit L. Hall and Eric W. Rise, *From Local Courts to National Tribunals: The Federal District Courts of Florida, 1821–1990* (Brooklyn, N.Y.: Carlson Publishing, Inc., 1991).

10. The literature on American federalism is extensive. For a small but significant sample, see Harry N. Scheiber, "Federalism and the American Economic Order, 1789–1910," *Law and Society Review* 10 (Fall 1975), 57–100; Idem, "Federalism, the Southern Economy, and Public Policy Since 1865," in David J. Bodenhamer and James W. Ely, Jr., eds., *Ambivalent Legacy: A Legal History of the South* (Jackson: University of Mississippi Press, 1984); Daniel J. Elazar, *American Federalism: A View from the States*, 3rd ed. (New York: Harper and Row, 1984); William Graebner, "Federalism in the Progressive Era: A Structural Interpretation of Reform," *Journal of American History* 64 (1977), 331–357.

11. See Morton Keller, *Affairs of State: Public Life in Late Nineteenth Century America* (Cambridge, Mass.: Harvard University Press, 1977); Idem, *Regulating a New Economy: Public Policy and Economic Change in America, 1900–1933* (Cambridge, Mass.: Harvard University Press, 1990); Idem, *Regulating a New Society: Public Policy and Social Change in America, 1900–1933* (Cambridge, Mass., and London: Harvard University Press, 1994).

12. *U.S. Constitution*, Eighteenth Amendment, Sec. 2.

13. Norman H. Clark, *Deliver Us from Evil: An Interpretation of American Prohibition* (New York and London: W. W. Norton & Company, 1976), 133–134.

14. Richard F. Hamm, *Shaping the Eighteenth Amendment: Temperance Reform, Legal Culture, and the Polity, 1880–1920* (Chapel Hill and London: University of North Carolina Press, 1995), 220, 255.

15. For example, see *Ellis* v. *State*, 6 So. 768 (Fla. 1889); *Theisen* v. *McDavid*, 34 Fla. 440 (1894); *Bueno* v. *State*, 40 Fla. 160 (1898).

16. John H. F. Shattuck, *The Rights of Privacy* (Skokie, Ill.: National Textbook Co., 1977), xiii.

17. Ibid., x; Paul L. Murphy, "Societal Morality and Individual Freedom," in Kyvig, ed., *Law, Alcohol and Order*, 67–80, 69. Besides Shattuck's book, see Alan F. Westin, *Privacy and Freedom* (New York: Atheneum, 1967); Edward Landynski, *Search and Seizure and the Supreme Court* (Baltimore: Johns Hopkins University Press,

1966); David J. Bodenhamer, *Fair Trial: Rights of the Accused in American History*, Bicentennial Essays on the Bill of Rights (New York: Oxford University Press, 1992); Paul Finkelman and Stephen E. Gottlieb, eds., *Toward a Usable Past: Liberty Under State Constitutions* (Athens: University of Georgia Press, 1991).

18. Kenneth M. Murchison, *Federal Criminal Law Doctrines: The Forgotten Influence of National Prohibition* (Durham, N.C., and London: Duke University Press, 1994), 21; Idem, "Prohibition and the Fourth Amendment: A New Look At Some Old Cases," *Journal of Criminal Law and Criminology* 73 (Summer 1982), 471–532.

19. Murchison, *Federal Criminal Law Doctrines*, 18, 102–103, 183.

20. Richard F. Hamm, "Review of Federal Criminal Law Doctrines" in *Law and History Review* (forthcoming).

21. Shattuck poses similar questions in his general treatment of search and seizure law. *Rights of Privacy*, 5.

22. James W. Ely, Jr., *The Guardian of Every Right: A Constitutional History of Property Rights* (New York: Oxford University Press, 1992), 3, 115, 176.

23. Murchison, "Property Forfeiture in the Era of National Prohibition: A Study of Judicial Response to Legislative Reform," *Buffalo Law Review* 32 (1983), 417–463.

24. Ibid., 419, 450, 452.

25. Lender, "The Historian and Repeal," 177.

26. For these reasons, see Clement E. Vose, *Constitutional Change: Amendment Politics and Supreme Court Litigation Since 1900* (Lexington, Mass.: Lexington Books, 1972), 101–102.

27. Ibid., 137.

28. See David E. Kyvig, *Repealing National Prohibition* (Chicago: University of Chicago Press, 1979); Fletcher Dobyns *The Amazing Story of Repeal: An Exposé of the Power of Propaganda* (Chicago: Willett Clark, 1940).

29. Levine, "The Birth of American Alcohol Control," 96–101.

30. For a more recent examination of the urban-rural dichotomy of the 1920s, see Charles W. Eagles, *Democracy Delayed: Congressional Reapportionment and Urban-Rural Conflict in the 1920s* (Athens: University of Georgia Press, 1990).

31. Lender deserves much credit for crystallizing these and related issues in his essay, "The Historian and Repeal."

32. Urofsky, "State Courts and Protective Legislation," 63–91.

CHAPTER ONE

Local Option to National Prohibition, 1885–1920

In 1907 the Florida Supreme Court heard a case in which a state's witness who had purchased a quart of wine from a bootlegger testified, "It looked like wine and we called it wine." But he admitted that even after drinking copious amounts he felt little effect and remained sober. Another witness claimed that "a person might become drunk if they [*sic*] downed two or three quarts of the beverage." He confessed, however, that he had imbibed "a little whiskey" before drinking the wine. Perhaps seeing a hole in the prosecution's case, the accused said, "The boys buy this stuff from me when they are drinking whiskey, bring the whiskey out with them, and mix it with it. That is how they get drunk. The slop I make won't get them drunk." The plea failed to pass the court's muster. Instead, it found the testimonies of the witnesses that "the wine produced symptoms of alcoholic intoxication in them" sufficient evidence to prove the inebriating capacity of the booze.[1]

The above case provides a microcosm of the legal issues raised by the enforcement of the liquor laws in Florida. To assume a broader perspective, this chapter details how the Florida Supreme Court responded to those laws between 1885 and 1920. As the liquor laws in Florida went from local option to national prohibition, temperance advocates successfully lobbied the Florida legislature to pass various dry measures. They designed these laws to limit property rights in alcoholic beverages, regulate saloons, curb social drinking and, ultimately, ban intoxicants statewide. To that end, the dry forces in Florida waged a three-phase war against the wet resistance. From 1885 to 1907, during the first and longest phase of the dry crusade, proponents utilized local option, license laws, and other measures to rid the state of alcohol and the social problems engendered by its consumption. In this phase, the Florida Supreme Court initially supported the "dry spirit" of these laws by constructing them broadly. It accepted and even endorsed an expansion of the police power provided that the authority remained local in operation.

In 1907, Florida drys embarked on the second phase of their war against "demon rum" by agitating for statewide prohibition. Although they initially failed to achieve that goal, they successfully pressured the legislature to outlaw saloons in 1913. Four years later lawmakers further curbed social drinking when they banned the dispensing of spirits, wines, or beer in private clubs. With these restrictions in place, the judicial consensus on Florida's liquor laws began unraveling. Some judges perceived an onerous threat to fundamental rights and southern culture. As this extension of the police power proceeded, judicial opposition arose collaterally with each wave of expansion. Couching their early arguments in terms of property rights, these justices attempted to safeguard vested rights from an oppressive, arbitrary police state.

Phase three began about 1918 when the legislature, by way of a constitutional amendment, banned intoxicating liquors throughout the state. At this point, the judicial opponents of the liquor laws became increasingly wary and continued attacking prohibition because of the threat it posed to property. However, in 1920 the U.S. Supreme Court upheld the National Prohibition Act and defined, rather ambivalently, the principle of concurrent powers. The same opponents to prohibition then began advancing state sovereignty as a bulwark against further erosion of constitutional foundations.

Over the course of the dry crusade, the Florida Supreme Court, by virtue of the power of judicial review, extended its reach beyond the judiciary and performed an important policy-making function as it supervised the state's executive and legislative branches. And as liquor regulation became more restrictive and passed from local to state to national control, Florida's high tribunal even attempted to check the escalation of federal jurisdiction. Similar to other politicians in the Progressive Era, some Florida judges "supported centralization within the state, [but] could not fully condone the increasing concentration of powers in the federal government."[2] As Kermit L. Hall has argued: "Judges had a large and active hand in the governance of a rapidly changing society."[3]

The Florida crusade against liquor paralleled the prohibition campaign in other southern states. One of the most vigorous and fervently supported social reforms in the South during the Progressive Era, prohibition "proved remarkably versatile in its effect upon southern sensibilities and yearnings." The movement, according to historian Dewey W. Grantham, brought together a constellation of tendencies, including Christian evangelicalism, humanitarian concern for social justice, and the dominant group's desire to control an African American population that anxious whites perceived as undependable at best and criminally inclined at worst. While each of these factors contributed to the demand for prohibition, the specter of racial unrest might have exacerbated white anxiety and created a sense of urgency that the others failed to achieve. A contemporary claimed: "The frightful race riots at Atlanta [in 1907], which sprang from the dives and were carried to such excesses of unreasoning ferocity by men who were inflamed by drink, may well enough have been in the minds of the Georgia legislators when they enacted state prohibition."[4]

Tantamount to racial anxieties, however, stood a provincial suspicion of external intrusions on local institutions coupled with a republican fear of factions. During the Progressive Era, one of the most ominous factions became personified by the liquor interests and manifested in the saloons. The southern prohibition campaign, and its Florida component, thus stemmed from a font of underlying social forces that began to coalesce about the turn of the century.[5]

For the most part, the early years of the temperance campaign went well for Florida's prohibitionists. The legislature passed laws restraining the sale of liquor and the supreme court threw its judicial weight behind these measures. In 1883, for example, the senate's Committee on Temperance drafted a liquor license law that permitted only "men of good moral character" to retail liquor. The bill passed in both houses. The court upheld the measure, claiming that the statute represented a police regulation established for the prevention of destitution and crime. By restricting sellers of liquor to persons who possessed sufficient intelligence and character, the law supposedly assured that licensed agents would not carelessly dispense intoxicants.[6]

Two years later the prohibitionist crusade achieved one of its basic aims when Article XIX of Florida's 1885 constitution made local option consonant with organic law.[7] By altering the constitution in this fashion, the state hoped to remit to the registered voters of each county the resolution of whether the sale of intoxicating liquors, beer, or wine should be prohibited within the county. In a sense, the local option article illustrated the republican ideal of home rule. The law gave to one-fourth of the electorate of any county the power to require an election once every two years to decide public sentiment concerning the liquor question. If most voters in a county or election district approved prohibition, the sale of alcohol became illegal until a subsequent election occurred in which the majority of voters decided against prohibition. To enforce this article, the Florida legislature enacted several statutes in 1887 that made it a misdemeanor for any person to sell (or cause to be sold) booze in a dry county. Upon conviction, violators could be fined or imprisoned or both.[8]

Local option removed exclusive liquor licensing power from county commissioners and conferred it on the public.[9] But unlike the liquor license law, the local option legislation operated as a prohibition and not merely as a restriction. Since the two systems of law proved repugnant to each other and unenforceable in the same locality simultaneously, the supreme court ultimately resolved several unanticipated problems concerning the exercise of each law. In *Butler and Chapman* v. *State* (1889), Florida Chief Justice George P. Raney concluded that in counties that had voted to adopt it, the local option ordinance, once effective, served to repeal all laws and parts of laws conflicting with it. Raney qualified his position, noting that the adoption of local option suspended rather than repealed the General Revenue Statute. And if the local option article ceased to function, Raney wrote, "those provisions of the revenue act which had been suspended by the enforcement of the article will resume their sway in the county or precinct."[10]

Between 1901 and 1907, the Florida legislature enacted several other statutes that complemented the local option ordinances. In 1901, the legislature passed a bill that authorized law enforcement officers to enter and search without warrant any building, booth, or other place within their jurisdictions, provided they had reasonable cause to suspect the illegal safekeeping of intoxicating spirits. Another law forbade giving away liquor within one mile of voting booths on election days. In 1907, the state legislature made it illegal to sell liquor to habitual drunkards.[11]

With Florida's local option, license, and other liquor laws in place, the temperance forces had laid a legal foundation for a dry commonwealth. At that point, the prohibition question shifted from the legislature to the judiciary. The state's highest tribunal therefore became poised to determine the scope of the liquor laws. Serving as a court of last resort, the Florida Supreme Court sat at the apex of the state judiciary. During the years 1885 to 1920, a chief justice and between two and five associates heard only the most important liquor cases that arose on appeal from the lower courts. The Florida Constitution of 1885 called for the election of three justices to the court and stipulated that they would choose the chief justice by lot. A constitutional amendment adopted in 1902 increased court membership from three to six. Following Justice Charles B. Parkhill's resignation in 1912, the court consisted of five members. This situation lasted until 1923, when Governor Cary A. Hardee appointed Glenn Terrell as a sixth justice.[12] In any event, the higher court reviewed the rulings of the lower courts, and if it reversed a decision, the supreme court usually returned the case to the trial court for a rehearing.[13]

As the dry crusade advanced in Florida, the supreme court initially supported the liquor laws by construing them broadly according to the framers' original intent and desired effect. Moreover, in the early appeals stemming from their enforcement, attorneys for convicted violators exploited any legal or procedural error they found or imagined. In one case a bootlegger had sold a handkerchief to another person for twenty-five cents and gave his "customer" a quart of wine as a complimentary gift. His counsel argued that the circuit court had erred in ruling this transaction an illegal liquor sale. Noting that a jury could have easily concluded that the defendant sold the handkerchief under false pretenses as a subterfuge and that the accused did sell a quart of wine, the supreme court sustained the lower court's judgment.[14]

In the above case and in others that followed, the accused often staked its defense on the prosecution's failure to adduce that the wine in question, if consumed, could produce an intoxicating effect. The court found it superfluous to prove wine's inebriating capacity. "In principal," the court declared, "the rule plainly is that under the very common term 'intoxicating liquor' in the statute, the indictment may simply mention by name any liquor which the court judiciously knows to be intoxicating. . . . It is a matter of common knowledge that wine is intoxicating."[15] And the court took judicial note. So in future cases the defense would have to prove that the substance sold was non-intoxicating.[16]

The modern national prohibition movement began in the South with the passage of Georgia's statewide liquor ban in August 1907. Following Georgia's lead, South Carolina and Alabama each went dry. Temperance developments in Florida shadowed these regional trends.[17] Fearing that liquor dealers in bordering states would attempt to sell their surplus intoxicants in Florida, dry advocates began pressuring the legislature to place a prohibitory referendum before the electorate. Baptists led the crusade for prohibition and mounted an intensive lobbying effort to get the measure enacted. Likewise, Methodists proved "equally persistent in their quest to make . . . Florida dry territory."[18]

One secular proponent, Judge Thomas Porter of Grand Ridge, publicly advocated the proposed bill. In a letter sent to the *Pensacola Journal*, Porter congratulated the editor for supporting prohibition and thanked "God that we had a man of such principle and such courage at the helm of [the] paper. With all my heart and hands, I . . . will help in every way I can."[19]

Echoing Porter, Judge Francis B. Carter of the state's first judicial circuit and a former state supreme court justice, penned an argument for the Escambia County Prohibition League in which he endorsed the proposed statewide ban. Appointed to the Florida Supreme Court in 1897, Carter resigned in 1905 to accept a more active position as a circuit judge. Two years later, he stepped down from the bench to practice law.[20] Carter believed that for prohibition to succeed in the South, the dry forces had to counter potent defenses for personal liberty. Many southern whites found prohibitionist rhetoric similar to the arguments of the abolitionists in the 1850s.[21] The South therefore, according to Carter, quite naturally drifted into thinking that like abolition, prohibition represented an intrusion on the sanctity of property. But southern concern for property, Carter pleaded, "should not prevent our doing what we believe to be right . . . for . . . our people."[22]

To promote the best interests of the commonweal, Carter called for the extermination of saloons. He regarded "grog shops" as odious institutions that served as "the greatest aider and abettor of shiftlessness and moral depravity that our civilization has evolved. . . . They give their customers nothing substantial," Carter declared, "in return for what they receive." Pressing his argument, Carter stressed that prohibition neither prescribed a penalty for drinking nor outlawed personal consumption. It simply made it a crime to sell liquor. He added that many laws then in force deprived individuals of their personal liberty in matters less harmful than retailing liquors. "Most all criminal laws are restraints upon the personal liberty to do what one pleases, and many of them are restraints on such liberty in respect to moral questions." Any citizen who voted for the legalization of liquor traffic because he feared governmental encroachment on personal liberty, Carter concluded, voted for the death of the commonweal. "Ardent spirits," he thundered, caused harmful effects to the family, the community, and the state.[23]

Although such pleas failed to muster adequate support to get statewide prohibition enacted in 1907, Florida's temperance forces remained steadfast in their mission. Indeed, drys even started playing the race card to further the cause. To illustrate the point, a contributor to the *Tampa Tribune* claimed that prohibition in the South "has some relation to the Negro question." Despite the Emancipation Proclamation, the writer said, blacks remained slaves. They had only changed their masters. Instead of having "gentle, kind, and loving masters," blacks found themselves bound to the liquor dealers, "none of whom cared a thrip [*sic*] for the negro, except to get his money and debauch him." It therefore behooved southerners to complete the task of emancipation. "The South," he continued, "has learned that no southern home is safe which harbors the licensed saloon." With that in mind, he reflected on the antebellum era and imagined slaves as "docile, harmless, and affectionate" servants to their masters. Those virtues and their dependability, he added, stemmed from their sobriety. Unfortunately, with freedom many former slaves became familiar with the white man's whiskey. Through this experience, a deadly deviant bent on the commission of countless crimes emerged, he claimed, and has consequently "blackened the fair name of every southern state." Happily for him: "In God's good providence the white men of the South have wakened [*sic*] to the fact that in order to save their women and their homes they must adopt prohibition." For once the saloon was eradicated "from the negro belt," he concluded, "there will be no more burning of criminal negroes at the stake by drunken mobs."[24]

Such racism aside, a plurality of factors motivated prohibitionists in the Sunshine State. In 1908, for example, Florida drys invited America's foremost opponent of saloons, Carry A. Nation, to embark on an extensive speaking tour of the state. According to historian Samuel Proctor, "the peppery crusader attracted large crowds wherever she spoke." In Tampa she told her audience, "I am not in favor of local option, but believe in the policy of annihilation by not allowing a drop of liquor to be manufactured." She also endorsed enfranchising women because she opposed "taxation without representation." Since women are people and the Constitution "says that the nation shall be governed by the will of the people," she concluded that women should vote.[25]

After exciting zealots in west Florida, Nation traveled south to Miami to assist locals in drying up the "wicked little city." Although Miami was born dry in 1896, public drinking flourished in the city due to numerous loopholes in its anti-saloon ordinance. As incidents of public drunkenness, violence, and related vices increased, a potent temperance force led by the Woman's Christian Temperance Union (WCTU) and the Anti-Saloon League emerged to restore order. In October 1907, with the support of a major newspaper, *The Metropolis*, the drys managed to call a special local option election for Dade County, which they ultimately lost. The margin of victory, however, was so slim that drys felt encouraged to try again. Toward that goal, they organized rallies in which many prominent temperance leaders (including Nation) participated.[26]

After arriving in Miami, Nation gave pep talks to enthusiasts in a tent pitched across the street from the courthouse. Because of these lectures, *The Metropolis* reported that those "who thought Mrs. Nation [was] simply a sufferer from a certain form of dementia Americana . . . are daily changing their opinions." In addition to giving speeches, Nation accompanied WCTU officials on unannounced tours of the Miami vice scene. Appalled by these tours, Nation said there was plenty of crime and corruption in Miami. Her allegations stirred county solicitor (and future circuit judge) H. Pierre Branning to subpoena Nation and her entourage for information concerning criminal activities in Miami. A few hours after reporting to Branning, Nation addressed an audience exceeding two thousand people. In her usual manner she quoted select Biblical passages on the evils of alcohol, and then, unexpectedly, Nation declared that official corruption had contributed to Miami's wickedness. These charges led a perturbed Branning to mount the platform, decry the allegations, and challenge Nation to produce the evidence. On that cue, she withdrew two bottles of whiskey from the folds of her dress and shouted, "These were purchased [in] north Miami on Sunday." Such antics goaded her audience to roar with cheers and laughter. At the end of her stay, the *Morning News Record* (a harsh critic of Nation) said despite her visit, Miamians would "continue to be almost as good as ever and no better." Whatever the case, Nation had an apparent impact on the city. Arrests for liquor violations increased, and locals organized a new county civic association to promote "good morals, good government, [and] temperance." In addition, the city council passed more stringent liquor laws that closed saloons at ten o'clock on weeknights and midnight on Saturdays, and banned women and children from entering saloons. Before long, even the *Morning News Record* was urging citizens to rid the city of vice and bad saloons. Nonetheless, Dade County would not approve local option until 1913.[27]

In 1908, as Carry Nation toured Florida on behalf of the dry crusade, prohibition became a major issue in that year's gubernatorial campaign. During the primary elections, three leading candidates each declared their support for prohibition. John Stockton and the future chief justice of the Florida Supreme Court, Jefferson B. Browne, both endorsed statewide prohibition. But Browne announced that he did not espouse the cause for political gain, for to do so would have cost him "the support of many men who are my warm personal friends, without the assurance of any corresponding gain." Candidate Albert Gilchrist, in contrast, favored local option. With the candidates' positions on the liquor issue clearly defined, Gilchrist prevailed in the Democratic primary and defeated the Republican Stockton in the general election for governor by a vote of 32,465 to 23,291.[28]

The election returns suggest that the majority of Floridians still preferred local to state control of liquor. To be sure, by 1908 local option and other liquor laws had served the temperance cause quite well. Thirty-four of Florida's forty-seven counties had gone dry, and within the entire state only 330 saloons still operated.[29] Regardless, dry advocates—to whom the only good saloon was a closed saloon—intensified their efforts during the second phase of the dry crusade in Florida. The WCTU joined forces with the Anti-Saloon League in 1910 and launched a forceful but ultimately unsuccessful campaign to place a statewide prohibition amendment before the electorate. Don C. McMullen, an official with the Anti-Saloon League of Hillsborough County, claimed, "few respectable people voted on the whiskey side." The proposed statewide ban went down in defeat because "the bulk of the [wet] vote in this county was ignorance, foreigners, and negroes." Likewise, according to the Anti-Saloon League's analysis of the election returns, "the defeat of prohibition [in Florida] was due to the negro vote, which was handled by the liquor interests." The four counties containing the largest block of African American votes provided a majority of over forty-nine hundred against the amendment. Those numbers spelled defeat for the dry cause.[30]

Drys did succeed, however, in pushing through the legislature several bills aimed at social drinking in general and saloons in particular. Before 1913, the state had permitted open saloons. But in 1913, the legislature enacted a bill that limited social drinking to private clubs, which had paid a tax to serve and distribute alcoholic drinks to members or non-resident guests. The same act—ostensibly directed at persons of moderate means—prohibited the open saloon.[31] Frank Lewinsky tested the statute in November 1913, after a Monroe County court had found him guilty of selling liquor to a female and of maintaining side entrances and screens to his barroom. On both counts, the defendant argued that the cited laws represented class legislation that required invalidation by the court.[32]

Challenging Lewinsky's premise, Justice Robert S. Cockrell claimed that legislation could exclude certain groups of people. Most states, for example, prohibited the sale of alcoholic beverages to minors and habitual drunkards. Florida's law, in contrast, went one step further in that it prohibited liquor sales to females. "A class," according to Cockrell, "associated in [most] matters of legislation with infants and others in need of special protection." Since no women at the time complained that the legislation deprived them of rights by not permitting them to drink at public bars, Cockrell concluded that Lewinsky's contention of class legislation did not stand. Besides, Cockrell saw a need for discriminatory legislation. In *Lachman* v. *Walker* (1906), he endorsed a Tampa liquor license tax that made the cost of permits there double that in most other counties. "Tampa, with its large foreign population," according to Cockrell, "required a larger tax, not only for policing, but also for revenue." Cockrell's statement might have been more objective than prejudicial. A sympathetic study of Latin culture in Tampa claims that Italians enthusiastically and with immigrant resolve dominated the city's illicit liquor trade during prohibition.[33]

In any case, on his second point Lewinsky asserted that a clause in the statute exempting hotels with one hundred rooms or more represented an arbitrary classification. The court should therefore strike it down as class legislation. Still, the court validated the law, for in a sense all legislation is classification. The court rationalized that, unlike smaller hotels where the liquor trade may be of principal economic importance, in larger hotels the bar is secondary and "the hotel management, under constant supervision of the state, will see . . . that the bar is conducted in an orderly, decent manner." The court further stressed that the act did not grant any specific privilege to hotels of one hundred rooms but merely exempted such lodgings from certain restrictions. Since the law did not invade Lewinsky's constitutional rights, the court dismissed the charge of class legislation and unanimously upheld the judgment against him.[34]

In addressing the issue of class legislation, the court failed to cite any of Florida's Jim Crow laws. This omission seems odd. In *Galloway, Sheriff* v. *Strauss* (1914), the same bench ruled that a statutory provision requiring a permit for all liquor retailers should be construed considering the recognized segregationist policy of the state. Like most southern states, Florida had institutionalized a system to keep people of different races from commingling in public places, such as restaurants, hotels, or railroad depots. The white legislature justified this form of discriminatory legislation as a police power intended to prevent friction between the races and thus preserve the peace.[35]

In the immediate case, a liquor dealer named Maurice Strauss operated a bar in Ocala, which served both black and white patrons. On payment of one thousand dollars, the Marion County tax collector granted Strauss a liquor license. However, upon learning that he catered to both races, the county attempted to collect an additional thousand dollars. The tax collector's actions suggest that the county designed its liquor license fee to suppress public drinking, rather than to raise additional revenue. If Strauss, for example, who failed or refused to pay the second fee, lost his case, his profits would have suffered due to his diminished share of the market. Without the additional profits earned from a racially diverse clientele, Strauss might have found the first license fee beyond his means. His business would have failed. Still, the court ruled in Strauss's favor, claiming that his bar operated as a single business. Even though he had maintained adequate separation of the races (separate entrances, separate counters, and partitions between sections so that customers of one race could not see customers of the other race) the court found the single permit sufficient. Strauss remained in business.[36]

Until 1913, according to the Anti-Saloon League, the liquor interests defeated almost every effective temperance bill proposed to the Florida legislature or succeeded in adding provisions to the measures that tended to make the laws ineffective. After 1913, however, the drys started winning the battles over liquor legislation. In 1913 the legislature enacted an anti-shipping and "blind tiger" (illicit liquor dealer) search and seizure law. Two years later the Davis Package Law went into effect. It banned all liquor sales in Florida except those of a half pint or more in sealed containers and outlawed consumption of booze on the premises where it was purchased.[37]

Soon after it became operable, Florida wets arranged the arrest of a Jacksonville liquor dealer to test the constitutionality of the Davis Package Law. In the case that followed, *Ex parte Pricha* (1915), attorneys hired by the state's liquor dealers alleged that the open-container law violated the Florida Constitution by depriving citizens of certain inalienable rights, including acquiring, possessing, and protecting property, without due process. In a split decision, with four separate opinions ranging from ten to twenty pages in length, the court discharged the writ. Speaking for the majority, Justice Thomas M. Shackleford found the liquor dealers' assertion untenable. Shackleford had sat on the state supreme court from 1902 to 1917. During his tenure he served two terms as chief justice and maintained close ties with the Anti-Saloon League of Hillsborough County. Claiming every regulation is of necessity a restriction, Shackleford concluded that the purpose of the statute in question, as well as other liquor legislation in Florida, remained regulation and not prohibition of the liquor traffic. "They operate as a check or restraint, upon the sale, not as an absolute inhibition, and are in the strictest sense regulations. They regulate by prohibiting the sale at certain times, to certain persons, and in certain places." According to Shackleford, the court's function under the separation of powers required a liberal construction of legislation. Only in clear cases should the judicial branch invalidate a statute.[38]

In a forceful dissent, Justice William H. Ellis said the dispute raised the fundamental question of whether the state constitution recognized the liquor trade as a legitimate business that every individual had a right to engage in, subject to reasonable regulations. Such regulations, he believed, included only those that the legislature might impose in the exercise of its police power, or the people of a county could institute through a majority vote in an election held solely for the purpose of prohibiting the sale of alcohol. According to Ellis, the legislature could no more prohibit the sale of intoxicating spirits in quantities of less than half a pint than it could forbid their sale in quantities of less than half a barrel. If the legislature did hold such power, he wondered, "Where [was] the line of demarcation beyond which the courts may say constitutionally thus far shalt thou go and no further?" In Ellis's view, as long as the Florida Constitution recognized the traffic in, or sale of, intoxicants as a legitimate occupation, the legislature lacked the authority to destroy such commerce entirely or partially. He further asserted that courts should stop frittering away "constitutional privileges by finespun theories and hairsplitting distinctions in order to sustain an act of the legislature which has for its purpose the complete destruction of one phase of the traffic and the regulation of what is left."[39]

Concurring with Ellis, Chief Justice R. Fenwick Taylor found the entire act unconstitutional. On its face, Taylor argued, the law represented a cleverly constructed attempt under the guise of regulation of the traffic in intoxicants to establish prohibition in Florida through legislative enactment. Instead, the people of the counties should have resolved the question by way of a direct vote.

From Taylor's perspective, if the legislature had the constitutional right to establish partial prohibition in one instance, then that body with equal right could prohibit all sales in any quantity. Believing in the sanctity of property, Taylor cast a dissenting vote.[40]

Shortly after the court handed down its ruling in *Ex parte Pricha*, the *Tallahassee Daily Democrat* reported that the decision would prompt more stringent enforcement of the Davis Package Law in "Jacksonville, Tampa, and Pensacola where clubs and next door restaurants abound to such an extent that the act is practically useless."[41] However, for those businesses that managed to skirt the Davis Law, the legislature enacted another statute in 1917, which curbed social drinking by prohibiting the dispensing of ardent spirits, wines, or beer in private clubs.[42]

Many enterprising individuals did their best to avoid the "club laws." J. G. Hilliard of Pensacola, for example, received and stored his customers' booze at his restaurant. He served his patrons their liquor whenever they so desired between the hours of six in the morning and seven in the evening. Hilliard did this until the Escambia County sheriff, J. C. Van Pelt, entered the restaurant on October 8, 1917 and seized all the liquors stored inside the premises. Filing for an injunction against Van Pelt, Hilliard claimed he had obtained all the permits necessary to operate his kind of business. The sheriff, he argued, had seized property that belonged to Hilliard's customers. If the sheriff continued doing this, it would destroy Hilliard's profitable business because his customers would refuse to entrust their liquors to him for storage. Finally, since Van Pelt had admitted openly that he intended to confiscate "all liquors which might be sent to Hilliard's place of business by his customers," the accused wanted the court to place a restraining order on the sheriff. The county court granted a temporary injunction ordering Van Pelt to stop seizing liquors at Hilliard's place of business or interfering with him in serving such spirits. A week later Van Pelt filed an appeal with the supreme court. Charging that the lower court erred in granting the injunction, he claimed Hilliard deserved no decree at all.[43]

Besides challenging the constitutionality of the law, this case raised questions concerning the construction of words and the interpretation of statutes. In addressing the meaning of words, the supreme court stated that if a word lacked a definite or widely accepted popular understanding, "or the connection in which it is used is ambiguous, then the court must construe such word and give to it such meaning as is reasonable and will carry out the legislative intent." Because the court failed to find a popular and definite meaning for the word "club," and neither counsel for either party furnished the bench with an authority that provided one, the court assumed the task. In doing so, it assigned the word a meaning that would harmonize with the letter and spirit of the law. The court agreed that a place "where persons in large numbers deposit with a proprietor of a restaurant [who] holds himself out as ready to receive such liquor and dispense it to such patrons for pay for such service, furnishing glassware, ice, milk, etc., . . . for making such liquors palatable and such persons frequently by day and night resort to such place, engage in discussing current events . . . and have intoxicating liquors served to them, though each person is served only with his own liquor, is a club." In construing this statute, the court noted that state policy prior to the act had been to prevent people from congregating and imbibing spirits in the open saloon, even though such restrictions did not apply to private clubs. With the latest law, the court claimed that the legislature had removed club exemptions to further discourage social drinking. By upholding the constitutionality of this act, the court found Hilliard guilty of operating an illegal business.[44]

Speaking for the majority, Justice James T. Wills claimed the legislature had the power to pass any statute deemed beneficial to the general public. This included any reasonable regulation of the conduct of a business or occupation. For occupations that might become damaging to the community, Wills reasoned that the legislature could ban them altogether, permit them only in certain localities under specified terms, or grant the privilege of pursuing them to some persons while denying it to others. "Individual interests," Wills wrote, "must yield when they are in opposition to the public good." The court therefore ruled in Van Pelt's favor, reversed the lower court's decision, dissolved the injunction, and dismissed the bill.[45]

As the intoxicating liquor cases ascended to the Florida Supreme Court, judges, time and again, facilitated the creation of a dry commonwealth. In the process, the bench provided judicial meaning to words, such as "intoxicating liquor," "whiskey," and "club," and construed inexplicit temperance legislation to make such laws effective. Such decisions, however, seemed mere quibbling when compared to the paramount issue of property rights that began to emanate as violators of the liquor laws staked their defense on substantive rights and constitutional law.

The judicial consensus continued fraying as the legislature proposed an amendment to the state constitution regarding ardent spirits and passed enabling legislation in a fashion that engendered an ambiguous division between legal and illegal activities. In April 1917, for example, the assembly placed greater restrictions on the liquor traffic, when it approved a bill intended to "promote temperance and suppress the evils of intemperance" by prohibiting the manufacture of alcoholic and certain *non*-intoxicating liquors.[46]

Less than a year after its passage, Joseph M. Fine challenged the statute on several counts. Fine charged that the act could not stand because it did not apply in general. And because the bill's title embraced more than one subject matter, Fine's counsel claimed that the state constitution rendered it void. The supreme court ruled, however, that only the subject needed expression in the title. This act clearly embraced a singular subject matter concerning traffic in intoxicating and non-intoxicating beverages. Accordingly, the topics of manufacturing, production, distribution, and handling adequately related to the subject of trade in that commodity. The court summarized that the law's title might contain numerous parts related to the general subject, and if the state banned one kind of beverage, the act could include several varieties of beverages. Speaking for the majority opinion, Justice Ellis wrote: "The state, in the exercise of its police powers, may consider not only the effect of the beverage upon the life and health of the individual, but the fact that it may be used as cover to violations of the law." Therefore, the act was "a lawful exercise of the police power." In a split decision, with Chief Justice Jefferson B. Browne dissenting, the court found no error in the record and affirmed the prior judgment.[47]

Browne's failure to concur with the majority opinion's "loose construction" of this law may have surprised some, since he had sought the Democratic gubernatorial nomination in 1908 as an advocate of statewide prohibition. Even so, by the late 1910s, Browne had reversed his earlier position on prohibition and had emerged as the Florida Supreme Court's champion of property rights.[48]

The Well's Quart Law, approved in May of 1917, prompted further litigation in which Browne advanced the sanctity of property. Designed by drys to supplement local option, the law stipulated that persons living in dry counties could order no more than one quart of liquor per month to slake their thirst.[49] In August 1918, James Francis challenged the statute in the Florida Supreme Court on several counts including that (1) the law sought to terminate without just compensation the private ownership of spirits; (2) prohibition of keeping, receiving, or possessing alcohol was not a legitimate exercise of the police power; (3) the state's seizure and subsequent destruction of Francis's property had denied him due process of law; and (4) the statute violated the Fourteenth Amendment to the U.S. Constitution.[50]

In *Ex parte Francis* (1918) the court's majority was quick to claim that features of the law clearly violated Florida's Declaration of Rights as well as parts of the local option article to the state constitution. Speaking for the majority, Justice Taylor said the local option article empowered county residents "to prohibit the sale only of intoxicating liquors, not their ownership, possession, or individual use by the citizen." If the legislature went beyond the realm of law directed "at prohibiting the unlawful sale of such liquors by inhibiting their private ownership, possession, or personal use," according to Taylor, "it transcends its authority under the constitution and its act is void." He noted that the traffic and not the liquor itself was subject to the police power. The property right, the privilege to satisfy personal tastes and appetites, Taylor asserted, remains "inviolate." Since Francis had received in dry territory one quart of liquor for personal use and not for sale or any other illegal purpose, Taylor concluded that "Dade County held the defendant in custody without authority of law and he should be and [was] hereby discharged at the cost of the state." Splitting three to two, the court ruled the statute unconstitutional.[51]

Concurring with Taylor, Chief Justice Browne found justification neither in the constitution nor in a valid exercise of the state's police power for the "discrimination made by this act between the quantity of intoxicating liquors a person may have for his own use in the different counties." Although some courts held that limiting the amount of liquor a person could have in his possession represented a legitimate exercise of police power to safeguard the individual from self-destruction, Browne disagreed. If protection was the purpose of the statute and it permitted possession for personal use in some counties but not in others, Browne wondered whether a person needed protection from himself in dry Santa Rosa county but not in wet Escambia County. He thought "clearly not." Noting that local option related only to the sale of intoxicants and not to their possession, he argued that when the legislature enacted the Well's Quart Law, it prohibited property rights in ardent spirits in counties that had voted against the sale of liquor. By doing this, the legislature, according to Browne, had "attempted to amend the Constitution by legislative enactment."[52]

Justice James B. Whitfield dissented. Appointed to the Florida Supreme Court in 1904, Whitfield became Chief Justice a year later. He held this position three times during a thirty-nine-year career on the bench, in which he penned a record 1,958 opinions. Whitfield viewed the constitution as "a living reality to be interpreted by the neon light of the present rather than the tallow dip of antiquity."[53] No wonder he claimed: "All property rights are subject to lawful governmental regulations under the police power . . . to conserve the . . . general welfare of the people." When the state, using the police power for public benefit, appropriately regulates the use of property, there occurs "no deprivation or taking of property within the inhibition of the Constitution, state or federal," even if such regulations circumscribe the use of property. Whitfield justified such limitations by noting that property rights in dangerous or harmful articles differed from those in useful or harmless ones.[54]

Moreover, Whitfield found the statute congruous with the Fourteenth Amendment. "The guarantee under the state constitution that all men are equal before the law and have inalienable rights to acquire, possess, and protect property," Whitfield wrote, "does not so differ from the rights secured by the federal [constitution] as to make individual rights in the use of intoxicating liquors superior to the state organic right of the public to have governmental regulations for the protection, security, and benefit of the citizens of the state." Whitfield maintained the ancient principle of the common law expressed in the Latin maxim, *Salus populi est suprema lex* (the welfare of the people is the supreme law). The legislature therefore could alter or amend the laws whenever the commonweal required such measures, provided the enactment did not conflict with some controlling provision of the state or federal constitution.[55] In Whitfield's view, liquor represented a class of property that both the legislature and the dominant public opinion regarded as detrimental to the health, peace, and morals of the people. Simply put, liquor was "subject to appropriate regulation under the police power of the state."[56]

On October 23, 1918, two months after the court invalidated the Well's Quart Law, Governor Sidney J. Catts published a letter endorsing a proposed state prohibition amendment, the fate of which would be determined in the upcoming general election. Two years earlier in a highly contested and disputed Democratic primary, party regulars with judicial endorsement had denied candidate Catts the party's gubernatorial nomination. A vindictive Catts accepted the Prohibition Party's nomination, however, and won the election. During the campaign, he attacked the "corrupt Democratic machine" and "them infernal judges, the five little tin gods on the Supreme Court." Riding high on the heels of this victory, Catts undoubtedly felt motivated to crush the liquor interests conclusively. "History," Catts wrote, "demonstrates that no people can attain its highest destiny so long as open saloons encourage the liberal use of malt and vinous beverages." To provide the children of Florida an opportunity to earn their salvation and to impress upon them a lasting lesson in sobriety, Catts proclaimed November 1, 1918 "Temperance and Educational Rally Day." He asked all teachers in public schools to observe the occasion in ways that would "create sentiment," in favor of the adoption of the prohibition amendment.[57]

Unlike a decade earlier, in 1918 the political winds then favored the drys, and state prohibition had sufficient support to become law. Besides Catts, newspapers like the *Tallahassee Daily Democrat* endorsed the amendment with headlines urging readers to vote for prohibition. Meanwhile, Florida's WCTU, anticipating the triumph of their cause in the forthcoming election, observed Sunday November 3 as a day of prayer and praise. As they expected, two days later the drys prevailed. On November 5, 1918, in a joint resolution the legislature amended the local option article of the state constitution so that "the manufacture, sale, barter, or exchange of all alcoholic or intoxicating liquors and beverages, whether spirituous, vinous, or malt, are hereby forever prohibited in the State of Florida." Reveling in the victory, Catts noted that "the mighty forces of temperance, sobriety and prohibition," have captured the spirit of the age and have voted "to forever free our magnificent state from the toils of inebriation, drunkenness, riot and death." The Florida prohibition amendment, he promised, "will put the Land of Flowers and God's Eternal Sunshine into the dry columns forever."[58]

Three weeks later, Catts summoned a special session of the legislature to pass an enabling bill for the state's prohibition amendment. In an interview with a reporter for the *Tallahassee Daily Democrat*, Catts explained why he called the extra session. Realizing that those who preferred loose enforcement of the liquor law would criticize his action, Catts defended it as serving the best interests of Florida. He insisted that the state should enforce prohibition without the assistance of federal authorities or national statutes. A firm believer in the "time honored principles of states' rights," Catts deemed it crucial to call the legislature to secure for Floridians the protections necessary "to prevent the wholesale desecration of the sacred rights of our people, by those who seek to profit by the unwholly [*sic*] traffic in liquor." Without stringent legislation rigidly enforced, he feared whiskey would "be brought in, and clandestinely distributed among us to cause so much murder, rape and arson, the prosecution of which would cost many times what the special session cost, to say nothing of the sorrow and grief that would follow." Spurred by Catts, the state senate voted eighteen to four and passed an enabling measure. Effective January 1, 1919, the statute coupled with the new amendment would make local option a dead issue. Meanwhile, on December 4, Catts had signed an emergency prohibition law, which effective December 9, dried up the state for the remainder of the year.[59]

With those laws enacted, the prohibitionists had prevailed during the second phase of their crusade and Florida became a dry state. Immediately prior to enactment of the state prohibition law, all but two counties had local anti-liquor ordinances. More significantly, when the state submitted the prohibition amendment to the people, every county returned a majority vote favoring statewide prohibition. Still, the clarification of any legal ambiguity resulting from this change would fall upon the courts.[60]

The initial test of state prohibition launched the third phase of Florida's dry crusade. The case arose after Sheriff Van Pelt arrested Antonio Marasso for possessing thirty-six gallons of alcoholic liquors on January 14, 1919. Marasso sought a discharge from custody on grounds that the revised statute violated his inalienable right to property. As in *Ex parte Pricha*, the justices disagreed about whether the state could impose restrictions on certain kinds of property. A polarized court split three to two and upheld the constitutional restriction on liquor as a proper exercise of the state's police power.[61]

The majority insisted that the state's police power extended to all matters affecting the individual and collective welfare of the people. Such power, Justice Whitfield opined, had potential application "to all the environments and activities of human life in the family home, as well as in business and public places." He concluded that "the exercise of the police power of the state [could] not be stayed by the acquisition of property that is subject to such power."[62]

In a six-page dissent, Chief Justice Browne developed the argument Justice Taylor presented in *Ex parte Pricha* and Browne himself had made in *Ex parte Francis*. That is, property rights remain inviolable. This task proved formidable for Browne, for he devoted much time, thought, and energy to reach what he considered was the right conclusion. As he deliberated, Browne found himself unable to make his convictions square with his "inclination to sustain a law which [sought] to lessen the evil caused by the excessive use of intoxicating liquor." Yet in the end, Browne's personal desire for a sober society succumbed to his constitutional and judicial principles.[63]

True to the rational conservatism of his namesake and political idol, Jefferson B. Browne viewed the integrity of the states as the main bulwark of natural rights against the encroachment of federal power. Like Jefferson, Browne believed state governments safeguarded "the liberties of the people from the excesses of a radical democracy on one hand and the despotism of a highly centralized federal government on the other." Therefore, according to Browne, every "nationalist" from Alexander Hamilton and John Marshall to Theodore Roosevelt posed a threat to human liberty. Indeed, Browne possessed a keen sense of history and realized that the case before the court raised questions extending well beyond the limited scope of the liquor issue.[64]

Implying that the adoption of the Eighteenth Amendment to the U.S. Constitution would supersede all state and local prohibition laws, he warned that if the court upheld the government's limitations on property rights in any manner, the bench would establish an extremely dangerous precedent. Such decisions, Browne asserted, would authorize further inroads upon private property. "We cannot blind ourselves," he wrote, "to the socialistic conditions prevailing in other countries, and rapidly winning adherents here, whereby the rights of property and the rights of persons are ruthlessly destroyed, justified by the doctrine of public welfare." Reminiscent of President James Buchanan's comments just before the Supreme Court handed down its ruling in the famous *Dred Scott* case, Browne added: "If this decision could be limited in its effect to intoxicating liquors, it would be harmless as a precedent, [because] the liquor question will soon be as completely removed from political consideration as the question of slavery." Like the "great jurist" Roger B. Taney, Browne sanctified property rights. Quoting Taney, Browne said, "spirits and distilled liquors are universally admitted to be subjects of ownership and property."[65]

Browne believed that those advocating the destruction of private property for the sake of the commonweal predicated their viewpoint upon Marxist ideology. Cognizant of political trends in Europe at the time, Browne feared "the proletariat [would] use its political supremacy to wrest by decrees all capital from the bourgeoisie." According to Browne, the framers of free government in the United States knew that when sovereignty passed from kings to the people, the people became vested with the same despotic power. To protect both human and property rights from the unbridled will of the "new sovereign," the framers placed limitations in the constitutions that they considered ample checks against a tyranny of the majority. That said, instead of referring to a specific Marxist work, Browne paraphrased the words of Supreme Court Justice Oliver Wendell Holmes, Jr. In *Noble State Bank* v. *Haskell* (1911), Holmes ruled that police power "may be put forth in aid of what is sanctioned by usage, or held by the prevailing morality or strong and preponderant opinion to be greatly and immediately necessary to the public welfare."[66] To Browne, this represented the apotheosis of the police power at the expense of all constitutional privileges, including freedom of speech, freedom of conscience, and freedom of religious worship.[67]

Although Browne admitted that the state by due process of law could preempt life and liberty, he claimed it could not do so by mere legislative enactment. Browne failed to see how a rule could be made concerning property that did not apply to life and liberty. He wrote, "It is a short step from outlawing property to outlawing a person; and if a legislative enactment is 'due process of law' in one instance, it is in the other." Nor did Browne concede that an amendment to a constitution could deprive citizens of their inalienable rights to life, liberty, and the pursuit of happiness. Such rights, he claimed, are inherent and had existed well before the adoption of the Constitution. "To preserve these rights," Browne concluded, "the spirit as well as the letter of the Constitution must be unflinchingly enforced."[68]

On January 16, 1920, the letter of the Constitution was changed when the Eighteenth Amendment became operative under the Volstead Act. It outlawed the manufacture, sale, or transportation of intoxicating liquors in the United States for beverage purposes. To no one's surprise, the WCTU in Florida and elsewhere "sounded their jubilee" in launching the nation's first saloonless year. Meanwhile, William Jennings Bryan agreed to deliver a series of lectures in southern cities to solicit funds for assisting prohibition enforcement. Bryan devoted one week in February exclusively to speeches in Florida, where he had earlier taken up winter residence. The "Great Commoner" assumed that the Democrats would accept prohibition as the permanent policy of the nation. Because three-fourths of the Democrats in the Senate plus two-thirds of the Democrats in the House endorsed the Eighteenth Amendment, and every state controlled by Democrats voted for ratification, Bryan found it inconceivable that his party would antagonize the moral sense of the country. "John Barleycorn is dead," Bryan cheered, hence the Democratic Party could not "tie itself to a corpse or become the champion of an outlawed traffic."[69]

To be sure, the temperance crusade had prevailed—the United States had become a dry nation. But the result was not "cut and dried," for the courts still had to clarify some legal ambiguity and confusion resulting from the concurrent operation of local, state, and national liquor law. In June 1920, for example, W. H. Neisel appealed a county court's decision that convicted him for possessing ninety-seven quarts of whiskey and transporting it from an undetermined point on the line of the Florida East Coast Railroad running from Jacksonville to Miami. Neisel unsuccessfully sought his release from custody on grounds that the court had convicted him under an invalid law. "It was not proposed, submitted, and ratified in accordance with . . . the State Constitution," Neisel's counsel asserted, "in that the legislature in proposing the amendment to Article XIX (local option) did not determine upon the submission of the amendment to the people for ratification or rejection."[70]

The Florida Constitution required that the legislature's proposed constitutional amendments shall "be agreed to by three-fifths of all members elected to each house," that "such proposed amendments shall be entered upon their respective journals with yeas and nays," and that "the same shall be submitted to the electors of the state for approval or rejection." Basing his opinion on this amendment procedure, Justice Whitfield spoke for the majority. He ruled that the constitution did not require "proposed amendments to contain express provisions for their submission to the electors." According to Whitfield, the general election law authorized placing any proposed amendments on the official ballots cast at general elections. Moreover, the appropriate state and county officials had authority to submit duly proposed amendments to the constitution to the electorate for endorsement or rejection. In Whitfield's view, the state prohibition article "was legally proposed, submitted, and adopted as a part of the Constitution."[71]

In affirming the constitutionality of state prohibition, Whitfield quashed Neisel's notion that the enabling statute extended beyond the legislature's power to enact laws. Noting that the Florida Constitution stipulated that the "legislative authority of this state shall be vested in" the legislature, Whitfield claimed that the state constitution did not grant particular lawmaking powers to the legislative body but imposed specific limitations upon that body's power to legislate. Those limitations permitted "the passage of statutes of the nature here considered." If a statute did not violate the constitution, according to Whitfield, it became the law of the land and required an interpretation that facilitated its purpose, rather than one that mitigated its intent or diminished its efficiency. "Otherwise, the legislature, as the lawmaking power, would not be a co-ordinate department of the government."[72]

To bolster his argument, Whitfield compared Florida's prohibition article to the recently adopted Eighteenth Amendment to the national Constitution. Whitfield viewed the Eighteenth Amendment as an added rather than a substituted article. Since three-fourths of the states had ratified the amendment, he regarded "national prohibition" as part of the federal Constitution before it became operative. "Statutes for enforcing the article proper," Whitfield opined, took "effect and become operative concurrently with the added article."[73]

On the other hand, Whitfield viewed the state prohibition article as a substitute article. Effective January 1, 1919, it replaced the original local option article of the constitution. Although local option remained in effect until January 1, Whitfield said it did not limit the authority or the function of the legislature in December 1918 to pass anticipatory statutes to enforce the amended Article XIX (that is, state prohibition), which had previously "been adopted at the polls in November, 1918." Whereas the original measure limited the lawmaking power of the legislature to prohibition of liquor sales, its provisions did not place limitations on the power of the legislature to enact anticipatory statutes to fulfill the requisites of an amendment to Article XIX that had been adopted to replace the original local option article. Whitfield therefore concluded that the statute here considered did not conflict with the original article, since it did not operate when the original local option article stood in force.[74]

In specific terms, Whitfield interpreted the Eighteenth Amendment as a grant of lawmaking power to Congress, authorizing it to enact laws regulating the sale or manufacture of intoxicating spirits in the states. Yet the state legislature, according to Whitfield, held plenary power to enact such laws, except where restrained by the Florida constitution. Because Neisel failed to show beyond a reasonable doubt that the law he broke violated any constitutional provisions, and the majority proved unable to find the statute palpably arbitrary or oppressive, the court, voting three to two, affirmed the order and remanded him to the custody of the lower court.[75]

In dissent again, Chief Justice Browne took issue with the notion that the state prohibition article, when adopted, became an operable part of the Florida constitution. According to Browne, an amendment that stipulated for it to become effective on a date after its adoption by a majority vote of the electorate represented a positive constitutional enactment. That is, the amendment did not become part of the constitution immediately upon its adoption. Browne declared that an amendment to a constitution could not become effective without being a part of the constitution, and conversely, it could not be a part of it without taking effect.[76]

On rehearing, Justice Whitfield maintained the majority decision on three points. First, he noted that the constitutional right to acquire, possess, and protect property did not enjoin the state from regulating property that is harmful in its use. Second, Whitfield said that a statute had not *ex proprio vigore* (in and of itself) any force until it became the law of the land, and that occurs when "by its terms, it takes effect, and it is to be understood as speaking from the time it goes into operation, and not from the time of its passage." Third, Whitfield argued that a statute that was valid when enacted and made effective did not become invalidated due to a subsequent amendment to the constitution, unless the legislature designed the amendment to have that effect.[77]

The enabling act for state prohibition remained valid then, "for the reason that the Legislature may enact any statute that is not forbidden by the state or federal Constitutions." Besides, Whitfield insisted that nothing in the original article, or in any other provision of the Florida Constitution, or in the federal Constitution, barred the legislature from enacting statewide prohibition "in December, 1918, to take effect only after original Article 19 had ceased to be a part of the organic law of the state."[78]

With the judicial endorsement of state prohibition and the ratification of the Eighteenth Amendment, the dry forces in Florida could claim victory. The hard fought battles from local option to national prohibition had ended to their advantage. As court records illustrate, the Florida Supreme Court played an important mediating role in this campaign. Initially, justices advanced loose interpretations of the intoxicating liquor laws and lent strong support to the dry cause. But once the legislature began to modify existing statutes and enacted new ones that further limited property rights in alcoholic beverages, the court's support for such measures began to wane. The more restrictive the statute, the greater the division on the bench. On one side stood justices who viewed the liquor laws as legitimate expansions of the state's police power. Opposed to them stood those who believed in a strict interpretation of law in general and the constitution in particular. In Jeffersonian fashion, the strict constructionists assumed the position that certain substantive rights remained inalienable and therefore beyond the scope of police regulation. In their minds, an unbridled federal police power such as the Volstead Act established an extremely dangerous precedent and posed a particular threat to white southern culture.

Indeed, two months after national prohibition became law, in a speech before the University of Florida's law class, Chief Justice Browne demonstrated remarkable foresight when he warned that an unchecked national government, through its police power, could desegregate schools and other public facilities, abolish miscegenation laws, or, even worse, place state and/or local elections under federal control. From this, Browne deduced that the ratification of the Eighteenth Amendment to the Constitution had promoted the destruction of the "reserved sovereignty" of the states and marked the beginning of the end of the American constitutional republic.[79]

NOTES

1. *Nussbaumer* v. *State*, 54 Fla. 87 (1907).

2. Samuel Proctor, *Napoleon Bonaparte Broward: Florida's Fighting Democrat* (Gainesville: University of Florida Press, 1950), 271.

3. Kermit L. Hall, *The Magic Mirror: Law in American History* (New York: Oxford University Press, 1989), 227.

4. Dewey W. Grantham, *Southern Progressivism: The Reconciliation of Progress and Tradition* (Knoxville: University of Tennessee Press, 1983), 161; Frank Foxcroft, "Prohibition in the South," *Atlantic Monthly* 101 (May 1908), 627–634, 632. For similar accounts, see John E. White, "Prohibition: The New Task and Opportunity of the South," *South Atlantic Quarterly* 7 (April 1908), 130–142; Josiah William Bailey, "The Political Treatment of the Drink Evil," *South Atlantic Quarterly* 6 (April 1907), 109–124; Booker T. Washington, "Prohibition and the Negro," *Outlook* 88 (March 14, 1908), 587–589.

5. For a brilliant interpretation that views consumption of liquor through the lens of republicanism, see Mark Edward Lender and James Kirby Martin, *Drinking in America: A Revised and Expanded Edition*, 2nd ed. (New York: Free Press, 1987).

6. Ch. 3413, *Florida Acts*, 1885; Ch. 3700, *Florida Acts*, 1887; *State* v. *Smith Tax Collector*, 7 So. 848–850 (Fla. 1890).

7. *Florida Constitution*, Article XIX (1885).

8. Ch. 3700, *Florida Acts*, 1887; *State* v. *Smith Tax Collector*, 848–850.

9. Thomas R. Pegram, "The Dry Machine: The Formation of the Anti-Saloon League of Illinois," *Illinois Historical Journal* 83 (Autumn 1990), 173–186, esp. 181; Norman H. Clark, *Deliver Us from Evil: An Interpretation of American Prohibition* (New York and London: W. W. Norton & Company, 1976), 97–103, 107–113.

10. *Butler and Chapman* v. *State*, 25 Fla. 347, 354–358 (1889).

11. Ch. 4832, *Florida Acts*, 1901; Ch. 5190, *Florida Acts*, 1903; Ch. 5689, *Florida Acts*, 1907.

12. *Florida Statutes* 3 (1941), 219–220; James M. Carson, "Historical Background of Florida Law," *Miami Law Quarterly* 3 (1949), 254–268; Manning J. Daur and William C. Havard, "The Florida Constitution of 1885—A Critique," *University of Florida Law Review* 8 (Spring 1955), 1–92. On the organization of state court systems

in general, see Merlin Lewis et al., *An Introduction to the Courts and Judicial Process* (Englewood Cliffs, N.J.: Prentice-Hall, 1976), 19–50.

13. See Frank Buckley, "Prohibition Survey of Florida," in U.S. Senate, *Official Records of the National Commission on Law Observance and Enforcement*, 71st Cong., 3rd sess. (Washington, D.C.: GPO, 1931), 111.

14. *Caldwell* v. *State*, 43 Fla. 545 (1901).

15. Ibid., 549–550.

16. See, for example, *Nussbaumer* v. *State*, 54 Fla. 87 (1907); *Purcell* v. *State*, 61 Fla. 43 (1911).

17. Grantham, *Southern Progressivism*, 161.

18. Frank Alduino, "The 'Noble Experiment' in Tampa: A Study of Prohibition in Urban America," (Ph.D. diss., Florida State University, 1989), 6.

19. *Pensacola Journal* [Florida], September 15, 1907.

20. Pensacola, *The Public Record*, May 24, 1941; *Tampa Tribune*, January 11, 1937; Henry S. Marks, *Who Was Who in Florida* (Huntsville, Ala.: Strode, 1973), 60.

21. According to Joseph R. Gusfield, "the identification with antislavery was strong enough to stifle completely the organization of the Temperance Movement in the South." *Symbolic Crusade: Status Politics and the American Temperance Movement* (Urbana: University of Illinois Press, 1963), 54.

22. Francis B. Carter, "A Powerful Argument and Plea for Prohibition," Escambia County Prohibition League, September 16, 1907, Manuscript Collection, Box 58, P. K. Yonge Library of Florida History, University of Florida, Gainesville, hereinafter cited as Yonge Library; E. Dixie Beggs, "A History of the Pensacola Law Firm of Beggs & Lane," *Florida Supreme Court Historical Society Review* 2 (1986), 5–10.

23. Carter, "A Powerful Argument and Plea for Prohibition."

24. *Tampa Tribune*, March 6, 1908.

25. Ibid., January 22.

26. Proctor, *Napoleon Bonaparte Broward*, 280–281; Gene M. Burnett, *Florida's Past: The People and Events that Shaped the State*, vol. 3 (Sarasota, Fla.: Pineapple Press, Inc., 1991), 222–224.

27. Ibid.

28. Proctor, *Napoleon Bonaparte Broward*, 280–284; Ric A. Kabat, "Everybody Votes for Gilchrist: The Florida Gubernatorial Campaign of 1908," *Florida Historical Quarterly* 67 (October 1988), 184–203, esp. 195, 197; Jacksonville *Florida Times Union*, November 15, 1907; Tallahassee *Weekly True Democrat*, November 22, 1907.

29. See Foxcroft, "Prohibition in the South," 631; Proctor, *Napoleon Bonaparte Broward*, 280.

30. See Ernest Hurst Cherrington, ed., *The Anti-Saloon League Yearbook, 1911* (Westerville, Ohio: Anti-Saloon League of America, 1912); Frank Alduino, "Prohibition in Tampa," *Tampa Bay History* 9 (Spring/Summer 1987), 17–28; Don C. McMullen to Albert Roberts, November 18, 1910, Manuscript Collection, Box 60, Yonge Library.

31. Ch. 6516, *Florida Acts*, 1913; *Van Pelt, Sheriff* v. *Hilliard*, 75 Fla. 792, 801–802 (1918). For the saloon's social significance, see Perry R. Duis, *The Saloon: Public Drinking in Chicago and Boston, 1880–1920* (Urbana and Chicago: University of Illinois Press, 1983).

32. *Ex parte Lewinsky*, 66 Fla. 324 (1913).

33. Ibid., 325–326. See Gary R. Mormino and George E. Pozzetta, *The Immigrant World of Ybor City* (Urbana and Chicago: University of Illinois Press, 1988), 9, 284–285.

34. *Ex parte Lewinsky*, 326.

35. *Galloway, Sheriff* v. *Strauss*, 67 Fla. 426 (1914). For the definitive study of Jim Crow in Florida, see Jerrell H. Shofner, "Custom, Law, and History: The Enduring Influence of Florida's 'Black Code,'" *Florida Historical Quarterly* 55 (January 1977), 277–298.

36. *Galloway, Sheriff* v. *Strauss*, 426, 432.

37. Ch. 6516, *Florida Acts*, 1913; Ch. 6860, *Florida Acts*, 1915.

38. *Ex parte Pricha*, 70 Fla. 265 (1915); *Tampa Daily Times*, September 22, 1927; *The Daily Democrat*, November 5, 1915.

39. *Ex parte Pricha*, 265, 287–290. On due process see Lawrence M. Friedman, *A History of American Law*, 2nd ed. (New York: Simon and Schuster, 1986), 342–345.

40. *Ex parte Pricha*, 293–295.

41. *The Daily Democrat*, November 5, 1915.

42. Ch. 7287, *Florida Acts*, 1917.

43. *Van Pelt, Sheriff* v. *Hilliard*, 795–797.

44. Ibid., 798, 797, 804–807; Ch. 7287, *Florida Acts*, 1917.

45. *Van Pelt, Sheriff* v. *Hilliard*, 813.

46. Ch. 7283, *Florida Acts*, 1917.

47. *Fine* v. *Moran, Sheriff*, 74 Fla. 417–418, 420, 434, 438–440 (1917); *Florida Constitution*, Article III, section 16 (1885).

48. See Kabat, "Everybody Votes for Gilchrist," 195–197; *Florida Times Union*, November 15, 1907; *Tallahassee Weekly True Democrat*, November 22, 1907.

49. *The Daily Democrat*, August 14, 1918.

50. *Ex parte Francis*, 76 Fla. 304, 305–306 (1918).

51. Ibid., 314–316. For the particular provision, see *Florida Constitution*, Article XIX, section 1 (1885).

52. *Ex parte Francis*, 317–318.

53. See Julia Whitfield Neeley and Randolf Whitfield, "Our Father, James Bryan Whitfield," *Florida Supreme Court Historical Society Review* 3 (1987–88), 1–12.

54. *Ex parte Francis*, 319–321.

55. Ibid., 322, 336.

56. Ibid.

57. *The Daily Democrat*, October 23, 1918. For the complete story of the 1916 Democratic primary, see Wayne Flynt, *Cracker Messiah: Governor Sidney J. Catts of Florida* (Baton Rouge: Louisiana State University Press, 1977), 63–93, 164, 180–186.

58. *The Daily Democrat*, October 23, November 1, 5, 7, 1918.

59. Ibid., November 22, 1918; Flynt, *Cracker Messiah*, 63–93, 164, 180–186.

60. See Ch. 7736, *Florida Acts*, 1918; Ch. 7733, *Florida Acts*, 1918; Buckley, "Prohibition Survey of Florida," 109.

61. *Marasso* v. *Van Pelt, Sheriff*, 81 So. 529 (Fla. 1919); Ch. 7736, *Florida Acts*, 1918.

62. *Marasso* v. *Van Pelt, Sheriff*, 530, 532.

63. Ibid., 533–539.

64. See E. Ashby Hammond, "Foreword," in Jefferson B. Browne, *Key West: The Old and the New* (Gainesville: University of Florida Press, 1973), vii–xxii; Jefferson B.

Browne, "The Super-Constitution," *The American Law Review* 54 (May–June 1920), 321–350; Idem, "The American Law Institute, Its Organization and Purpose," *Proceedings of the Florida State Bar Association* (Miami 1923), 85–102.

65. *Marasso* v. *Van Pelt, Sheriff*, 534; *License Cases*, 46 U.S. 504 (1847).

66. *Noble State Bank* v. *Haskell*, 219 U.S. 104, 111 (1911); Browne, "The American Law Institute," 85–102.

67. *Marasso* v. *Van Pelt, Sheriff*, 538.

68. Ibid.

69. *Daily Democrat*, January 9, 14, 1920; *Tampa Tribune*, January 16, 18, 1920.

70. *Neisel* v. *Moran, Sheriff*, 80 Fla. 98, 100 (1919).

71. Ibid., 105, 106.

72. Ibid., 108–109.

73. Ibid., 112–113. *U.S. Constitution*, Eighteenth Amendment.

74. *Neisel* v. *Moran, Sheriff*, 113.

75. Ibid., 114. Besides *Hawke* v. *Smith* 253 U.S. 221 (1921), for subsequent litigation similar to *Neisel*, but national in scope, see *National Prohibition Cases*, 253 U.S. 350 (1920); *Dillon* v. *Gloss*, 256 U.S. 376 (1921); *Leser* v. *Garnett*, 258 U.S. 130 (1922).

76. *Neisel* v. *Moran, Sheriff*, 120, 121, 123.

77. Ibid., 128, 136, 138, 142.

78. Ibid., 144–145.

79. Browne, "The Super-Constitution," an address delivered to the law class of the University of Florida, Gainesville, March 16, 1920, Special Collections, Yonge Library.

CHAPTER TWO

Concurrent Enforcement of the Liquor Laws, 1905–1922

Soon after the Eighteenth Amendment and the Volstead Act became law, the U.S. Supreme Court heard seven test cases. In the combined *National Prohibition Cases,* the plaintiffs contended chiefly that the Eighteenth Amendment invaded the sovereignty of the various states by sequestering their police powers and infringing their right of local self-government. "[I]f the so-called Eighteenth Amendment be lawful, then the states are not in truth indestructible," charged the distinguished counsel and former Secretary of State Elihu Root before the Court. "It must be manifest that the precedent necessarily erected by a holding that the Eighteenth Amendment is constitutional would authorize the complete subversion of our dual and federal system of government."[1]

Root's argument proved to no avail. The Court wasted little time finding both measures constitutional and concluded that national prohibition had become part of the nation's fundamental law. Accordingly, the Eighteenth Amendment operated throughout the territorial boundaries of the United States and invalidated "every legislative act," wrote Justice Willis Van Devanter, "whether by Congress, by a state legislature, or by a territorial assembly which authorizes or sanctions what [it] prohibits." Finally, regarding Section 2 of the Amendment (the concurrent power clause), Van Devanter concluded merely that concurrent power enabled Congress and the states to enforce prohibition "by appropriate means."[2]

The decision sparked dissent. Justice Joseph McKenna found the phrase "concurrent powers" ambiguous at best and paradoxical at worst. He wrote: "A concurrence of power in the states and Congress excludes the idea of supremacy in either. Therefore, neither principle nor precedent sustains the contention that Section 2, by giving concurrent power to Congress and the states, gave Congress supreme power over the states." And even though Justice James C.

McReynolds concurred with the majority, his opinion perhaps best predicted the powerful constitutional and legal contradictions provoked by the concurrent enforcement of national prohibition. Uncertain about which construction of the Eighteenth Amendment to advance, McReynolds stated somewhat presciently, "A multitude of questions will inevitably arise and demand solution here. In the circumstances, I prefer to remain free to consider these questions when they arrive."[3]

McReynolds apparently realized that the concurrent power clause, as explained in the Eighteenth Amendment and as construed by his associates on the Supreme Court, remained tenuous and subject to further interpretation. The fundamental problem concerned the division of police powers between the states and the national government in regard to jurisdiction over liquor. In other words, did the Eighteenth Amendment allocate an equivalent power to each level of government and, by that, mandate that state and federal authorities equally assume the burden of prohibition enforcement?[4] If so, the establishment of concurrent police powers dramatically increased the likelihood that a citizen could be tried twice for the same crime, once by the state and once by the federal government. The Fifth Amendment's provision that "No person shall be . . . subject for the same offense to be twice put in jeopardy," thus stood directly at odds with Section 2 of the Eighteenth Amendment.[5]

The burden of mitigating such constitutional stress ultimately fell upon the courts. This chapter examines the judicial rulings in state and federal prosecutions that dealt specifically with liquor law and the doctrine of concurrent power. Covering the years 1905 to 1922, the analysis ferrets out the constitutional and case law that judges drew on to formulate their concepts of concurrent power. It also illustrates how the courts fitted judicial precedent with constitutional change by focusing on the exclusive power of Congress to regulate interstate commerce.

As early as 1847, the Supreme Court recognized that the states enjoyed rather expansive authority under their police power "to regulate the importation of alcoholic beverages into the state." In *License Cases*, Chief Justice Roger B. Taney held that "even though the shipment of liquor into a state was part of interstate commerce and thus within reach of the federal commerce power, state regulation of such commerce was valid as long as it did not conflict with any law of Congress." In 1890, however, the Court turned back Taney's judgment, asserting that "commerce among the states is placed under Congress's exclusive authority by the Constitution unless Congress has acted to place it [under the states]."[6] Prompted by these rulings, Congress passed the Wilson Act (1890) and the Webb-Kenyon Act (1913) to unleash the restraints of the commerce clause and to place regulation of liquor trade firmly within the police power of the states.[7] This meant that courts would determine when interstate commerce in intoxicants became intrastate trade in liquor and therefore subject to the reserved police power of the state.

Wrestling with that issue, judges also had to consider the dual sovereignty exception to double jeopardy. According to this principle, an individual who committed a singular act might theoretically violate the law of two separate jurisdictions. Under such circumstances, each authority could bring the culprit to trial without violating the constitutional protection against double jeopardy.[8]

Section 2 of the Eighteenth Amendment created an ideal setting in which to test what limitations, if any, the judiciary imposed on the idea of concurrent power. As it happened, both the state and federal judiciaries discovered antecedents for concurrent power in the traditional ways of allocating governmental authority. These customary methods included diversity jurisdiction,[9] dual sovereignty, and the interstate commerce clause.[10] With this body of law in mind, and perhaps failing to grasp that Section 2 authorized a sharing of unequal power instead of a proportional division, each court system validated the new federal order. Serious constitutional questions then followed, because the exercise of concurrent powers often impinged on the double jeopardy provision of the Fifth Amendment. Perceiving this affront to constitutional guarantees as a dangerous inroad, judicial dissonance arose. State and federal judges then began backpedaling. And as their support for the concurrent power doctrine wavered, these same judges became increasingly attentive to the courts' traditional role as protector of individual liberties.

District courts represent the first rung of the federal judicial system. These trial courts have jurisdiction over cases that arise under federal law, involve representatives of foreign nations, and affect citizens of different states. Between the Supreme Court and federal district courts, the circuit courts operate as appellate courts that limit the caseload on the Supreme Court. To do this they hear appeals from the district courts.[11] During the prohibition era two federal judicial districts served Florida. The Northern District encompassed twenty-two counties in the northwestern and gulf regions of the state. In this district, justices held court at Pensacola, Marianna, Tallahassee, as well as Gainesville. The Southern District's boundaries extended from Duval County in the northeastern section of Florida southwest to the Keys. Courts for this jurisdiction presided at Jacksonville, Ocala, Tampa, Miami, and Key West. One judge, one U.S. attorney, and one assistant attorney served the Northern District, while three judges with the aid of one U.S. attorney and three assistants administered the Southern District.[12]

The constitutional framers originally conceived the federal courts to address matters concerning national issues, while the appropriate state courts would hear questions involving their laws. Until the Civil War, the division of power seemed to provide a solution to the problem of centralized versus local control.[13] During the half century that preceded national prohibition, however, the United States underwent a remarkable transformation as business, industry, labor, and government organized on a national scale.[14] At the same time, the states and federal governments found it requisite to rearrange the balance of power.[15]

In similar fashion, the post-bellum drive for temperance became national in scope. As the anti-liquor crusade blossomed into a full-fledged movement, prohibitionists used the interstate commerce doctrine to further their cause. That is, temperance reformers in Congress attempted to mold the American federal system so that federal law would serve as an important adjunct to state and local liquor statutes. Ideally, no conflict of authority would occur. Instead, the national government would work in harmony with the sovereign states, enforcing the law, preserving order, and promoting the general welfare of the people.[16]

With this republican concept of federalism in mind, in 1905 Florida Representative Frank Clark sponsored a bill that would prohibit internal revenue collectors from receiving special taxes from individuals who intended to engage in the retail liquor trade in communities that had passed ordinances outlawing such business. According to Clark, federalism, as contemplated by the founders of the republic, had given way to what he termed "departmental government." Under this bastardized system, federal agencies such as the Internal Revenue Service had largely "usurped the functions of the Congress and ha[d] prescribed rules and regulations entirely at variance with the spirit and letter of Congressional enactment."[17]

To make his point, Clark cited a federal statute that required internal revenue collectors to conspicuously post for public inspection an alphabetical list of the names of all persons who had paid the special tax within their district. By providing these names to state authorities, the law, according to Clark, was intended to "aid the local authorities in the enforcement of their local laws."[18] Yet despite its intent, the Commissioner of Internal Revenue had issued an order that instructed collectors to withhold information regarding payments of the federal liquor tax from state and local authorities engaged in criminal prosecutions of liquor dealers.[19]

In Clark's view, such departmental orders nullified federal legislation designed to promote the general welfare by helping the states enforce their police regulations. Clark inferred that a notorious partnership between the national government and the liquor interest existed with the intent to defy the authority and trample underfoot the laws of the sovereign states. "There is no escape from the proposition," Clark groused, "that the federal government . . . for a few paltry dollars [has] . . . form[ed] an alliance with persons who are openly defying the laws of the different states."[20]

Clark then turned to conditions in Florida, where two-thirds of the state's counties had passed local option ordinances. Despite these laws, illicit liquor dealers (the so-called blind tigers) still operated and as a rule paid the federal revenue tax required "to carry on their nefarious business." Clark went so far as to suggest that the blind tigers served as a prolific source of lawlessness and contributed to nine-tenths of the crimes committed in Florida. Yet if the federal revenue service prohibited collectors from receiving taxes from persons in dry communities, he claimed, "we would soon have a true and genuine prohibition in such communities." Clark based this conclusion on his assumption that liquor traffickers were "mortally afraid" of federal courts.[21]

Although Clark neither specified nor illustrated why liquor violators feared the federal courts, he seemed to have suggested that state and local courts provided far less support for the internal revenue law than their federal counterparts. Though impressionistic, Clark's account seems to hold up when compared to fresh scholarship. In Wilbur R. Miller's study of federal liquor law enforcement in the mountain South, he has shown that the universal hostility of state officials posed one of the most serious difficulties that revenue collectors confronted. In addition, Miller suggested that the widespread introduction of state and local prohibition laws around the turn of the twentieth century exacerbated the complexities surrounding the ever changing federal system. State and local bans on liquor, for example, clearly deprived the federal revenue bureau of a major source of tax money. Ironically, as a black market expanded in response to the demand for liquor in *de jure* dry areas, revenuers became hard pressed to combat the increased numbers of illicit manufacturers.[22]

In Florida too, state and local prohibition measures agitated state and federal relations. Conflicts emerged over the division of governmental powers and also over jurisdictional matters between state, federal, and municipal courts. As the lower courts addressed these issues during the early 1900s, judges provided a somewhat coarse judicial understanding of "cooperative federalism" well before the U.S. Supreme Court's rulings in the *National Prohibition Cases*. Yet in the end, unlike the Supreme Court, the lower courts construed concurrent power to mean separate and equal. That is, the lower judiciary acknowledged federal authority without compromising state sovereignty.[23]

Long v. *Southern Express Co.* (1912), decided in a federal court for the Southern District of Florida, showed clearly that state legislation designed to restrict property rights in ardent spirits confounded the notion of American federalism. A group of Jacksonville liquor dealers claimed that the Southern Express Company had violated a Georgia statute that prohibited intrastate liquor trade. By breaking that law, the Georgia firm had managed to offer much lower rates than the licensed Florida dealers. Because the Southern Express Company's unlawful trade did serious damage to Jacksonville's legitimate liquor commerce, the latter sought an injunction against the former's illicit enterprise.[24]

In considering this case, the federal district court assumed jurisdiction because the litigants were residents of different states. The next important question concerned whether that court could enjoin Southern Express from committing the acts complained of in Georgia. A careful analysis of federal case law led District Judge John M. Cheney to sustain the proposition. "Where the property injured is within the jurisdiction of the court," he wrote, "a nuisance can be enjoined in another state or district if the court has jurisdiction of the offending party." In response to the notion that the agents of the company could not distinguish illegal shipments from lawful ones, Cheney applied a rule of reasonableness. "If the party presented fifty packages consigned to as many different parties, and daily made such offerings for shipment," Cheney opined, "it might well convince him as a reasonable person that the party offering such shipments was selling liquor."[25]

The court dismissed the claim that the injunction represented a judicial grant of monopoly. According to Cheney, the Jacksonville liquor dealers had a right to sell liquor in Georgia but had to compete with a lower express rate offered by an illicit operation. Such illegal commerce inflicted a monetary damage on the Florida dealers and entitled them to the relief sought. Cheney then issued a restraining order that barred Southern Express Company from receiving or transporting "liquors of any class or kind from any person or persons engaged in the liquor business within the state of Georgia to persons resident within the [same]."[26]

Undaunted, Southern Express appealed Cheney's ruling to the Fifth Circuit Court, where Judges Don A. Pardee, David D. Shelby, and William T. Newman reversed the decree on several counts. For one, they noted that the district court had based the injunction on grounds that the carrier's business violated the prohibition laws of Georgia. But according to Justice Shelby, Georgia, for all practical purposes, had repealed those laws by non-enforcement. "Can the citizens of Florida, whether liquor sellers or not," he asked, "make Georgia's failure to enforce these statutes the basis of a bill in equity?" Shelby thought not.[27]

Furthermore, the circuit court rejected the notion that the express company's illegal sales to persons who would otherwise buy from the Florida dealers damaged the latter and constituted a nuisance. "When it is considered that no names are given of shippers or buyers, or of the plaintiff's former customers, and that it is not stated that they have the same customers," Shelby reasoned, "the interest of the plaintiffs, as asserted, is too . . . vague and general to show with the requisite certainty, pecuniary interest and damage." The court concluded that the mere transporting of the liquors did not constitute a nuisance.[28]

Before the ratification of the Eighteenth Amendment, Florida's Supreme Court had heard numerous cases addressing questions of jurisdiction between separate sovereigns. In addition to establishing a judicial record on concurrent power, the court addressed other constitutional matters. These included double jeopardy; indictments, acquittals or convictions in other states; and the interstate commerce clause.[29]

In *Theisen* v. *McDavid* (1894), for example, a circuit court had convicted the plaintiff of violating a municipal ordinance that banned beer sales on Sundays. In appeal, Theisen claimed that the existence of a municipal statute identical in wording to the state law had subjected him to double jeopardy. Rejecting this argument, the Florida Supreme Court countered that "municipal governments are regarded as separate and distinct bodies politic from the government of the state." Therefore, "the same act may be a violation of, and consequently a crime against, the laws of both governments." In words foreshadowing William Howard Taft's opinion in *United States* v. *Lanza* (1922), the court clearly enunciated the dual sovereignty exception to double jeopardy. It concluded that the state "constitution does not prohibit a second jeopardy for the same act but forbids the second jeopardy for the same offense."[30]

Five years later, in *Sligh* v. *Kirkwood, Sheriff* (1913), the Florida Supreme Court construed federalism in general and the commerce clause in particular. S. J. Sligh appealed a judgment convicting him of violating a Florida statute that prohibited the selling, shipping, or delivery of any fruit unfit for consumption. Sligh, who had shipped "immature fruit" to a party in Georgia, appealed on the premise that the Florida law trespassed upon the exclusive power of Congress to regulate interstate trade. Additionally, he claimed the statute conflicted with the Pure Food and Drug Act of 1906.[31]

In addressing the latter objection first, the court saw no conflict between the state and federal laws. Under the Pure Food and Drug Act, Congress banned commerce in filthy, decomposed, or putrid vegetable products. This included citrus fruit. And according to the court, green or immature fruit posed as great a health risk to the public as the same fruit in an overripe or rotted condition. Since the federal law enjoined the latter but said nothing about the former, the high court left "the field of deleterious immature fruit" open to state resolutions.[32]

What is more, the court found the disputed statute in accord with the interstate commerce clause. Recognizing that the Florida law did incidentally affect interstate commerce by prohibiting green citrus fruits produced within the state's borders from becoming subjects of shipments or sale, the Florida Supreme Court considered the legislation a proper exercise of the state's police power to protect the public health. Speaking for a unanimous court, Justice R. Fenwick Taylor acknowledged that the state could not directly regulate or burden interstate commerce under the cover of exerting its police power. Still, a police regulation that had real relation to and proper protection of the people and remained reasonable within its terms, Taylor insisted, would not conflict "with any valid act of Congress."[33] Two years later, the Supreme Court sustained Taylor's construction of the commerce clause. According to Justice William R. Day, green or immature fruit did not fall within the federal act. Unless Congress legislated "upon the subject," the state remained free to enter the field.[34]

In 1890 Congress passed, and President Benjamin Harrison signed into the law, the Wilson Act. A Republican-sponsored measure, it was designed to "extend congressional permission for the states to control foreign and interstate liquor shipments." It essentially granted states a local option "to do as they please in regard to the liquor question." The Wilson Act piqued constitutional discussions concerning the federal commerce power and state police power that replicated notions advanced in the courts, Congress, and law journals. Senator Richard Coke, a Democrat from Texas, for example, conceded that "the Constitution conferred upon Congress the power to regulate commerce," but countered that Congress could not "abdicate power" as it was proposed in the bill and delegate it to the states. The Supreme Court disagreed. The day after the Wilson Act passed, a syndicate of Chicago brewers and liquor dealers financed a test case heard before the Supreme Court. Speaking for the majority, Chief Justice Melville Fuller said Congress could enumerate certain commodities in interstate trade as "governed by a rule that divests them of that character at an earlier period of time than would otherwise be the case." By upholding the law, the Supreme Court assured that temperance would remain a state matter.[35]

After the Wilson Act but before national prohibition, no dry law was more important for the crusade than the Webb-Kenyon Act. Passed by Congress in 1913, this act banned shipments of liquor into states that had adopted state or local prohibition laws but permitted liquor shipments into states that recognized the right to import booze for personal use. Moreover, it lacked provisions for implementing federal enforcement because drys had always intended that the states would enforce it. The Webb-Kenyon Act, according to historian Richard F. Hamm, "implemented the prohibitionist idea of concurrent exercise of national and state power against liquor, and its passage awakened drys to the possibility of enacting national prohibition." The Supreme Court validated the law in *Clark Distilling Co.* v. *Western Maryland Railway Co.* (1917).[36]

On the heels of this dry victory, in March 1917 Congress attempted to rectify some legal problems concerning interstate commerce in liquor. In the process, the legislature made a significant concession to the dry states. Under the Reed Bone Dry Amendment to a postal appropriation bill, Congress banned interstate shipments of alcohol into states that had outlawed the manufacture or sale of alcohol therein regardless if they permitted importations for personal use. With that measure, Congress effectively converted all dry states to "bone dry" states. Moreover, the bill's passage revealed a great deal about the state of the prohibition movement in 1917. It illuminated the Anti-Saloon League's adept political skills while exposing the potency of the "bone dry" concept. All of this, according to Hamm, helped shape the Eighteenth Amendment.[37]

As drys awaited national prohibition, Florida's federal courts responded favorably to the new liquor regulations. *Ex parte Westbrook* (1918), for example, involved two men who had obtained intoxicants from a Jacksonville dealer, loaded the spirits into their automobile, and began heading to Albany, Georgia. Less than two miles into their trip, police officers stopped the car and arrested both men. While confessing that they owned the liquor, the petitioners countered that they did not consummate the crime charged in the affidavit. Theirs was merely an attempt. Unswayed, the district court advanced a loose construction of the Reed Act and broadly construed the words "interstate commerce" to include "transportation by automobile from one state to another." According to Judge Rhydon Mays Call, a Baptist Democrat, the testimony proved sufficient in demonstrating probable cause. It thus justified holding the defendants on "the prohibitions contained in the act."[38]

Call's judgment in *Ex parte Westbrook* fits the general pattern set by earlier judges in similar interstate commerce cases. In the two decades that preceded the national prohibition era, Florida's state and federal courts had established a judicial record on concurrent powers based primarily on the doctrines of separate sovereigns and the interstate commerce clause. In attempting to balance local demands with federal concerns, judges interpreted concurrent power to mean separate and equal. By that they protected state sovereignty from federal encroachment. Judicial actions in Florida thus suggest that courts limited the reach of the federal government well into the twentieth century.[39]

The day national prohibition became law, the *Tampa Tribune* reported that enforcement would be left largely to state, county, and municipal officials. With that in mind, the Florida Educational and Temperance League launched a fundraising campaign for assisting the enforcement of state, local, and federal prohibition laws in all parts of Florida. The individuals backing the fund raiser planned to allocate $75,000 of the contributions for south Florida's quota. The league expected that they would easily secure the funds. According to a spokesperson, "Floridians generally recognize the difficulty and necessity of wiping out the sale of intoxicants in the state and are strongly behind our work." District Chair Tom Alexander added, "South Floridians are [entering] the enforcement fight with characteristic enthusiasm." Because of this, he anticipated success in upholding the laws and securing the funds. If such expectations failed to materialize, however, Prohibition Commissioner John F. Kramer warned that federal authorities would step in and see that the law was enforced in any states hostile to national prohibition.[40]

With the national prohibition laws in effect, the concurrent power doctrine faced new challenges. To cooperate with the federal government, states had to yield—to a certain degree—local autonomy to national authority. Under those circumstances, upholding federal law without completely surrendering state sovereignty became problematic for the courts. The Florida Supreme Court, for example, had endorsed the doctrine of concurrent power well before the Eighteenth Amendment took effect. The court, however, based its decision that federal law superseded Florida law on a hypothetical situation. The question concerning how judges would respond in a real case involving real people still lingered.[41]

During the interim, the justices of the Florida Supreme Court had an opportunity to consider the concurrent power doctrine and attempt to come to terms individually with the issue. Jefferson B. Browne had already assumed his position in the debate when the controversy arose. In his speech to the University of Florida's law class of 1920, as previously noted, he argued that judicial rulings in both state and federal courts had eased the rapid extension of the police powers. Tyranny, under the guise of progressivism, according to Browne, had replaced the traditional American constitutional arrangement of shared powers and governmental limitations.[42]

To underscore his point, Browne cited *Ruppert* v. *Caffey* (1920), in which Louis Brandeis argued that the state's police power over the liquor traffic included the authority to prohibit the sale of intoxicating liquors. "[I]t is a single broad power to make such laws, by way of prohibition," said Brandeis, "as may be required to effectively suppress the traffic in intoxicating liquors." But according to Brandeis, federal authority remained paramount. "When the United States exert[ed] any . . . powers conferred upon it by the Constitution, no valid objection can be based upon the fact that such exercise may be attended by the same incidents which attend an exercise by a state of its police power." Although he was a longtime champion of civil liberties, Brandeis tolerated government actions under prohibition enforcement that "he almost undoubtedly would have refused to countenance in other contexts."[43]

At any rate, Browne demurred to such judicial rulings. To him, Brandeis's unbridled federal power established an extremely dangerous precedent and posed a particular threat to American republicanism. In his mind's eye such disregard for constitutional limitations could ultimately usher in the dictatorship of the proletariat. That possibility Browne found repugnant. He therefore dedicated much of his intellect to developing a forceful ideological countermeasure to stem the flow of absolutism.[44]

Browne's opportunity arrived in *Hall* v. *Moran* (1921). The case originated four days after national prohibition became law. Dade County Sheriff D. W. Moran arrested Walter Hall for possessing forty quarts of liquor—a quantity permitted under federal law, but a direct violation of state law. Following his conviction in circuit court, Hall appealed and placed before the Florida Supreme Court the problem of defining the new constitutional relationship established by the concurrent enforcement of prohibition. In the litigation that ensued, a wide range of constitutional questions arose: Did the Eighteenth Amendment restrain or annul the existing state laws even if appropriate for enforcement? Did the Eighteenth Amendment ban property rights in liquor? How did the Eighteenth Amendment affect federalism in general and the reserved powers of the states in particular? Finally, what became of state laws that conflicted with the Volstead Act?[45]

Responding to such queries, the Florida Supreme Court upheld all state liquor laws operative before the Eighteenth Amendment that proved appropriate for enforcement. But it nullified any of those that conflicted directly with the Volstead Act. Acknowledging that the concurrent power clause permitted statutory prohibitions of the possession of liquor as a means to aid enforcement, the court said such statutes could not violate any applicable provision of paramount law. Nor could the state exercise its reserved powers, the court insisted, in any way that violated the Constitution.[46]

After reviewing both the Eighteenth Amendment and the Volstead Act, Florida's high court agreed unanimously on the meaning of each. The justices found the Eighteenth Amendment *sui generis* (unique). Whether called a national police or other sovereign power, Justice James B. Whitfield wrote, "It is the paramount law of the United States on the specified subjects." The Eighteenth Amendment governed the operation of all provisions of the Constitution that conflicted with its expressed mandates. Instead of rendering inoperative any state regulations befitting for enforcement, Whitfield claimed that the prohibition amendment merged similar state measures into the paramount federal prohibitions. In short, state and federal powers operated in unison to prevent the manufacture, sale, transportation, importation, and exportation of liquors for beverage purposes.[47]

Furthermore, the Florida Supreme Court agreed that the Eighteenth Amendment did not destroy property rights in intoxicants. Rather, it permitted unlimited possession in one's private home for lawful family purposes. The court believed that with this measure, Congress had bestowed a privilege on American citizens that state authority could not deprive. Such provisions, however, did not preclude a state from exercising under appropriate circumstances its inherent police power to conserve the general welfare. Still, according to Whitfield, these provisions became unenforceable if they impaired, curtailed, denied, or abridged the federal privilege by limiting the quantity of alcoholic beverages that an individual could legally possess. Whitfield reasoned that such laws violated the due process clause of the Fourteenth Amendment. Since federal law stood paramount, it rendered inoperative any conflicting state legislation.[48]

Based on this understanding of the new federal relationship, the Florida Supreme Court ruled that the state law that Hall had violated expressly limited the quantity of liquor that one might possess.[49] The Volstead Act, in contrast, permitted unlimited private possession of liquor for personal consumption.[50] Since the Eighteenth Amendment did not control the difference in the statutes, the Fourteenth Amendment became operative and thus nullified the Florida law because the latter violated the former. In short, Hall's possession of forty quarts of intoxicating spirits "was legal under exceptions that are protected by the dominant law."[51]

Still, the Florida Supreme Court noted that the burden of proof fell upon the possessor to demonstrate that they had legally acquired the alcoholic beverage in question. During the same session, in *Burrows* v. *Moran* (1921), the court heard its first appeal under the altered assumption of guilty until proven innocent. Earlier, on June 15, 1920, a Dade County court had indicted and convicted Timothy Burrows for possessing forty quarts of Canadian Club whiskey. Burrows pleaded guilty, and the court sentenced him to a three-month confinement at hard labor in the county jail. His counsel challenged (as did Hall's) the conviction claiming that the charge of possessing a specific quantity of liquor conflicted directly with federal law, and thus invalidated the state law.

Such reasoning failed to pass the court's muster and it resolved the matter in short order. Because the defendant pleaded guilty and offered nothing to show that his possession was legal under the Constitution, Judge Whitfield claimed, "the plea of guilty gave to the statute its full force." If the possession proved legal under a difference in the statute, Whitfield concluded, "it was incumbent upon the defendant to show it by evidence." Since Burrows failed to do this, his prior conviction stood.[52]

The Florida Supreme Court, however, had more to say on the matter and moved the debate concerning concurrent powers to a higher plane. In reviewing Burrows's appeal, Whitfield and his associates attempted to clarify some ambivalence surrounding the legal meaning of concurrent power. According to the court, the precept was not new. For instance, under the legislature's interstate commerce clause, Congress had conferred upon the state and federal courts concurrent jurisdiction. Such authority, Whitfield claimed, neither dominated nor subordinated in either court, "though the law when enforced remained preponderant."[53]

To make his point, Whitfield suggested that Congress, under its commerce clause, could confer upon adjacent states concurrent power to enforce their respective law on boundary waters, such as rivers, without reference to the precise territorial borderline on land under the waters. This concurrent jurisdiction represented to Whitfield a "separate, equal, co-ordinate power of adjoining sovereignties to enforce their respective laws." Accordingly, such power had reference to a government's jurisdiction beyond its territorial limits and to matters not particularly within the province of another authority. In Whitfield's view, "the Compact between the states with the consent of Congress control[ed] the nature and extent of the concurrent jurisdiction."[54]

Considering the question of dual enforcement, Whitfield anticipated the issue of double jeopardy. Two distinct governments, he asserted, each held power within its jurisdiction to separately enforce its commanded prohibitions. Violators of the specified prohibitions therefore answered to the authority that first attained jurisdiction or the other if the former did not act. This "first come first served" construction, Whitfield argued, gave "harmonious, natural and logical effect to every word of the Eighteenth Amendment." It made the enforcement of prohibition "practicable and universal in every portion of the United States, without conflicting with any provision or principle of organic law." So the idea of concurrent power, in Whitfield's view, proved consonant with the Tenth Amendment's clause that reserved certain powers for the states.[55]

The Florida Supreme Court then summarized its judicial understanding of national prohibition in *Wood* v. *Whitaker* (1921). As in the preceding cases, the court interpreted the Eighteenth Amendment in a way that broadened the scope of federal police power and did so with little dissent. Considering Chief Justice Browne's strong defense of property rights before 1920 and his adamant concern for state sovereignty, the court's consensus then seemed surprising.

Browne, who had likened himself to a man destined to reverse the onslaught of tyranny, for the most part remained silent. In his stillness the aggrandizement of federal authority marched onward. The court, for example, concurred that the Eighteenth Amendment represented an innovation in the dual system of government. Not only did it expand federal power to intrastate control of intoxicating liquors for beverage purposes, but as paramount law it invalidated all conflicting state laws.[56]

In *Ex parte Ramsey* (1920), the U.S. District Court for the Southern District of Florida heard its first significant test of the Eighteenth Amendment's concurrent power clause. A Duval County court had tried and convicted two white men, E. H. Ramsey and Clyde White, and one African American, Rufus Grant, for possession of one thousand quarts of liquor. It sentenced each violator to six months of hard labor. The same three men subsequently petitioned the District Court for a writ of *habeas corpus* on nine counts. In particular, they charged that the Florida law that they purportedly violated had become invalid once the Eighteenth Amendment became operative. From this they deduced "that they were and [remained] beyond the scope of state jurisdiction."[57]

The case unfolded like a comedy of errors. On or about July 2, 1920, C. H. Nesle, a federal revenue agent, seized a forty-foot sea skiff laden with one thousand quarts of liquor at a point offshore near New Smyrna in Volusia County. Nesle arrested the crew for violating the federal liquor law. He then brought his prisoners from the place of arrest to, and up, the St. Johns River to a point near Jacksonville. While en route, a group of Duval County deputy sheriffs intercepted the boat and forced it to shore within the Jacksonville city limits. The deputies then seized the liquor, arrested Nesle and his prisoners, and placed all four in the county jail. Shortly after that, Nesle secured his release. Meanwhile, during the arraignment, a deputy sheriff convinced the other three rumrunners that if they pleaded guilty as charged the court would fine them a small fee, release them, and drop further state prosecution. Perhaps unaware of their legal rights, Ramsey, White, and Grant each pleaded guilty. The criminal court then promptly convicted all three and sentenced them to six months on the county chain gang.[58]

The three bootleggers eventually hired an attorney who sought their discharge based on the fact that when the state authorities arrested the men "they were then in the custody of a revenue agent of the United States government." Because the case concerned federal law and involved a federal officer, Federal Judge Call assumed jurisdiction to inquire into the cause of detention. After considering the Supreme Court's then recent decision in *National Prohibition Cases*, Call perceived no jurisdictional discord. Although violators of the Volstead Act suffered the penalty of forfeiture while the Florida statute imposed either a fine or imprisonment on convicted violators, such differences, according to Call, did not constitute a conflict. He even suggested that the Volstead Act may have been copied from Florida's older liquor law.[59]

Regarding the state's authority to enforce federal legislation, Call said that the Eighteenth Amendment vested certain powers in the states to carry out prohibition. Besides, it made little difference whether the state legislative action preceded the effective date of the amendment and its enabling law. Under the concurrent power clause a state could pass legislation to enforce the Eighteenth Amendment if such laws jibed with federal legislation. Yet regardless of the circumstances, Call concluded that the federal amendment prevailed over prior state legislation. He ordered the three defendants discharged from custody.[60]

In a later federal case involving allegations of conspiracy to violate the National Prohibition Act, Judge Henry D. Clayton (a progressive Democrat and author of the Clayton Anti-Trust Act) reaffirmed the district court's position on concurrent power. Clayton claimed the Eighteenth Amendment simultaneously granted plenary power to Congress to enact legislation appropriate for its enforcement. The amendment did not provide the means for making it effective; that "duty [was] conferred upon the Congress and within the scope of the amendment the legislative branch [could] enact such laws as it may deem proper." Of course, Clayton realized that Congress could not transcend the fundamental law. The amendment, for example, did not authorize Congress to pass legislation that denounced the bare intrastate possession of liquors. "To do this," Clayton asserted, "would be an illegal protrusion."[61]

Even so, Clayton believed that Congress had the power to prohibit the possession of intoxicants, "if the possession [was] inhibited for . . . rendering effective the expressed prohibitions of the amendment." But Congress could not do this, Clayton countered, with the intent of adding a new prohibited act to the constitutional law. "The amendment neither by expression nor implication denounce[d] the simple possession of liquors."[62]

Referring to the Court's opinion in *United States* v. *Jin Fuey Moy* (1917), Clayton attempted to address the above issue indirectly by way of analogy. In the cited case, the Court said: "If opium is produced in any of the states, obviously the gravest question of power would be raised by an attempt of Congress to make possession of such opium a crime."[63] In Clayton's view, congressional limitations of property rights in the less dangerous substance—liquor—raised as serious questions as congressional restrictions of possession of the more harmful substance—opium. The language of the Eighteenth Amendment, Clayton declared, never empowered Congress to make the mere possession of liquor a crime.[64]

By the end of 1921, the concurrent enforcement of prohibition had not worked out as envisioned by the drys. A wet federal judge, William B. Sheppard, castigated prohibition officers "for combing dockets of state courts to find violators of local statutes and bring[ing] them into federal court on identical charges." In addition, the top federal prohibition officer in the state, Judge O. P. Hilburn, said that his officers in Florida had confiscated about $3 million worth of property, made over five hundred arrests, and destroyed over one million gallons of booze. Nonetheless, he noted that federal agents had received "very little cooperation from county officers anywhere in the state." To remedy this situation, Hilburn called on the Methodist ministers of Florida "to see that sufficient sentiment in favor of [liquor] law enforcement [was] created."[65]

Evidently, the Methodist ministers rose to the occasion and had some success in cultivating a favorable public opinion toward enforcement. In fiscal year 1922, the Prohibition Department reported making 564 arrests, seizing 261 distilleries, and convicting 307 offenders in Florida. At the same time, they imposed fines of $34,664 on violators and confiscated property valued at $270,376 in the Sunshine State. And although a few state and county officers had opposed enforcement, according to the Anti-Saloon League, by 1923 conditions had improved compared to the pre-prohibition period. There had occurred "a general tightening up of enforcement . . . in response to healthy public sentiment."[66]

Meanwhile, the courts continued working out cooperative federalism. In the process, they re-negotiated jurisdictional relations between states, municipalities, and the national government. Municipal reform, as Dewey W. Grantham has noted, became manifest in a wide range of moral crusades that included the temperance drive against urban taverns. To achieve their dry objectives, cities passed ordinances that regulated ardent spirits. The courts then became poised to determine whether municipal prohibition harmonized with the Eighteenth Amendment.[67]

In one such action, Mamie Wright filed a petition against Tampa Judge C. Edmund Worth. A municipal judge as well as temperance activist, Worth believed that the citizens of Tampa remained as determined to enforce prohibition as they were to get the measure enacted. The immediate case arose after police officers arrested Wright and charged her with violating the city's liquor ordinance. Wright claimed that the federal government alone had the power to make the possession of inebriating spirits a criminal offense. While conceding that the federal government and the states shared exclusive power to enforce the Eighteenth Amendment, Wright's counsel countered that the states did not have the authority to delegate to city governments power or jurisdiction to enforce the "Eighteenth Amendment or to legislate thereon." In short, Tampa lacked power to adopt or enforce a prohibition ordinance because such laws abridged individual privileges and immunities guaranteed under the Fourteenth Amendment.[68]

A sharply divided Florida Supreme Court ruled that the charge against Wright appeared to comply sufficiently with the statute. Since Tampa lacked the authority to make the possession of liquors an offense punishable in the municipal court, the majority concluded that the state could authorize its cities to enforce prohibitions by ordinances that remained consonant with state and federal law.[69]

After months of restraint, Chief Justice Browne finally arose to voice a dissenting opinion. "The ordinance of the city of Tampa," said Browne, "is but another move in the direction of destroying constitutional guarantees . . . lately inaugurated by the great public thinkers of the country." A person placed in jeopardy in federal court for a violation of the Volstead Act, Browne reasoned, could not again "be placed in jeopardy for the same offense without violating the Constitution of Florida."[70]

Pressing his argument, he claimed that neither the state nor a municipality could divest the federal courts of jurisdiction to try violators of the Volstead Act by simply assuming jurisdiction of such cases. To do this, Browne repeated, would place a person in double jeopardy. The city prohibition ordinance that Wright had supposedly transgressed, in Browne's view, deemed punishable the same offense created by an act of Congress. If so, the plaintiff had become subject to a second prosecution for the same offense.[71]

The double jeopardy issue also started to unsettle the district courts. As this litigation worked itself out, like their counterparts on the state supreme court, federal judges learned quickly that the issue of dual prosecutions proved more problematic than questions of jurisdiction. In *United States* v. *George Adams* (1921), for example, the defendant had challenged a federal indictment charging him with unlawful distribution of liquor, because a jury in a county court had previously convicted him on the same allegations and had fined him $500. After Adams defaulted on payment of the fine, Judge W. S. Graham ordered him "confined in the county jail . . . at hard labor of sixty days." In view of this conviction, Adams charged that the federal prosecution had placed him in double jeopardy.[72]

The Adams case presented the court of Justice Call a hard question to resolve. To Call, the facts showed that the defendant had definitely violated the liquor laws: in one instance a state law, and in the other a federal law. Yet the judge concluded that both indictments charged Adams with the commission of the same crime. Even though he maintained that the state and federal courts held concurrent jurisdiction, Call agreed with Adams. The second prosecution constituted double jeopardy.[73]

Although Call had initially endorsed the concurrent enforcement of liquor law, he appeared less supportive when the use of this broadened police power encroached upon the constitutional protection against double jeopardy. Perhaps a dearth of relevant past judicial rulings caused him to hesitate before responding to Adams's pleas. Or maybe Call realized that his decision would have broad implications. Whatever his reasoning, after much deliberation Call acted prudently and left the question of double jeopardy for another judge to resolve.[74]

It was former President and then Chief Justice William Howard Taft who settled the matter. His decision in *United States* v. *Lanza* (1922) reaffirmed the established principles that related to the law of dual prosecutions. In this dispute, a district court in Washington state had brought charges against Vito Lanza for violating the Volstead Act. The defendant entered a plea of prior conviction in a county court for the same actions but in violation of the state's prohibition law. Lanza based his defense on the grounds that the two punishments for the same crime, one under federal law, the other under state law, constituted double jeopardy.[75]

The district court sustained Lanza's plea only to see the Supreme Court reverse that decision. Under the immediate circumstances, according to Chief Justice Taft, there existed two sovereignties that derived power from different sources. Yet each remained capable of dealing with the same subject matter within the same territory. "Each may, without interference by the other," Taft wrote, "enact laws to secure prohibition." In addition, Taft suggested that each government determined "what shall be an offense against its peace and dignity" and in doing so exercised "its own sovereignty, not that of the other."[76]

Taft then deduced that whenever national and state governments jointly denounced an act as a crime, such actions violated the peace, dignity, and law of each, and both could impose punishment on transgressors. Trial and conviction in the state court, accordingly, did not preclude a prosecution in the federal court nor place the defendant in double jeopardy. The defendant committed two different crimes by the same act. Voting seven to two, the Supreme Court upheld the prohibition amendment, ambiguously defined the concept of concurrent power, and endorsed the dual sovereignty exception to double jeopardy.[77]

With that resolved, after 1922 pleas of *autrefois convict/acquit* (previously convicted/acquitted) arising from prohibition enforcement virtually disappeared from Florida court dockets. Accordingly, neither Browne nor Call, nor any other justice in Florida, felt obliged to object to a dual prosecution instituted under national prohibition. This regional pattern seems to fit the broader national trend for the same period. In his study of the dual sovereignty exception to double jeopardy during the prohibition era, Kenneth M. Murchison noted that few, if any, "decisions reported during the last years of prohibition discuss the dual sovereignty issue." Murchison gave several reasons for this phenomenon. First, some states had repealed their prohibition statutes, which made "successive prosecutions by federal and state authorities" highly remote. Second, other states enacted laws that enjoined state prosecutions pursuant to a federal prosecution for the same act. Third, due to the increased docket entries, "both federal and state prosecutors faced more prohibition cases than they could handle effectively." Therefore they proved unwilling to "risk adverse publicity by prosecuting persons already convicted by another government when large numbers of defendants had never been prosecuted by anyone." Murchison concluded that the dual sovereignty issue almost never arose in litigation, hence "the Lanza rule survived the prohibition era intact."[78]

The evidence in Florida supports Murchison's third proposition, but his conclusion appears overdrawn. Even though the dual sovereignty exception to double jeopardy disappeared in prohibition cases, judges and prosecutors continued applying the doctrine in other areas of law where the states and federal governments held concurrent power. In *Ex parte Sirmans* (1927), for example, Florida Supreme Court Justice Rivers Buford, speaking for a majority, echoed Whitfield's earlier ruling in *Burrows*. "Courts of concurrent jurisdiction are of equal dignity as to matters so cognizable, and the uniform rule in both state and federal jurisdictions is," he insisted, "in cases of concurrent jurisdictions in different tribunals, the one first exercising jurisdiction acquires control to the exclusion of the other."[79]

Even as late as 1968, Florida law provided "little protection for an accused about to be tried a second time unless the prior prosecution was in the same court or one of concurrent jurisdiction."[80] In *Waller* v. *State* (1968) the Florida Supreme Court ruled that "if a person has been tried in a municipal court for the identical offense with which he is charged in a state court, this would not [preclude] . . . prosecution of such person in the proper state court."[81] Likewise, the Florida Supreme Court reaffirmed its position on dual prosecutions in *Hilliard* v. *City of Gainesville* (1968). "An act committed within municipal limits may be punished by city ordinance even though the same act is also proscribed as a crime by a state statute." The court added that "an offender may be tried for the municipal offense in the city court and for the crime in the proper state court. Conviction or acquittal in either does not bar prosecution in the other."[82]

Ultimately, however, the Fifth Amendment prevailed. The Supreme Court overturned the *Theisen* precedent in *Waller* v. *Florida* (1970). Chief Justice Warren Burger wrote, a person "could not lawfully be tried both by the municipal government and by the State of Florida." In this context, the "dual sovereignty theory is an anachronism and the second trial constituted double jeopardy."[83]

In the last analysis, one thing seems certain. The double jeopardy issue stemming from prohibition enforcement proved short-lived, for the threat posed to the Fifth Amendment by the Eighteenth Amendment's concurrent power clause rarely materialized after 1922. On the other hand, the Fourth Amendment, which protects citizens against unreasonable searches and seizures, faced perhaps its greatest challenge during the prohibition era. Yet unlike the double jeopardy issue, the right to privacy controversy did not disappear from judicial dockets. Instead, from 1920 to 1933, courts continuously heard prohibition cases in which the litigation centered on those liberties that the Fourth Amendment guaranteed.

NOTES

1. *National Prohibition Cases*, 253 U.S. 350, 367 (1920).
2. Ibid., 387.
3. Ibid., 401, 392. For more on this see Clement E. Vose, *Constitutional Change: Amendment Politics and Supreme Court Litigation Since 1900* (Lexington, Mass.: Lexington Books, 1972), 95.
4. Department of Treasury, *State Cooperation and State Responsibility under Concurrent Power* (Washington, D.C.: GPO, 1930), 2, 3, 5.
5. *U.S. Constitution*, Fifth Amendment.

6. *License Cases*, 46 U.S. 504 (1847); *Leisy* v. *Hardin*, 135 U.S. 100 (1890).

7. For brief discussions on the interstate commerce law, see *Report of the Attorney General of the State of Florida* (1919), 211–212; Richard S. Mandel, "Liquor Advertising: Resolving the Clash between the First and Twenty-First Amendments," *New York University Law Review* 59 (1983–84), 157–186.

8. In general, the literature on these topics is more legal than historical. See Earl M. Barker, Jr., and Donald J. Hall, "Multiple Prosecution: Federalism vs. Individual Rights," *University of Florida Law Review* 20 (1968), 355–368; Jay A. Sigler, "A History of Double Jeopardy," *Journal of American Legal History* 7 (1963), 283–309; E. H. Decker, "Double Jeopardy in Cases Coming under Both the Eighteenth Amendment and State Prohibition Laws," *Oregon Law Review* (1923), 124–128; J.A.C. Grant, "The Lanza Rule of Successive Prosecutions," *Columbia Law Review* 32 (1932), 1309–1331; Idem, "The Scope and Nature of Concurrent Power," *Columbia Law Review* 34 (June 1934), 995–1040; Kenneth M. Murchison, "The Dual Sovereignty Exception to Double Jeopardy," *New York University Review of Law and Social Change* 14 (Spring 1986), 383–435; Idem, *Federal Criminal Law Doctrines: The Forgotten Influence of National Prohibition* (Durham, N.C., and London: Duke University Press, 1994), 104–125, 177–179, 186–187, 190–194, 237.

9. See Henry J. Friendly, "The Historic Basis of Diversity Jurisdiction," *Harvard Law Review* (1934), 483–510.

10. On dual federalism and the interstate commerce clause, see Edward S. Corwin, *The Twilight of the Supreme Court* (New Haven, Conn.: Yale University Press, 1934); Idem, *The Commerce Power versus States' Rights* (Princeton, N.J.: Princeton University Press, 1936).

11. Merlin Lewis, Warren Bundy, and James L. Hague, *An Introduction to the Courts and Judicial Process* (Englewood Cliffs, N.J.: Prentice-Hall, 1978), 51–74. See also Rayman L. Solomon, "The Politics of Appointment and the Federal Courts' Role in Regulating America: U.S. Courts of Appeals Judgeships from T.R. to F.D.R.," *American Bar Foundation Research Journal* (1984), 285–343; Idem, "Regulating the Regulators: Prohibition Enforcement in the Seventh Circuit," in David E. Kyvig, ed., *Law, Alcohol, and Order: Perspectives on National Prohibition* (Westport, Conn.: Greenwood Press, 1985).

12. Frank Buckley, "Prohibition Survey of Florida," in U.S. Senate, *Official Records of the National Commission on Law Observance and Enforcement*, 71st Cong., 3rd sess. (Washington, D.C.: GPO, 1931), 117.

13. Lewis et al., *An Introduction to the Courts and Judicial Process*, 63–65.

14. See Robert H. Wiebe, *The Search for Order, 1877–1920* (New York: Hill and Wang, 1967); Alfred D. Chandler, Jr., *The Visible Hand: The Managerial Revolution in American Business* (Cambridge, Mass.: Harvard University Press, 1977). Some organizational scholars have utilized similar analytical concepts to better evaluate the temperance movement. See K. Austin Kerr, *Organized for Prohibition: A New History of the Anti-Saloon League* (New Haven, Conn.: Yale University Press, 1985).

15. See Solomon, "The Politics of Appointment and the Federal Courts' Role in Regulating America," 299.

16. Richard Francis Hamm, "Southerners and the Shaping of the Eighteenth Amendment, 1914–1917," *Journal of Southern Legal History* 1 (Spring/Summer 1991), 81–107, 102.

17. *Congressional Record*, 59th Congress, 1st sess., 2861–2863.

18. Ibid., 2862.

19. Ibid. See also *In re Weeks*, 83 Fed. 729 (1914) in which the court found the Commissioner's instructions valid and in accordance with the federal laws.

20. *Congressional Record*, 59th Congress, 1st sess., 2863.

21. Ibid.

22. Wilbur R. Miller, *Revenuers & Moonshiners: Enforcing Federal Liquor Law in the Mountain South, 1865–1900* (Chapel Hill: University of North Carolina Press, 1991), 2, 4, 108–109. In addition, see Stephen Cresswell, *Mormons & Cowboys, Moonshiners & Klansmen: Federal Law Enforcement in the South and West, 1870–1893* (Tuscaloosa: University of Alabama Press, 1991), 154.

23. However, the U.S. Supreme Court shared the lower court's view on dual federalism as late as 1917. See *Clark Distilling Co.* v. *Western Maryland Railway Co.* 242 U.S. 311 (1917).

24. *Long* v. *Southern Express Co.*, 201 Fed. 441 (1912).

25. Ibid., 444.

26. Ibid. According to court records, the Southern Express Company caused a loss to each of the plaintiffs of a sum in excess of $3,000. The record did not tell how long it took to incur these damages.

27. *Southern Express Co.* v. *Long*, 202 Fed. 463 (1913).

28. Ibid.

29. See, for example, *Alford* v. *State*, 6 So. 857 (Fla. 1889); *Ellis* v. *State*, 6 So. 768 (Fla. 1889); *Bueno* v. *State*, 40 Fla. 160 (1898). In *Osborne* v. *State*, 14 So. 588 (Fla. 1894), the court ruled, "The Southern Express Company may carry on any and all business that constitutes interstate or foreign commerce, free from regulation by or under our laws; but business strictly of a state or local character cannot be exempted from our laws, or put beyond our authority, by its engaging at the same time in interstate or foreign commerce." Fourteen years later, in *State* v. *Atlantic Coastline Railroad Co.*, 47 So. 879 (Fla. 1908), the court ruled that "the regulation of intrastate transportation by common carriers is the exercise of the inherent and reserved power of the state. While the Constitution expressly authorizes the regulation of common carrier corporations, it also expressly provides for the protection of property rights against unlawful invasion, whether under the guise of regulation of a public service or otherwise."

30. *Theisen* v. *McDavid*, 34 Fla. 440, (1894). See also *Strobhar* v. *State*, 55 Fla. 167 (1908).

31. *Sligh* v. *Kirkwood, Sheriff*, 65 Fla. 123, (1913); Ch. 6236, *Florida Acts*, 1911.

32. *Sligh* v. *Kirkwood, Sheriff*, 125.

33. Ibid.

34. As quoted in Grant, "The Scope and Nature of Concurrent Power," 1020.

35. Richard F. Hamm, *Shaping the Eighteenth Amendment: Temperance Reform, Legal Culture, and the Polity, 1880–1920* (Chapel Hill and London: University of North Carolina Press, 1995), 79–80, 84, 88–89, 91.

36. Ibid., 212; Norman H. Clark, *Deliver Us from Evil: An Interpretation of American Prohibition* (New York and London: W. W. Norton & Company, 1976), 119; *Clark Distilling Co.* v. *Western Maryland Railway Co.*, 242 U.S. 311 (1917); Webb-Kenyon Act, *Statutes at Large*, 34 (1913).

37. Post Office Appropriation Act, *Statutes at Large*, 39 (1917); Clark, *Deliver Us from Evil*, 127; Hamm, *Shaping the Eighteenth Amendment*, 236–243, 256.

38. *Ex parte Westbrook*, 250 Fed. 636 (1918); Harold Chase et al., *Biographical Dictionary of the Federal Judiciary* (Detroit: Gale Research Co., 1976), 41; "Memorial to Judge Rhydon Mays Call," *Florida State Bar Association Law Journal* 1 (February 1928), 3–8.

39. See Morton Keller, *Affairs of State: Public Life in Late Nineteenth Century America* (Cambridge, Mass.: Harvard University Press, 1977).

40. *Tampa Tribune*, January 16, February 5, 1920.

41. See *Neisel* v. *Moran, Sheriff*, 85 So. 346 (Fla. 1919).

42. Jefferson B. Browne, "The Super-Constitution," an address delivered to the law class of the University of Florida, Gainesville, March 16, 1920, Special Collections, Yonge Library.

43. Ibid. *Ruppert* v. *Caffey*, 251 U.S. 264 (1920); *Hamilton* v. *Kentucky Distilleries & Warehouse*, 251 U.S. 146 (1919). For Brandeis's position on liquor law, see Natalie Wexler, "The Prophet Stumbles: Brandeis, the Bill of Rights, and Prohibition," *Cardozo Law Review* 13 (December 1991), 1355–1368.

44. Browne, "The Super-Constitution."

45. *Hall* v. *Moran, Sheriff*, 81 Fla. 706 (1921).

46. Ibid., 707.

47. Ibid.

48. Ibid. For the Supreme Court's construction of the Fourteenth Amendment's due process clause see *Slaughterhouse Cases*, 16 Wall. 36 (1873).

49. Ch. 7890, *Florida Acts*, 1918, approved May 17, 1919, amended Ch. 7736.

50. National Prohibition Act, *Statutes at Large*, 41 secs. 1, 3, and 33, Title 2 (1919).

51. *Hall* v. *Moran, Sheriff*, 712.

52. *Burrows* v. *Moran, Sheriff*, 89 So. 111 (Fla. 1921).

53. Ibid., 112.

54. Ibid.

55. Ibid. See also *Johnson* v. *State*, 89 So. 114 (Fla. 1921).

56. *Wood* v. *Whitaker*, 89 So. 118 (Fla. 1921).

57. *Ex parte Ramsey*, Case File No. 1094, Box No. 12, U.S. District Court, Southern District of Florida, July term 1920, Federal Records Center, East Point, Ga. (hereinafter FRC).

58. Ibid.

59. Ibid.

60. Ibid.

61. *United States* v. *Dowling*, 278 Fed. 630 (1922). Clayton served as a member of Congress from 1897–1914. In his last two terms, he served as chairman of the committee on the judiciary. Chase et al., *Biographical Dictionary of the Federal Judiciary*, 52. On the drafting of the Clayton Act, see Thomas K. McCraw, *Prophets of Regulation: Francis Adams, Louis D. Brandeis, James M. Landis, Alfred E. Kahn* (Cambridge, Mass.: Belknap Press, 1984), 119–127.

62. *United States* v. *Dowling*, 637.

63. *United States* v. *Jin Fuey Moy*, 241 U.S. 394, 401 (1917).

64. *United States* v. *Dowling*, 637.

65. See Kermit L. Hall and Eric W. Rise, *From Local Courts to National Tribunals: The Federal District Courts of Florida, 1821–1990* (Brooklyn, N.Y.: Carlson Publishing Inc., 1991), 74–75; *The Daily Democrat* [Tallahassee], December 4, 19, 1920.

66. See Ernest Hurst Cherrington, ed., *The Anti-Saloon League Year Book, 1924* (Westerville, Ohio: Anti-Saloon League of America, 1925), 83, 89; Idem, *The Anti-Saloon League Year Book, 1925*, 112–113.

67. Dewey W. Grantham, *Southern Progressivism: The Reconciliation of Progress and Tradition*. 2nd ed. (Knoxville: University of Tennessee Press, 1983), 167. See also Edward Ayers, *The Promise of the New South: Life after Reconstruction* (New York: Oxford University Press, 1992), 169, 171, 178–180.

68. *Wright* v. *Worth, Municipal Judge*, 91 So. 87 (Fla. 1922); *Tampa Tribune*, February 6, 1920.

69. *Wright* v. *Worth, Municipal Judge*, 89. See also *Matthews, Chief of Police* v. *Holloway*, 90 So. 924 (Fla. 1922); *Bailey* v. *Poitier*, 86 Fla. 160 (1923).

70. *Wright* v. *Worth, Municipal Judge*, 87, 89.

71. Ibid., 91.

72. *United States* v. *George Adams*, Case File No. 550, Box No. 5, U.S. District Court, Southern District of Florida, March term 1921, FRC.

73. Ibid. For similar handling of the double jeopardy doctrine, see *United States* v. *Leo Day*, Case File No. 539, Box No. 5, U.S. District Court, Southern District of Florida, March term 1921, FRC.

74. *United States* v. *George Adams*.

75. *United States* v. *Lanza* 260 U.S. 377 (1922); Decker, "Double Jeopardy in Cases Coming under Both the Eighteenth Amendment and State Prohibition Laws," 124.

76. *United States* v. *Lanza*, 382.

77. Ibid.

78. See Murchison, "The Dual Sovereignty Exception to Double Jeopardy," 404–405.

79. *Ex parte Sirmans*, 94 Fla. 832 (1927).

80. Barker and Hall, "Multiple Prosecution: Federalism vs. Individual Rights," 361–362.

81. *Waller* v. *State*, 213 So. 2d 623 (Fla. 1968).

82. *Hilliard* v. *City of Gainesville*, 213 So.2d 689 (Fla. 1968).

83. *Waller* v. *Florida*, 397 U.S. 387 (1970).

CHAPTER THREE

Prohibition and Privacy Rights, 1921–1930

In 1924, the Florida Supreme Court overturned a lower court's conviction against a black woman named Ida Belle Jackson who had allegedly obstructed justice. According to court records, a deputy sheriff and another officer had secured a warrant to search the room of a boarder who lived in Jackson's house. When they arrived at her home, Jackson let them in, directed the officers to the boarder's room, and watched as they searched the premises. Finding no moonshine and annoyed by Jackson's presence, the officers repeatedly ordered her to leave the room. She refused their demands and one of them tried to eject her. Jackson resisted by "biting him on the arm and taking hold of his person in a rude, angry, and threatening manner." Her tooth prints remained on the officer's arm for several days after the incident.[1]

Justice Glenn Terrell wrote the court's opinion in this case. Terrell viewed law as an instrument that served the interests of all citizens. In deciding any case, instead of merely settling a dispute he strove to mete out justice fairly for all parties involved. By doing so, Terrell believed he would attain a proper balance between the power of government and the rights of its citizens.[2] In *Jackson* v. *State* the plaintiff had challenged the legality of the search. Terrell responded that American law "is the child of our Anglo-Saxon liberty which holds every man's house . . . is his castle and which declares that it must not be invaded or [searched] except by a duly qualified [and warranted] officer." Even warranted searches, he noted, were restricted by constitutional safeguards. Small wonder Terrell claimed that when the officers attempted to eject Jackson, she had a perfect right to resist with equal force. The actions of the officers had thus provoked Jackson's violent but justifiable attack.[3]

The above case raised questions concerning the Fourth Amendment's clause: "The right of the people to be secure in their persons, houses, papers, and effects, against unreasonable searches and seizures, shall not be violated and no warrants shall issue but upon probable cause."[4] This wording at once protects individuals against unreasonable searches, while recognizing that the government has authority to conduct reasonable searches based on probable cause. The same clause, when construed narrowly, guarantees what Louis D. Brandeis called the "right to be left alone—the most comprehensive of rights and the right most valued by civilized men."[5]

Despite Brandeis's clear articulation, the right to privacy suffers from considerable ambiguity. Nowhere was this uncertainty greater than in the judicial construction of search and seizure law during the prohibition era. Indeed, the enforcement of prohibition raised many questions pertaining to the Fourth Amendment. For instance, what was the scope of an individual's right to privacy within the context of prohibition enforcement? Did such a privilege extend beyond the home to protect a person operating a private automobile on a public highway? Also, if the right to privacy provided less protection to businesses, how did it apply to persons maintaining an enterprise within their home? Perhaps most important, what constituted a reasonable search?

Steeped in common law traditions, judges grappled with these questions and attempted to reconcile the constitutional stress. Toward that end, they established guidelines for regulating lawful searches, and by that defined the grounds on which the state could seize contraband. As the process unfolded, the courts not only influenced the efficacy of prohibition but, more significantly, they set parameters under which the right to privacy doctrine operated. When applying the doctrine to private residences or vehicles, judges generally assumed a libertarian outlook and advanced a strict construction of the Fourth Amendment.[6] On the other hand, in cases involving restaurants where the division between public authority and private space appeared less clear, judges couched their rulings in republican terms. By broadening search and seizure law for the good of the commonweal, judicial actions ostensibly allowed police officers wider latitude. Even so, the expanded police power proved more symbolic than real, for courts continued to exercise discretionary authority to overturn any search that they found unreasonable. Put succinctly, the courts secured the right to privacy by maintaining taut reins on the police power of the state.[7]

In 1901, Florida's anti-liquor advocates persuaded a bare majority of the legislature to pass a law that empowered police officers "to enter any building, booth, tent, or other place . . . without warrant, in which they had good cause to suspect that . . . liquors were kept for sale contrary to law." A proviso exempted any persons keeping reasonable amounts of booze in their "private residence for private use." Perhaps exemplifying the pluralistic nature of the legislative process, the statute's ambiguous wording limited the bill's dry intentions. The courts ultimately decided how much comprised a reasonable quantity, leaving the judges either to broaden or narrow the scope of the police powers.[8]

To the discontent of the drys, the bill found little support on the bench. In the two decades that followed its passage, the Florida Supreme Court usually secured individual liberties from arbitrary government. The rights of the accused proved no exception, as judges made certain that police officers did their duties within the bounds of constitutional law. Such limitations included the constitutional protection against illegal searches. Florida's highest court interpreted this fundamental right to the letter by ruling unlawful any arrest made without a proper warrant.[9]

In *Tillman* v. *State* (1921), for example, the Florida Supreme Court advanced a strict construction of the right to privacy doctrine and checked an expansion of the police power made possible by the 1901 statute. A Manatee County court had tried and convicted Will Tillman, an African American, of assault with the intent to murder deputy sheriff C. D. Blackwelder. Tillman, in testimony, denied the charges and claimed to have been home when the shooting supposedly took place. The victim, who was the only witness to the incident, provided a different account. He testified that while proceeding in his car, he saw a "negro" carrying something under his arm as he walked along the road. Blackwelder described the package as a gallon jug and suspected that it contained moonshine. He drove up beside Tillman, stopped the car, and asked what he had under his arm. Tillman responded unintelligibly to Blackwelder. Then without a warrant and without disclosing his official character, the deputy got out of his car, walked up to Tillman, reached under the suspect's arm, and demanded to see the package. Wary of Blackwelder's intimations, Tillman pulled out a pistol, pointed it at the deputy, and stated: "You damned son-of-a-bitch, you have been getting it from some of them, but you will never get it from me." Blackwelder then grabbed for the pistol and the two men fought. During the altercation, the gun discharged twice. One bullet passed through the deputy's hat and the other missed completely.[10]

Considering this reconstruction of the events, the Florida Supreme Court found several grounds for reviewing the case. Chief Justice Jefferson B. Browne opined: "No such offense as an assault with intent to commit murder in the third degree existed, because the presence of an intent precludes the commission of that offense." With that matter resolved, the court considered whether an officer without a warrant had "the right to stop anyone on a public highway, particularly in the night time, and demand that he surrender what he has in his possession, or take it from him without his consent." Browne found no justification for such actions. "It is true that in this instance the person who was to be searched, and whose effects the officer attempted to seize without a warrant," Browne quipped, "belongs to a race who some seem to think have no rights that a white man is bound to respect." Yet "such a doctrine," Browne insisted, "has never been sanctioned by this court or any of the courts of this country."[11]

Browne firmly believed that constitutional guarantees protected all classes and races alike. "It is but a step, and a short one," he said, "from violating the rights of negroes to violating the rights of white persons." No matter how enthusiastically an officer performed his duties, "he should not forget," Browne asserted, "that his oath to support, protect, and defend the Constitution precludes his seizing property in violation of the Constitution." On that note, the high court overturned the original judgment.[12]

Even so, the enforcement of national prohibition engendered as many questions concerning privacy as those involving property. In fact, judges often melded the two rights to fashion an ideological bulwark to protect the citizenry from what some judges deemed obtrusive legislation. Such judicial actions were traditional in that property and privacy go hand in hand. According to some constitutional scholars, "search and seizure" in the Fourth Amendment relates to the laws of trespass and tangible property. Brandeis's "right to be left alone" therefore stemmed from the inalienable right to property.[13]

In any case, the privacy issue emanating from a violation of the Volstead Act first reached the Florida Supreme Court in November 1921. The bench reviewed a lower court's judgment against John Haile for unlawful possession of booze. The arresting officers had searched the defendant's home at night and found some moonshine whiskey. Haile's counsel claimed the officers' unwarranted actions violated the defendant's constitutional rights.[14]

Summarizing the case, the court noted that the Florida constitution forbade the legislature to enact laws that authorized unreasonable searches or seizures. It also enjoined shakedowns and confiscations by officers purporting to act under the laws that authorized reasonable searches. The court concluded unanimously that a reasonable law and a valid search are both ultimately for judicial determination. Furthermore, searches lacking proper warrants remain illegal, said the court, unless deemed reasonable as an incident to a lawful arrest.[15]

After heightening Haile's expectations for an acquittal, the court quashed his motion and seemingly provided the police greater latitude to facilitate enforcement. Since the possession of the moonshine in this case was "not disputed by the defendant," the court reasoned that Haile had violated both state and federal liquor law. Nevertheless, Justice James B. Whitfield stressed that the court could and would throw out any cases where the discretion of the arresting officer proved less than reasonable. In doing so, Whitfield clearly articulated the "rule of reason" that became the standard by which the courts upheld or dismissed police enforcement procedures. Flexing its judicial muscle, the high court seized the initiative, checked the legislature's authority to define the extent of the police powers, and reaffirmed its commitment to safeguarding individual liberties.[16]

Florida's dry-dominated legislature, however, would not sit idly by and watch judicial rulings thwart the spirit of the liquor laws. In 1923 the legislature passed several statutes that greatly strengthened the enforcement code of the state by enacting a more stringent search and seizure measure. And two years later the Florida legislature passed a new search law that authorized inspections of automobiles and other personal property for liquor under certain conditions.[17]

Yet despite these more stringent laws, police procedures ultimately had to pass a test of reasonableness. Because the courts administered the test, judges continued determining the reach of the police powers much as they had in the past.[18] In *Hart* v. *State* (1925), to illustrate, the Florida Supreme Court again curbed the legislature's expansion of the police powers. In effect, it restricted the authority to issue warrants to only certain judges or justices of the peace. The court heard this appeal after a jury had convicted G. L. Hart for unlawful possession of one quart of Scotch whiskey. In the original trial, a St. Petersburg city detective, George M. Hazard, testified that he and two police officers had entered Hart's home under the authority of a warrant but against the objections of Hart's wife. While the officers proceeded to search the residence, Mrs. Hart ran into the bathroom and slammed the door. Hazard then allegedly heard the sound of breaking glass coming from the bathroom. On that cue, he rushed to the door, threw his shoulder to it, and forced his entry. Once inside, Hazard witnessed Mrs. Hart and her little daughter destroying evidence by breaking bottles into the bathtub. Caught in the act and enraged, Mrs. Hart struck Hazard in the head with a quart bottle filled with liquor.[19]

After the other officers helped subdue Mrs. Hart, Hazard searched the rest of the premises. He found one quart of gin, two quarts of Scotch, and one broken bottle. Hazard wrapped these articles in a package and later placed it in a cell in the county jail. The parcel remained put until the morning of Hart's trial. On that day, a deputy sheriff delivered the package to the court. However, when introduced as evidence against Hart, the court learned that one full bottle of Scotch had disappeared. Despite the missing evidence, the jury convicted Hart as charged.[20]

Hart challenged the verdict on two points. First, he claimed the municipal judge lacked the authority to issue warrants. Second, he insisted that the court could not use evidence obtained under an unauthorized search, especially when a substantial portion of it had vanished. Responding to Hart's first premise, Judge Jefferson B. Browne agreed that a municipal judge lacked the authority to issue writs. "No officer other than those enumerated" by Florida law, Browne wrote, "has the power to issue a search warrant and any attempt to do so by any other person is a high-handed invasion of the sanctity of the home."[21]

In addressing Hart's second point, Browne felt obliged to quote Francis Wharton's *Criminal Evidence* (1882). "State courts, in some instances in express terms had stated their indifference to the methods used to obtain demonstrative evidence, and refuse to exclude it on the ground that it was illegally obtained. A different rule prevails in the United States Courts." Browne took issue with Wharton's inference that state courts proved less mindful of constitutional guarantees than the federal judiciary. When considering the decisions of Florida's high tribunal, Browne found Wharton's harsh criticism of state courts groundless. Browne then proved his point. Since the person who issued the warrant to investigate Hart's home lacked "authority to do so," Browne ruled the search illegal and Hart won his case.[22]

Legal scholar Rayman L. Solomon has argued that during national prohibition, the Supreme Court resolved major policy disputes that arose from the state and federal courts while the lower federal courts supervised the Bureau of Prohibition.[23] In Florida the district courts and the circuit courts played comparable parts in monitoring federal agents. Throughout the state, federal judges impressed on enforcement personnel that the bench would not tolerate improper police procedures and would dismiss any evidence seized unlawfully.

In March 1920, for example, a prohibition agent forcefully entered Wo Kee Law's home in West Palm Beach, searched the premises and seized eleven pints of whiskey and four pints of Chinese wine without the occupant's consent. The officer arrested Wo Kee Law for violating national prohibition. The accused filed a petition in federal court claiming that the agent had violated his Fourth Amendment privileges by failing to obtain a search warrant. After hearing the case, Judge Rhydon Call agreed and ordered the seized spirits returned to Wo Kee Law.[24]

Yet even an agent armed with a warrant found considerable judicial limitations restricting his subsequent actions. One month after the raid on Wo Kee Law's home, a U.S. commissioner authorized agent L. C. Devlin to search D. R. Armstrong's premises in Broward County. Devlin, however, changed the warrant without the commissioner's knowledge, making it apply to the suspect's house in Dade County. The officer searched the Dade County home, seized some liquor, and Armstrong subsequently petitioned for the return of his property.[25]

Citing the Volstead Act, Judge Call noted that the government could not issue warrants to search private dwellings.[26] He then quoted former Attorney General Philander Knox. "No warrant shall issue, but upon probable cause, supported in oath or affirmation, and particularly describing the place to be searched, and the person or thing to be seized. . . . [W]hether this requirement ha[s] been met and whether the warrant should issue in a particular case, is a highly responsible and important duty." Call then emphasized to the federal agents the sanctity of the home. "A man's private dwelling, being his castle," he charged, "should not be invaded, except and unless it was being partly used for the sale of intoxicating liquor." Since the facts did not show this, Call ruled the search of Armstrong's home illegal and ordered the return of his property.[27]

In *United States* v. *Alexander* (1922), another defendant sought the return of his liquor by contesting the validity of a warrant used against him. Insisting that the warrant's description of the suspect's residence proved too vague because it essentially authorized an investigation in any one of four places, the defense cited *United States* v. *Mitchell* (1921) to clinch its argument. In the earlier and similar case, the contested warrant had authorized a search of an apartment building that contained four units. The defendant lived in apartment number four. Before entering and searching the premises, the investigating agents telephoned the commissioner and received permission to insert in the warrant the phrase: "By order of Comm. Krull, this to specify Apt. 4, especially." Acting under the amended warrant, the officers then searched the place and seized a substantial amount of liquor. The court, however, restored the property to the defendant. The majority reasoned that, because search warrants trespass upon the most important rights of the people, they must "be properly issued in the first instance." When issued, they must be used promptly. "It should go without saying," declared the court, "that they are of such grave importance that they may be amended, if at all, only by the officer issuing them, and then only in conformity with the affidavits or depositions upon which they are based." An all encompassing warrant issued against an apartment house where many families reside, the court added, "is sufficient to condemn it, as it was never claimed that the whole premises should be searched."[28]

The reference to *Mitchell* moved Judge Henry D. Clayton to follow its precedent. Clayton noted that the search warrant used against Alexander failed to particularly describe the searched premises. Because the warrant lacked legal authorization, the search of Alexander's property violated his constitutional rights, making all legal proceedings prior to that warrant void. Yet ignoring his own words, Clayton refused to order the return of Alexander's moonshine because he had distillled it contrary to law. Instead he ordered the booze destroyed.[29]

Of course in many cases a district court's conviction marked the first, rather than the last, stage of litigation. Seeking recourse in the circuit courts, appellants based their petitions on myriad reasons. More often than not, they challenged the reasonableness of police procedures. In July 1922, for example, a U.S. Commissioner issued a warrant to R. F. Stearns and fellow prohibition agent L. R. Cobb authorizing them to search a barn on the premises of W. M. Sutton. The agents built their case on several letters informing them that Sutton stored liquor in his barn. After receiving the letters of complaint, but before the commissioner issued the warrant, agent Cobb, joined by a local deputy sheriff, observed Sutton's premises from a distance of about 125 feet on a moonless night. During the surveillance, the officers saw Sutton go into the barn and return with a small package under his arms. Soon after witnessing Sutton's "suspicious activity," Cobb requested a warrant to search the premises.[30]

Two days after receiving the warrant, Cobb, Stearns, and the deputy returned to Sutton's home. Arriving shortly before nine o'clock in the morning, they found Mrs. Sutton at home alone. She informed them that her husband was away for the day on business. Cobb told Mrs. Sutton the purpose of their visit and gave her a copy of the warrant. She offered no resistance and followed them to her husband's big wooden barn. They inspected the stalls and found several glass bottles plus a few five-gallon containers. The bottles contained whiskey and the other receptacles held a strong wine. The officers seized the liquor and gave Mrs. Sutton a receipt for the evidence.[31]

During the trial that followed, Sutton motioned to dismiss all evidence because the agents had acted under an illegal warrant. The court overruled the objection and the jury found Sutton guilty of violating national prohibition. The court fined him $300 and ordered the confiscated spirits destroyed. Sutton's attorneys then motioned for an appeal to the Fifth Circuit Court, which was granted.[32]

Before the circuit court, Sutton's attorneys again challenged the legality of the warrant. Justice Alexander L. King, however, found no cause for reversal. Cobb's complaint and affidavit proved adequate. The warrant as issued, positively stated and, according to King, "sufficiently described . . . the defendant's premises of which . . . a more particular description . . . was unknown." The court ruled the evidence admissible and affirmed the district court's judgment.[33]

Although Agent Stearns's police methods prevailed in *Sutton*, at times his efforts to enforce prohibition overstepped his warranted authority. On those occasions, the courts checked such high-handed actions. For example, on August 28, 1922, in Bagdad, a small town in the Florida panhandle, Stearns and two deputy sheriffs had entered Rome Pressley's home and searched the premises for intoxicants. In one room they found a gallon jug sitting next to a half-pint bottle. The officers believed each of these contained booze.[34]

Three months later, in the federal court at Pensacola, Pressley denied all charges against him. In addition, he asked the court to exclude all testimony and evidence against him, claiming the officers obtained the evidence illegally. Although the legality of Stearns's warrant remained questionable and though he lacked sufficient reason to suspect that Pressley possessed liquor contrary to federal law, the court refused to suppress the evidence. So began a legal contest that eventually ascended to the circuit court. Like their counterparts on the district courts, circuit judges also attempted to clarify what constituted reasonable searches and lawful seizures.[35]

During the original trial, Agent Stearns claimed that on the day of the arrest he had requested and received assistance from a county sheriff to carry out a liquor raid in Bagdad. When the officers reached the town, a deputy showed Stearns the place where Pressley lived and operated a small shoe store. According to Stearns's testimony, Pressley ran his shoe business in the front room "and the other rooms served as a home for Pressley and his family." In Pressley's absence, Stearns entered through the shop, searched the entire premises, and in one room found Mary, Pressley's paralytic, bedridden mother. Beside her on a table sat the jug and the bottle, which he suspected to contain liquor.[36]

At that point in the trial Pressley's counsel, Lewis V. Trueman, asked the court to strike the evidence due to the dubious validity of the warrant. "No sufficient affidavit . . . or deposition," he claimed, "had been made or submitted to the United States Commissioner." His objection denied, Trueman proceeded to cross-examine the government's witness:

> Q. Mr. Stearns, how and where did you get information that you would likely find intoxicating liquor on the premises of the defendant?

A. Through the mail, sir, I got a letter, sir.

Q. Mr. Stearns, please state whose name was signed to the letter informing you that you would likely find intoxicating liquor in Mr. Pressley's home.

The prosecuting attorney then objected, since the law, he asserted, did not compel federal prohibition agents "to disclose the source of their information in such cases." The judge agreed and sustained the objection.[37]

Upon further examination, Stearns admitted that several years earlier he had imbibed liquor freely but had since quit the habit. He also confessed that he had neither tasted the contents nor made a chemical analysis of it. Nonetheless, based on his experiences and familiarity with the odor of alcohol, he testified that the containers held ardent spirits. The government's second witness, Deputy Sheriff T. F. Hall, corroborated Stearns's account. Even though the deputy had never taken a drink of liquor in his life, in his opinion, both receptacles contained moonshine.[38]

For an expert witness, the government next called on Hal Scott, a former Internal Revenue Service official. During Scott's tenure with the revenue department, he became familiar with the use of a hydrometer—an instrument used to determine the alcoholic content of substances. The government had Scott analyze the evidence. The results of his tests concluded that the jug contained 83-proof and the bottle 82-proof alcohol. During cross-examination, Trueman mocked Scott's expertise:

Q. Mr. Scott, are you a chemist?

A. No, sir.

Q. Mr. Scott, is . . . the use of a hydrometer a means of arriving at the alcoholic contents of intoxicating liquor by specific gravity?

A. Yes, sir.

Q. Mr. Scott, what is specific gravity?

A. I don't know, sir.

Q. Would it be possible for the contents of this jug and bottle to contain a percentage of medicine, say, 2 percent medicine of some kind and 98 percent alcohol, and for you not to be able to determine the amount of medicine by the use of the hydrometer?

A. Yes, sir.

Q. Then you wouldn't say then that there is nothing else in the contents of this jug and bottle except alcohol and that it doesn't contain a percentage of medicine?

A. No, sir.[39]

Trueman obviously followed this line of questioning to suggest that the receptacles contained medicine and not moonshine. To prove this point, the defense called seven other witnesses. The first, Mae Pressley, the defendant's sister-in-law, told the court that shortly after Rome had married (about two years earlier), his father built an addition to his son's house. The father and his wife, Mary, then moved in with their son and his new bride. Rome's parents had previously lived with Mae and her husband. While living with them, "Grandma Pressley" (who suffered paralysis and pellagra) "took a treatment from an Indian doctor" named Wahoo. The Native American gave Grandma Pressley a medication, Mae testified, to take internally and to use while taking a bath. When Rome's mother moved into his home, she brought her medicine with her.[40]

The second witness for the defense, Rome's wife Ellen, claimed that when the officers searched the house, they found the jug and bottle in her mother-in-law's room. She described it as "a special room that Grandpa Pressley built and fixed up for her" shortly after Rome's wedding. "They have occupied that room ever since," and as Ellen put it, "Everything . . . in there belong[ed] to them." In short, the grandparents maintained complete control over their room. By this account, the officers had seized medicine in a room in a house that had served as a home within a home. The contraband did not belong to Rome, and the warrant failed to specify a search of his parents' home, which happened to be a room in his house.[41]

After three witnesses corroborated that the jug and bottle contained medicine, the defense produced two witnesses who had been familiar with Wahoo. One claimed he remembered a Native American doctor who had passed through the county in 1915 and who "was prosecuted for practicing medicine without a license." The last witness, Henry Thompson, a state attorney for the First Judicial Circuit of Florida, took the stand and announced that he had successfully prosecuted the case against Wahoo. The conviction stood and Wahoo ultimately left town. Having no other witnesses to call, the defense then rested its case.[42]

Judge William B. Sheppard presided in the court that heard Pressley's trial. Long known for his liberal decisions, the native-born Floridian was appointed to the district court by President Theodore Roosevelt in 1907. Sheppard had first captured national attention for his prosecution of several Florida peonage cases. His success in convicting and sending many of the worst offenders to prison led directly to his elevation to the federal court. As a jurist, Sheppard brought to the bench even-tempered wisdom and integrity. Although he believed that the excessive caseload that resulted from prohibition enforcement diminished the dignity of the federal courts, Sheppard would not allow his personal ideas to conflict with a legal decision. That said, he had favored the legalization of light wines and near beer, for he thought "insufficient judicial equipment had rendered [prohibition] enforcement futile." While to some contemporaries he seemed somewhat self-contradictory, reporters who were familiar with his court said Sheppard "believed in law enforcement regardless of changing public sentiment."[43]

Sheppard instructed the jury that Pressley had to prove that he had obtained the liquor before national prohibition became operative. And, having legally acquired it, he would have had to register the liquor with the proper officials. If the defendant showed that he had acquired the liquor on a prescription issued by a licensed physician, a conviction could not stand. The evidence here, Sheppard noted, tended to show that the liquor in question belonged to Grandma Pressley and that an Indian doctor had prescribed the substance for her. But the evidence did not show that Wahoo was licensed to practice medicine or give prescriptions for liquors in lawful quantities. A person violated national prohibition, Sheppard concluded, "if intoxicating liquor was on his premises, although not his property, if he knew it was there and allowed it to remain there after knowing it was there."[44]

The jury found Pressley guilty as charged. Subsequently, the defendant motioned for a new trial, claiming that the verdict was unsubstantiated and contrary to the evidence. The court, however, overruled his motion, entered judgment against Pressley, and fined him $200. Since "he was a poor pauper unable to prepay [court] fees or costs," as a last resort, Pressley brought error at the expense of the government.[45]

Pressley's appeal eventually reached the circuit court. There, Judge King was quick to rule that Stearns's warrant "to search a shoe shop" did not authorize an investigation of the premises where Pressley dwelled. King noted that the Espionage Act of 1917 provided the guidelines that authorized search warrants under the Volstead Act. He specifically cited the proviso: "A search warrant cannot be issued but upon probable cause supported by affidavit . . . and particularly describing the property and the place to be searched."[46]

King next cited the section of the Volstead Act that banned issuing warrants to search private dwellings. He noted that Congress supplemented this law with an act making it illegal for any employee, agent, or officer of the United States engaged in enforcing the federal prohibition law to search a private residence without a special warrant that directed such searches. With these laws in mind, King claimed the warrant failed to satisfy all legal requirements. The description of the premises proved too general, since any shoe shop in Bagdad would have fit the description given. And because the search was not within the scope authorized by the warrant, "the evidence," King concluded, "was illegally procured and should not have been received by the court. The evidence was material and its reception harmful error." Consequently, King reversed the district court's judgment and instructed it to grant Pressley a new trial.[47]

Unlike *Sutton*, where the contested search found approximately twenty-five gallons of liquor stored for illegal purposes in a barn outside a private dwelling, *Pressley* involved the search of a person's home that uncovered less than two gallons of an alcoholic substance used to treat a specific ailment. Those circumstances proved the deciding factors. According to King, the former case represented a reasonable search, since the quantity of liquor seized suggested that Sutton was a liquor trafficker. Moreover, because the latter case involved a reasonable quantity of liquor intended for private consumption in the home, the search of Pressley's premises had violated the law.

King's guideline in *Sutton* proved consonant with later U.S. Supreme Court decisions. In *Hester* v. *United States* (1924), Justice Oliver Wendell Holmes dismissed a convicted bootlegger's claim that the Fourth Amendment's protections included the open fields that surrounded his house.[48] In Florida cases, bootleggers often incorporated similar arguments to ground their defense. In 1926, for example, a district court convicted Robert Dexter on three counts against the Volstead Act and on a fourth for producing distilled spirits in an unauthorized building. Judge Lake Jones fined Dexter $100 on each of the first three counts and sentenced him to a year's imprisonment on the fourth. Dexter then appealed the judgment claiming that the arresting officers had seized his property without a lawful warrant.[49]

Based on the government's account, two prohibition agents walking down a public road had seen Dexter standing in his field. They stopped and asked Dexter if they could get a drink of water. Dexter said, "Yes." One agent entered the property and walked over to a pump located next to a shed. Inside the shed he noticed six barrels of mash and asked if Dexter owned them. Dexter admitted that he did. The agent then asked him if it would be necessary to get a search warrant. Dexter answered, "No." The officers proceeded to search the premises and found some additional containers of whiskey and a copper still in operation.[50]

Given the similarities between *Sutton* and the immediate case, the ultimate ruling in the circuit court came of little surprise. Judge Nathan P. Bryan, who once declared publicly, "the individual has . . . inalienable rights . . . which the whole power of the federal government cannot force him to yield up to the brute force of a numerical majority," considered both the quantity of liquor and the paraphernalia seized.[51] He claimed the officers had the authority to make the seizure without a search warrant "because the defendant did not refuse to grant the officers' permission to search the premises." Bryan noted, however, that Dexter "should not have been sentenced on the first and third counts," because the allegation of manufacturing liquors included the other two counts. Bryan sustained Jones's judgment but remanded the case for proper sentence.[52]

In view of the written and unwritten rules that limit government searches of private homes, the state and federal courts in Florida maintained a strict construction of the right to privacy in a home. Judges generally dismissed most cases involving a search of a person's dwelling in which the officer had either failed to secure a warrant, altered a commissioned warrant, or applied a warrant lacking semantic precision. Judges tended to bend the rule of reasonableness, however, in cases where the court believed that the alleged violator was illegally marketing intoxicating spirits. Under those conditions, the courts permitted the police greater discretion in search and seizure procedure.

Because a majority of Americans used the nation's highways for lawful activities, public roads became effective conduits for trafficking illicit liquor. To curb such crime, enforcement personnel throughout the nation faced a daunting task. According to historian David E. Kyvig, the "efforts to enforce prohibition led federal and state police officials to claim new rights of search and seizure," which empowered officers to stop automobiles of suspected bootleggers and examine them without a warrant.[53] But in Florida, judges applied strict guidelines to searches of automobiles on public highways and effectively checked the arbitrary police methods that Kyvig found elsewhere.

In one Florida case, the U.S. district attorney at Tampa filed charges against Tom Allen for unlawful transportation of liquor. Allen testified that near midnight on August 14, 1926, two prohibition agents, without warrent, stopped the defendant's automobile on a public highway in Hillsborough County. The officers searched the vehicle, found liquor, placed Allen under arrest, and seized the contraband.[54]

The prosecution offered the testimony of federal prohibition agent W. C. Crumley. He claimed that before stopping Allen, he had obtained information that some automobiles would be hauling whiskey over the road that night. Crumley's source told him to watch for a Ford coupe, a Dodge truck, and a Studebaker sedan that had blue headlights, a driving light in the center, and a broken window on the passenger side mended with tape. Acting on this information, Crumley and a second agent staked out an observation point near a bridge that crossed the Alafia River. From their lookout, they saw a Studebaker that matched the tipster's description, followed by a Ford coupe traveling about twenty miles per hour. Although the agents saw neither the driver nor the contents of the car, they still proceeded to follow. When asked whether he saw anything when pursuing the two cars that made him suspect that the Studebaker was then transporting liquor, Crumley stated, "It appeared to be loaded and it was rather dirty; it appeared to be on a long drive . . . [and] had mud on the back part of the spare tire cover and fenders." Because of this, Crumley and his assistant drove ahead of the Studebaker and forced the driver to stop the car. They immediately went up to the vehicle, found the liquor, and arrested Allen.[55]

In urging the admissibility of the seized liquors as evidence, the prosecution relied solely on Chief Justice Taft's ruling in *Carroll* v. *United States* (1925). This opinion established that only certain circumstances, such as reasonable suspicion, justified a warrantless search.[56]

In the district court, Lake Jones presided. Jones had a rather unusual background for a district judge. Following nearly two decades of work for the U.S. Post Office, he earned a law degree from Northwestern University at the mature age of forty-two. In 1909 he passed the Florida Bar and went on to establish a successful practice in Jacksonville. In 1924, President Warren G. Harding appointed Jones to a new judgeship created for the Southern District to alleviate its congested docket. Members of the bar and "the largest financial interests in the state" vigorously endorsed Jones's appointment. Drys, however, complained that Jones was "allied with the liquor interest."[57]

In any event, Jones emphasized that the facts in the immediate case had to measure up to the *Carroll* standard but concluded that they fell short. Unlike in *Carroll*, the arresting officers in *United States* v. *Allen* (1926) neither knew the suspect personally nor from past enforcement activities. The information about the Studebaker sedan that the agents had stopped ("the source of which or reliability of which was not disclosed"), Jones deduced, would have justified those officers "stopping and searching any and every Studebaker sedan automobile that might happen to have blue bulbs in the headlights, a driving light in the center, and with dirt on the back of it." According to Jones, when Taft sustained the seizure in the *Carroll* case, he did not intend to grant police officers such discretionary authority. "It would be intolerable and unreasonable," Jones quoted Taft, "if a prohibition agent were authorized to stop every automobile on the chance of finding liquor, and thus subject all persons lawfully using the highways to the inconvenience and indignity of such a search."[58]

Jones considered a federal officer's right to stop, inspect, and seize automobiles on public highways an important issue. As prohibition agents promiscuously stopped cars for inspection, Jones suggested that they inherently marched upon constitutionally guaranteed liberties. "It is unfortunate," Jones insisted, "that the average prohibition officer or agent appears to be under the impression that there is but one provision in the Constitution of the United States, and that is the Eighteenth Amendment." From his viewpoint, the other provisions deserved the same consideration and proved just as binding upon legal institutions of this country as the prohibition amendment. Jones found it "incumbent upon those empowered to enforce the Eighteenth Amendment to be careful at the same time not to violate the rights guaranteed under the Fourth Amendment." Because the facts of the case in question did not measure up to the guidelines set down in the *Carroll* case, Jones sustained the defendant's original objection and ruled the seized liquor inadmissible evidence.[59]

In applying search and seizure doctrine to homes or automobiles, judges had little difficulty in drawing a boundary between the private and public domain. In cases involving private businesses, such as restaurants that catered to an open clientele, judges soon learned that demarcating between the two spheres proved more difficult. Under those circumstances, judges faced a formidable task of reconciling private rights with public authority. As it turned out, the courts expanded the police powers by broadening the construction of reasonable search and probable cause. Yet, with one eye on the commonwealth and one eye on liberty, the courts proved ready, willing, and able to check arbitrary police methods.

In *United States* v. *Diego* (1929), to illustrate, the federal court at Tampa dismissed an officer's testimony because he had waited over a year before filing a bill to abate a nuisance at a Spanish restaurant, which allegedly served liquor and where he had found booze stored in the attic.[60] The government had filed a suit against Angelicio Diego, the owner of the premises, and Joe and Manuel Rubin, the proprietors of the restaurant. In describing the premises, the government charged that the owner had equipped the restaurant with bar fixtures to keep, sell, or barter ardent spirits. The government successfully sought a temporary restraining order that prohibited the use and occupancy of the premises for one year.[61]

The defendants denied all allegations. The premises came equipped with restaurant fixtures they claimed, to conduct a "high-class, respectable restaurant . . . catering to family trade and other high-class orderly and law-abiding patronage." Neither Diego nor the Rubins had violated any law.[62] But according to the government's story, on three or four occasions in late October 1928, an undercover agent working for the Tampa Police Department had purchased a bottle of liquor from an employee of the restaurant. Although the detective usually bought the alcohol in the kitchen out of the defendant's presence, twice the employee walked to another part of the restaurant and gave the cash payment to Joe Rubin.[63]

Besides the sleuth's statement, police officers testified that they had received many anonymous telephone calls, complaining that the Rubins sold liquor at their restaurant. One officer admitted, however, that after receiving such calls, he visited the premises and each time he found no liquor. As far as he could tell, the Rubins had conducted a "high-class, law-abiding restaurant catering to the public to sell food and not liquor."[64] A second police officer, over the objections of the defense, testified that a year earlier he had executed a search warrant at the same premises. During the investigation he found a significant amount of assorted liquors in the attic above the restaurant. The officer did not know who owned the liquor, however, and several days later when he served a second search warrant, he found nothing.[65]

In summarizing the case, Judge Jones made two points. First, all witnesses concurred that the defendants maintained a restaurant that served first-rate food and not ardent spirits. Second, Joe and Manuel Rubin each denied having knowledge or interest in the liquor seized on the premises the past year. Emphasizing that the officer found liquor in a portion of the premises that the Rubins did not occupy, Jones concluded that the evidence failed to demonstrate that the defendants had maintained a saloon. Jones dismissed the charges.[66]

In *United States* v. *Brown* (1929), a similar suit heard the same day, Judge Jones entered a disparate verdict. District Attorney William M. Gober filed a bill alleging that a Tampa building, equipped with a bar and barroom accessories, maintained a common nuisance. As in *Diego,* the government sought an injunction prohibiting the use or occupancy of the premises for one year.[67]

This time, testimony revealed that on June 6, 1928, a lawfully warranted prohibition agent had entered the building and ordered a drink of whiskey from a bartender named Cohen, who served him the drink. The agent then promptly seized the pitcher and placed Cohen under arrest. The same agent, with a different warrant, returned to the speakeasy the following September. Once inside, the agent heard a crashing sound coming from the back of the bar. Smelling an alcoholic odor, he investigated and found two bottles of beer. About six weeks later, two more undercover officers visited the same premises on two separate occasions and each time bought liquor from the proprietor, who was named Wolfe.

Wolfe testified that neither he nor anyone with his consent sold liquor at his place. He suggested instead that two sailors had managed to sneak the two bottles of beer into the restaurant without his knowledge. Regarding the restaurant's bar fixtures, Wolfe claimed that the previous occupants had installed them six years before he first signed his lease. He "sold soft drinks, sandwiches, and cigars and used the back of the place as a gymnasium where prize fighters trained and business men exercised."[68]

Judge Jones said that the facts here were different from those in *Diego*. In the earlier case the warrant proved too general. On the other hand, in *Brown* federal agents had reasonable cause to believe that illegal liquor transactions had occurred. The officers secured lawful warrants and seized certain quantities of booze under the specific guidelines stated in the warrant. Without a doubt, Jones determined, a nuisance existed. He issued an injunction closing the building's doors for a year.[69]

United States v. *Pirl Todd* (1929) perhaps best illustrates the willingness of courts to bend search and seizure doctrine to suit their concept of justice. The indictment charged Thomas M. Chevis with possession of one pint of whiskey and accused Pirl Todd of possessing fifty-nine bottles of home-brew beer. The indictment also stated that Todd and his accomplice, Leo Day, had intended to sell the same beer at their "drink stand" in Tampa.[70]

Leo Day owned and maintained two frame buildings in Tampa. The larger structure served ostensibly as a taxi stand. The rear of the building connected to a smaller structure that supposedly housed a tire shop. In reality the premises operated as a speakeasy and had established an ongoing and lucrative business.[71]

Due to Day's widespread reputation, prohibition agents had kept the buildings under constant surveillance. Evidently, Day's troubles with the authorities reached back at least to 1920, when a state court acquitted him of liquor violations. At that time, one of his employees had testified that Day "was in the bootlegging business and everybody knew it." The employee also informed the arresting officers that he intended to plea bargain because Day would take care of him. Moreover, a prohibition agent who had known Day for about fifteen years testified that three or four months before the raid on October 8, agents had arrested Day at his speakeasy. When placed under arrest, Day asked the officer "not to break the glass around there." He said that he would prepare a box for it, "which he did." Subsequently, he beat a federal prosecution on a plea of *autrefois acquit* (previously tried and acquitted).[72]

The morning of the raid, officer H. V. Colley observed Leo Day's place and saw Todd come out of the building, walk up to a car, and hand a package to the driver, Thomas M. Chevis, a Tampa city police officer. His suspicions piqued, Colley walked up beside Chevis's car and asked him what he had in the package. Before Chevis replied, Colley grabbed the bag and began to examine it. Despondent, Chevis confessed that the bottle contained whiskey and surrendered to Colley. Immediately after that, Colley saw Todd enter the building carrying a bottle. Colley followed him inside and saw the suspect throw a quart of Canadian Club out the window. The bottle shattered on an iron rod. Colley went to the rod, smelled the spilled contents, "determined that it was red whiskey," and arrested Todd. Calling for and receiving assistance, Colley went over to the building that Todd had earlier exited twice. Then without a warrant, the agents broke the door lock, went into the structure, and seized fifty-nine bottles of home brew beer in a tub on ice.[73]

In district court, Judge Sheppard found the search of the car unlawful. "We never yet sustained a case," he quipped, "where the officer had nothing to justify his search or seizure but the neck of a bottle." On the other hand, Sheppard overruled each objection that the defense raised concerning the introduction of evidence seized without warrant or probable cause. Instructing the jury, Sheppard attempted to clarify the Fourth Amendment's legal ambiguity. "The highest courts in the country," Sheppard claimed, have decided that "an automobile or vehicle cannot be searched on mere suspicion, there must be reasonable ground to believe that the party suspected, has in his possession in that car contraband." For this reason, Sheppard advised the jury to acquit Chevis. The bottle seized from him proved too common to raise reasonable suspicions.[74]

Even so, Sheppard claimed that after seeing the bottle of Canadian Club thrown from Day's premises, the officers had a right to investigate the building. "Just as much," Sheppard claimed, "as though they had been armed with all the search warrants in the country." According to Sheppard, any officer witnessing a crime automatically assumed probable cause and became authorized to investigate the violation without a warrant. Failing to see a contradiction in Sheppard's logic, the jury considered his instructions and after considerable deliberation acquitted Chevis but found Todd and Day each guilty as charged.[75]

Crying mistrial, Day and Todd appealed their convictions. They objected in particular to the court's permitting the government to admit as evidence the bottle of whiskey seized from Chevis and the fifty-nine bottles of home-brew beer found in the tire shop. Unmoved, the circuit court claimed the officers did not violate the appellants' constitutional rights. Colley had the right to seize the liquor "as incident to the lawful arrest of Todd, whom he had actually apprehended in an overt violation of the law."[76]

Undaunted, the appellants urged more vigorously (but to no avail) that the government's evidence, at best, showed merely the taking of orders for whiskey at the buildings; it did not show that any "was kept for sale or sold there." To bolster their claim, they noted that the law required the government to prove in essence that the accused maintained a common nuisance. The circuit court, however, believed the evidence had amply supported such a conclusion—the activities of Day and Todd had constituted a nuisance. The facts proved that they had used the office for taking orders and receiving payments for sales of ardent spirits. Furthermore, the evidence demonstrated that they had carried a portion of the liquors stored in the little building into the larger structure on the premises and through it for delivery. Finding no reversible error, the circuit court sustained the lower court's ruling.[77]

On some rare occasions, prohibition violators presumed an absolute right to privacy in the home, forcefully resisted a search of their premises, and killed the investigating officer. Yet this presumed absolute right to privacy in the home did not bear out in the courts. The state and federal judiciary shared similar legal viewpoints regarding justifiable homicide. If a violator took the law into his own hands and killed a prohibition agent in the line of duty, the demand for order superseded the demand for liberty. Accordingly, the courts narrowed the right to privacy while broadening the extent of the police powers.[78]

In *Buchanan* v. *State* (1928), for example, the Florida Supreme Court heard its first and only homicide case stemming from prohibition enforcement. A Taylor County jury had indicted and convicted J. W. Buchanan of first degree murder with a recommendation of mercy and sentenced him to life in the state prison. Claiming mistrial, Buchanan appealed to the high court. While more exceptional than typical, *Buchanan* spawned litigation that provides clues to the nature of prohibition enforcement in Florida. In addition to placing federal enforcers within their cultural and institutional contexts, an examination of this legal contest helps ground moonshiners within their local community.[79]

Buchanan and his wife shared a hardscrabble life in a four-room shack about fourteen miles from Perry, Florida, in Taylor County. One December morning in 1926, Buchanan left his home to go on a hunt. Accompanied by companion D. W. Blue, Buchanan returned home at mid-morning and asked his wife to prepare a lunch for the two men. As his wife made lunch, Buchanan noticed that two men in an automobile had arrived at their front gate. The driver, Jacob P. Brandt, sounded the car's horn and Buchanan stepped out to meet his visitors. After brief introductions, Buchanan invited Brandt and his partner Walter D. Mobray into the house. When the three men reached the front path, Buchanan told his guests to wait there while he informed his wife that they had company.[80]

At this point, Buchanan's account conflicted with the prosecution's reconstruction. According to the government's version, the two agents went to Buchanan's home "for the purposes of making a purchase of liquor, upon which to base the issuance of a search warrant." After the agents asked Buchanan about the liquor, he allegedly ran into his house, secured two guns, returned, and opened fire on both officers. Alarmed and wounded, Mobray tried to escape. He staggered a distance of about twenty-five feet, before falling dead to the ground. Brandt fared no better. Buchanan first shot him with a pistol in the left shoulder. Then as Brandt sought shelter under the house, Buchanan unloaded his shotgun on the helpless officer.[81]

In his initial trial, Buchanan claimed he had killed the officers in self-defense. Despite many contradictions in statement and in fact, Buchanan tried to reconstruct the events to justify the homicides.[82] He shot and killed Brandt because, as Buchanan put it, "he started to shoot me first and I had to shoot him for my own protection."[83]

Later testimony revealed the improbability of Buchanan's account. With the denouement of the courtroom drama, Buchanan's chances for acquittal deteriorated. A sheriff, several neighbors, and his hunting companion Blue testified against Buchanan. His neighbor J. P. Jones claimed that a week prior to the shooting he had asked Buchanan "if he was not afraid to have whiskey in the house." In response, Buchanan boasted that "he would walk over anybody that went to search his place."[84]

Following his conviction in the lower court Buchanan appealed the decision to the state supreme court, which found the original trial flawless. With this issue resolved, Buchanan still had to stand trial for killing agent Mobray. As expected, the second court drama replicated the first. A jury heard the same testimonies and arguments and after comparable deliberation, reached the same verdict. Buchanan again appealed his conviction claiming that the officers had unlawfully entered his home.[85]

The high court again found the appellant's position untenable. When the two men told Buchanan their business, and he acknowledged their mission, he in effect invited them to enter his home and search it. "This amounted," wrote Justice Armstead Brown, "to waiver of his right to demand the production of a legal search warrant and rendered the existence of such a warrant immaterial. It removed from the case the question of the lawlessness of their entry."[86]

Besides illuminating the selective nature of prohibition enforcement in Florida, *Buchanan* is significant for another reason. The case shows clearly that neither the state courts nor the local community impeded the enforcement of federal liquor law. The kind of state obstructionism of federal law enforcement that Wilbur Miller and others have found elsewhere failed to occur in Florida. In Buchanan's case, his peers and neighbors proved his harshest critics.[87]

The federal courts responded similarly to violent resistance of prohibition enforcement in Florida. In one such case, George W. Moore had shot and killed two prohibition agents on January 18, 1930, shortly after six o'clock in the evening. Like Buchanan, Moore tried to beat the charges against him based on the right to defend one's home. But Moore also discovered that, like the Florida Supreme Court, the federal courts found such rhetoric flawed. In short, the courts would not justify the killing of any federal officer performing the duties of his office. Under those conditions, every man's house was not his castle.[88]

The Federal District Court in Miami, under Justices Alexander Akerman and Halsted L. Ritter, tried Moore for using a deadly weapon to resist a prohibition agent in the execution of a search warrant. At the time, Akerman believed that no person had a right to have liquor in his home unless they could demonstrate that it was pre-Volstead booze. And in 1930, that supply, he mused, was "running pretty low." Nor did Akerman think that "the law intended that a man should make a brewery or distillery out of his home." His musings aside, a paper reported that "Akerman did not . . . tell prohibition agents to go raiding [Florida] homes" for he believed "the sanctity of the home is strongly guarded by the courts." As he put it: "A man's home continues to be his castle, if it may not be his brewery."[89]

During the trial, Moore claimed that, as he sat in the living room with his wife and daughter, he heard a commotion at the screen door. When he got up to investigate, his spouse cried out, "Look out, George, they are going to shoot you!" Then, according to this account, Moore saw a man crouching in the kitchen. Moore hastily reached for his gun, just as someone threw his weight against the door and shouted, "Shoot him, shoot him, shoot him!" Moore reacted quickly. He fired a shot through the front door killing the invader and then wheeled around and shot the other intruder as he crouched in the kitchen.[90]

Following closing statements and arguments, Akerman instructed the jury that "the Constitution protects the home of the citizen against illegal searches, but that does not authorize the citizen to carry on an illicit business in his home." And where sufficient probable cause existed, the judge asserted, "a man's home may be just as well searched as his place of business, or the woods behind his house." Though the law provides more protection to a man's home, such protection, Akerman wrote, did not license a person to assault willfully "and kill officers executing a valid process against that home. . . . [To] say I will shoot anybody that comes to my home . . . is not contemplated by the law." The jury then recessed, deliberated, and returned with a verdict of guilty. The court convicted Moore and imposed the maximum sentence of ten years.[91]

Prohibition violators who shot and killed federal officers often cloaked themselves in the common law maxim, "Every man's house is his castle." Yet such twisting of the doctrine provided little defense for staving off convictions. In both the Florida Supreme Court and the federal courts, judges agreed that the right to privacy did not license a person to indiscriminately shoot and kill any intruder (police officers in particular) who came to his or her home. The evidence also suggests, somewhat ironically, that if Buchanan or Moore had not responded to the officers with deadly force, they probably could have successfully contested the searches of their residences by invoking the Fourth Amendment. Instead, by shooting the federal agents, Moore and Buchanan each forfeited his right to privacy and suffered the crushing weight of the police powers when supported by the courts. Moreover, in striking a balance between individual liberty and governmental authority, the courts proved adept at moving in opposite directions, depending of course on the nature and circumstances that surrounded any particular case.[92]

In his study of prohibition and the Fourth Amendment, Kenneth M. Murchison discerned three changeovers in the Supreme Court's concept of search and seizure doctrine during national prohibition. In the pre-prohibition cases, the court advanced a loose construction of privacy rights. A strict construction came next in the early 1920s, followed by ambivalence, and finally returned to a broad construction at the end of the era. These shifts, according to Murchison, closely mirrored the changing public attitudes toward prohibition but also illustrate that "doctrinal growth is not always controlled by some internal logic or some special 'legal reasoning' that is the exclusive domain of the professional." Regarding prohibition's impact on the development of Fourth Amendment doctrines, Murchison claimed that basic rights survived unchallenged because the courts neither fully abandoned the property focus nor granted general warrants. The resulting litigation thus tended to keep the Fourth Amendment's meaning at the periphery.[93]

Although Murchison's interpretation contributes significantly to the literature on the legal aspects of prohibition, it still overlooks the persistence of tradition in American courts. Additionally, because his study assumed the vantage point of the U.S. Supreme Court, it slights the role that the lower courts played in shaping legal doctrines as well as maintaining search and seizure law during the 1920s.[94]

Florida's state and federal court records suggest that Murchison's thesis fails to capture the pliable essence of the right to privacy doctrine or the puissant "contradictions that have beset it."[95] While judges in Florida often determined the admissibility of evidence based upon the "manner in which it was obtained rather than its nature," such judicial procedure did not mark the ascendancy of legal realism. Instead, the use of broad discretionary power by judges when dealing with search and seizure law in Florida shows clearly that a traditional legal culture held sway. Succinctly put, judicial continuity characterized the period of prohibition enforcement in Florida.

Judges in Florida's Supreme Court and federal district courts rooted the Fourth Amendment guarantee against arbitrary searches in the common law maxim, "Every man's house is his castle." Occasionally, the courts did make exceptions and upheld unwarranted searches of private residences, but only if the residents granted permission to search and when the evidence uncovered therein clearly demonstrated a violation of law. Generally speaking, citizens' protection against unreasonable searches of their homes, though less than absolute, proved close to certain.

Such protection, however, diminished in varying degrees once the individual left the sanctity of the home. The courts, for example, permitted unwarranted searches of automobiles on public roads provided, of course, that the officer could convince the judge that he had reasonable suspicion. Businesses, where private and public space overlapped, had even less security against unwarranted searches, for the courts in such cases loosely interpreted probable cause. After a decade of litigation that pitted prohibition enforcement against privacy rights in Florida courts, one pattern seemed clear. Judges demonstrated more willingness to bend search and seizure doctrine in cases involving considerable amounts of liquor intended for illicit sales. The courts apparently found supply-side liquor violations far more contemptuous than demand-side transgressions. In other words, keeping or having a reasonable amount of liquor in the privacy of one's home or automobile for personal consumption proved tolerable, while keeping an unreasonable quantity to sell for profit did not. Because judges ultimately determined the quantity's reasonableness, the amount necessary to establish a violation varied from court to court.

Finally, the Fourth Amendment's ambiguous wording left the law wide open to judicial construction. In responding to enforcement, the courts, to illustrate metaphorically, considered a half-empty glass of liquor a reasonable quantity, while the same glass half-full proved unreasonable. Sometimes justices saw a glass half-empty; other times the glass appeared half-full. Clearly, judge-made law superseded statutory law. Such discretionary power thus enabled the courts to counterpoise pluralistic but contending interests for the sake of social harmony by utilizing common law principles.[96]

In those cases where judges perceived a "glass of liquor half-full," they tended to sustain the search and seizure and order the contraband forfeited. Such rulings, however, merely prompted further litigation, as property replaced privacy as the crux of the legal disputes stemming from prohibition enforcement. Under those circumstances, bootleggers often claimed that the government's seizure of their property had violated the Fifth Amendment's due process clause. In short, judges confronted a dilemma. Notions that condoned deeming private property a public nuisance and confiscating it in the name of the commonweal clashed with the ideal that placed property rights of individuals well beyond the reach of the state.

NOTES

1. *Jackson* v. *State*, 99 So. 548 (Fla. 1924).

2. Doris Terrell Johnson et al., "Portrayal of Terrell: Family Man, Mentor Jurist" *Florida Supreme Court Historical Review* 1 (Spring 1985), 1–13, 13.

3. *Jackson* v. *State*, 548.

4. *U.S. Constitution*, Fourth Amendment; *Florida Constitution*, Declaration of Rights, Section 22 (1885). For more on the right to privacy, see John H. F. Shattuck, *Rights of Privacy* (Skokie, Ill.: National Textbook Company, 1977); David J. Bodenhamer, *Fair Trial: Rights of the Accused in American History*, Bicentennial Essays on the Bill of Rights (New York: Oxford University Press, 1992); Paul Finkelman and Stephen E. Gottlieb, eds., *Toward a Usable Past: Liberty under State Constitutions* (Athens: University of Georgia Press, 1991). For more esoteric discussions, see "The Right to Privacy in Nineteenth Century America," *Harvard Law Review* 94 (1981), 1892–1910; Samuel D. Warren and Louis D. Brandeis, "The Right to Privacy," *Harvard Law Review* 193 (1890), 193–220.

5. *Olmstead* v. *United States*, 279 U.S. 849 (1925); quoted in Kermit L. Hall, *The Magic Mirror: Law in American History* (New York: Oxford University Press, 1989), 319.

6. An "understanding of the political significance of privacy seems to have been deep in ancient republicanism." According to one scholar, "although institutionalized in a way repellent to us: that is, in the idea of oikos, the dominated household to which the independent citizen retired for service (by noncitizens) to his bodily needs for sustenance and release, and his spiritual need for replenishment (by the daily experience of his domestic mastership) of his self-direction." See Frank Michelman, "Law's Republic" *Yale Law Review* 97 (July 1988), 1493–1538, 1535 at note 175.

7. For a counterpoint to this chapter's thesis, see William Cuddihy and B. Carmon Hardy, "A Man's House Was Not His Castle: Origins of the Fourth Amendment to the United States Constitution," *William and Mary Quarterly* 3rd Series, 37 (1980), 371–400. The authors argued that "the Fourth Amendment represented an American extension of the English tradition that a man's house was his castle." While they conceded that "aged British precedents supported an undefined right against unreasonable searches," they concluded that "the particular mechanism by which the Fourth Amendment defined and enforced that right was neither ancient nor British." Likewise, a more recent study contends that the American setting greatly modified the ancient English doctrine of the duty to retreat. According to this theory, a threatened party had a legal duty to retreat "to the wall" before fighting back. An individual therefore could not indiscriminately shoot an intruder in his home. Thus, a house was not always a castle. See Richard Maxwell Brown, *No Duty to Retreat: Violence and Values in American History and Society* (New York: Oxford University Press, 1992).

8. Ch. 4932, *Florida Acts*, 1901; Attorney General of the State of Florida, *Biennial Reports*, 1918.

9. See, for example, *Roberson* v. *State*, 43 Fla. 156 (1901).

10. *Tillman* v. *State*, 81 Fla. 558, 560–563 (1921).

11. Ibid., 564. Browne's comments serve as a foil to Roger B. Taney's ruling in *Dred Scott*. Blacks he said had "been regarded as beings of an inferior order, and altogether unfit to associate with the white race, either in social or political relations; and so far inferior, they had no rights which the white man was bound to respect." As quoted in Don E. Fehrenbacher, *Slavery, Law, and Politics: The Dred Scott Case in Historical Perspective* (New York: Oxford University Press, 1981), 189–190.

12. *Tillman* v. *State*, 564.

13. Shattuck, *Rights of Privacy*, 6.

14. *Haile* v. *Gardner*, 91 So. 376 (Fla. 1923).

15. Ibid., 376.

16. Ibid., 378. See also *Combs* v. *Lake City*, 112 So. 51 (Fla. 1927).

17. See Ernest Hurst Cherrington, ed., *The Anti-Saloon League Year Book 1925* (Westerville, Ohio: Anti-Saloon League of America, 1925), 83; Idem, *The Anti-Saloon League Year Book 1924*, 112.

18. For interpretations along this line, see Morton Keller, *Affairs of State: Public Life in Late Nineteenth Century America* (Cambridge, Mass.: Harvard University Press, 1977); Melvin I. Urofsky, "State Courts and Protective Legislation during the Progressive Era: A Reevaluation," *Journal of American History* 72 (June 1985), 63–91.

19. *Hart* v. *State*, 103 So. 633 (Fla. 1925).

20. Ibid., 633–634.

21. Ibid., 634. Browne cited, Ch. 9321, *Florida Acts*, 1923.

22. *Hart* v. *State*, 635.

23. Rayman L. Solomon, "Regulating the Regulators: Prohibition Enforcement in the Seventh Circuit," in David E. Kyvig, ed., *Law, Alcohol, and Order: Perspectives on National Prohibition* (Westport, Conn.: Greenwood Press, 1985).

24. *United States* v. *Wo Kee Law*, Case File No. 139, Box No. 1, U.S. District Court, Southern District of Florida, Spring term 1921, Federal Records Center, East Point, Ga. (hereinafter FRC).

25. *United States* v. *Armstrong*, 275 Fed. 506 (1921).

26. National Prohibition Act, *Statutes at Large*, 41 sec. 25, 305 (1919) reads: "No search warrant shall issue to search any private dwelling occupied as such unless it is being used for the unlawful sale of intoxicating liquors."

27. *United States* v. *Armstrong*, 506–508.

28. *United States* v. *Alexander*, 278 Fed. 308 (1922); *United States* v. *Mitchell*, 274 Fed. 128 (1921).

29. Ibid. For a guideline on the wording of warrants by Judge Jones, see *United States* v. *Smith*, 16 F.2d 788 (1927).

30. *United States* v. *Sutton*, Case File No. 269, Box No. 7, U.S. District Court, Northern District of Florida, Pensacola, November term 1922, FRC.

31. Ibid.

32. Ibid.

33. *Sutton* v. *United States* 289 Fed. 488 (1922).

34. *United States* v. *Rome Pressley*, Case File No. 320, Box No. 8, U.S. District Court, Northern District of Florida, Pensacola, November term 1922, FRC.

35. Ibid.

36. Ibid.

37. Ibid.

38. Ibid.

39. Ibid.

40. Ibid.

41. Ibid.

42. Ibid.

43. *The Pensacola Journal* April 22, 1934; *New York Times*, October 1, 1925; Kermit L. Hall and Eric W. Rise, *From Local Courts to National Tribunals: The Federal District Courts of Florida, 1821–1990* (Brooklyn, N.Y.: Carlson Publishing Inc., 1991), 74–75.

44. *United States* v. *Rome Pressley*.

45. Ibid.

46. *Pressley* v. *United States*, 289 Fed. 476 (1923). See Espionage Act, *Statutes at Large*, 40, 228 (1917).

47. *Pressley* v. *United States*, 479; National Prohibition Act, sec. 25.

48. *Hester* v. *United States*, 265 U.S. 57 (1924).

49. *Dexter* v. *United States*, 12 F.2d 777 (1926).

50. Ibid., 778.

51. Nathan P. Bryan, "Labor Day Speech at St. Augustine," September, 1917(?), Bryan Papers 1906–1935, Manuscript Collection, Box 19, P. K. Yonge Library of Florida History, University of Florida, Gainesville.

52. *Dexter* v. *United States*, 778.

53. David E. Kyvig, "Sober Thoughts," in *Law, Alcohol, and Order*, 14.

54. *United States* v. *Tom Allen*, Case File No. 1735, Box No. 18, U.S. District Court, Southern District of Florida, Tampa, December term 1926, FRC.

55. Ibid.

56. Ibid. See also *Carroll* v. *United States*, 267 U.S. 132 (1925).

57. "In Memoriam: Judge Lake Jones," *Florida State Bar Association Law Journal* 4 (June–July 1930), 60; Harold Chase et al., *Biographical Dictionary of the Federal Judiciary* (Detroit: Gale Research Co., 1976), 143; Hall and Rise, *From Local Courts to National Tribunals*, 61–63.

58. *United States* v. *Tom Allen*.

59. Ibid.

60. *United States* v. *Mrs. Angelicio Diego, Joe Rubin, and Manuel Rubin*, Case File No. 555, Box No. 110, U.S. District Court, Southern District of Florida, Tampa, March term 1929, FRC.

61. Ibid.

62. Ibid.

63. Ibid.

64. Ibid.

65. Ibid.

66. Ibid.

67. *United States* v. *Brown*, 31 F. 2d 307 (1929).

68. Ibid.

69. Ibid.

70. *United States* v. *Pirl Todd, Leo Day, and T.M. Chevis*, Case File No. 2593, Box No. 36, U.S. District Court, Southern District of Florida, Tampa, July term 1930, FRC; *Tampa Tribune*, October 9, 1929.

71. *United States* v. *Pirl Todd, Leo Day, and T.M. Chevis.*

72. *United States* v. *Leo Day*, Case File No. 539, Box No. 5, U.S. District Court, Southern District of Florida, Tampa, March term 1921, FRC.

73. *United States* v. *Pirl Todd, Leo Day, and T.M. Chevis.*

74. Ibid.; *Tampa Tribune*, October 9, 1929.

75. *United States* v. *Pirl Todd, Leo Day, and T.M. Chevis.*

76. *Todd* v. *United States*, 48 F.2d 530 (1931).

77. Ibid.

78. In ten years of prohibition enforcement in Florida, only nine federal agents died in the line of duty. See U.S. Congress, Senate, Committee on Law Observance and Enforcement, *Enforcement of the Prohibition Laws: Official Records of the National Commission on Law Observance and Enforcement* (Washington, D.C.: GPO, 1931).

79. *Buchanan* v. *State*, 95 Fla. 301 (1928).

80. Ibid., 303–306; U. S. Congress, *Enforcement of the Prohibition Laws*, 160–161.

81. *Buchanan* v. *State*, 305–306.

82. Buchanan maintained that he had "returned the officers' fire when he ordered them not to enter a room where his wife was dressing." See *Gainesville Sun*, September 17, 1927.

83. *Buchanan* v. *State*, 304; U.S. Congress, *Enforcement of the Prohibition Laws*, 160–161.

84. *Buchanan* v. *State*, 304–306.

85. Ibid., 309–311.

86. Ibid.

87. Ibid.

88. *United States* v. *George W. Moore*, Box No. 72, U.S. District Court, Southern District of Florida, Miami, January term 1930, FRC; *Moore* v. *United States*, 57 F.2d 840 (1932); *New York Times*, January 19, 1930.

89. *Tampa Tribune*, November 27, 1930.

90. *Moore* v. *United States*, 57 F.2d 840 (1932).

91. *United States* v. *George W. Moore*; *Moore* v. *United States* 840.

92. See also *Cooper* v. *State*, 143 So. 217 (Fla. 1932); *Jackson* v. *State*, 87 Fla. 262 (1925). For the court's handling of search and seizure involving aspects other than liquor laws, see *Chandler* v. *State*, 113 So. 91 (Fla. 1927).

93. Kenneth M. Murchison, *Federal Criminal Law Doctrines: The Forgotten Influence of National Prohibition* (Durham, N.C., and London: Duke University Press, 1994), 22, 46–104, 123–124, 150–153, 177–197, 222; Idem, "Prohibition and the Fourth Amendment: A New Look at Some Old Cases," *Journal of Criminal Law and Criminology* 73 (Summer 1982), 471–532.

94. Morton Keller, *Regulating a New Economy: Public Policy and Economic Change in America, 1900–1933* (Cambridge, Mass.: Harvard University Press, 1990), 5. See also Idem, *Regulating a New Society: Public Policy and Social Change in America, 1900–1933* (Cambridge Mass., and London: Harvard University Press, 1994), 125–148.

95. Hall, *The Magic Mirror*, 7.

96. Ibid., 223, 264–271. See also Keller, *Regulating a New Society*, 125–148.

CHAPTER FOUR

The Judicial Check on Property Forfeiture, 1921–1930

Forfeiture law is as old as the Mosaic Code: "If an ox gore a man or woman that they die; then the ox shall be surely stoned and his flesh shall not be eaten; but the owner of the ox shall be quit." Ancient cultures sanctioned forfeiture as the "punishment of the personified object for its guilt."[1] The doctrine's place within American legal culture remains moot. Some scholars have claimed that American jurisprudence since its inception found forfeiture "so repugnant to our ideas of justice" that the doctrine never established deep roots in the nation's common law traditions.[2] Others have found an American counterpart grounded in the theory that certain kinds of property can facilitate illegal activities and thus justify forfeiture.[3] Regardless of the debate, there is little doubt that during the prohibition era state and federal law enforcement personnel throughout the nation readily embraced forfeiture as a way to curb violations of the liquor laws. The burden of reconciling the tension between property rights and governmental power once again fell upon the courts.

In the 1920s, the legislative decision to authorize property forfeitures to enforce national prohibition prompted some confounding legal issues.[4] The fundamental question raised in numerous courtrooms nationwide became, under what circumstances could the government order private property forfeited?[5] Even when the contested property itself proved unlawful (that is, liquor) the courts struggled to resolve the matter. And if the property had served as an instrument utilized to violate the law—for example, automobiles transporting or concealing contraband—the legal puzzle became even more troublesome. To illustrate, the Volstead Act's forfeiture provisions protected an innocent owner's property rights, while the older revenue laws did not. Reasoning that forfeiture aided in the enforcement of the liquor laws, federal officers frequently invoked the revenue laws to confiscate the vehicles of innocent owners used to transport liquor. This enforcement strategy produced considerable debate in the various federal districts as innocent owners charged that the National Prohibition Act had repealed the forfeiture provisions of the Internal Revenue Law. If so, they reasoned that the confiscation of an innocent person's property remained beyond the reach of the federal police powers. As it turned out, however, Congress spared the courts the burden of answering this question by passing the Supplementary Act of 1921. This statute assured that the revenue laws remained in force. In short, liquor—though deemed illegal—remained taxable, while automobiles used to transport or conceal alcoholic substances became subject to confiscation despite the innocence of the owner.[6]

Although the two statutes seemed clearly in conflict, creating a situation in which the federal government taxed what it explicitly prohibited, the legal contradiction becomes less bewildering when placed in the context of the nineteenth-century political economy. The Civil War had prompted an expansion of the federal government by creating a need for "a far-reaching system of internal revenue taxation." After the conflict, Congress retained the wartime taxes on whiskey, tobacco, and other commodities for two reasons. First, the government sought revenue to help reduce the large national debt incurred to preserve the republic. Second, Congress needed additional money to finance the cost of expanded governmental operations during Reconstruction. According to Wilbur R. Miller, the "strongest arguments for retention of the taxes, which temperance advocates began to view as an evil of the revenue system, was that the income from liquor and tobacco excises became a significant and necessary component of government revenues." In short, the "war's huge public debt had to be paid off, and as the years went by the government owed more to citizens in the form of veteran pensions."[7]

Furthermore, when the legislature originally enacted the revenue law the American economy had not yet fully institutionalized the notion of consumer credit and the practice of buying on installments. So not surprisingly, when Congress passed the tax measure they showed little concern about possible hardship to innocent lienors. Since the law considered the vehicle itself the wrongdoer, the necessity of rigorously enforcing the revenue law justified absolute forfeiture. The Volstead Act, then, complemented the older revenue laws by constructing what one judge called "a secondary defense against a forbidden use and preclud[ed] evasions by dispensing with the necessity of judicial inquiry as to collusion between the wrongdoer and the alleged innocent owner."[8]

Still, an answer to the question of which federal law applied to vehicles used in liquor violations proved elusive. On the national level judicial rulings established at best a rudimentary guideline for lower courts to follow. For example, when enforcement officers seized a stationary automobile containing liquors and concealing the contraband to defraud the government of taxes, the car became subject to forfeiture under the revenue statutes. But if the driver of the same car had started the engine, released the clutch, and proceeded to move the car a distance covered by a one-quarter revolution of the wheels, the revenue law would not apply. Instead, by a quarter turn of the wheels, the driver would have transported liquor, making the National Prohibition Act operable.[9]

Other issues remained equally confusing, for customs law added to the legal incongruity. For instance, like the Internal Revenue Law, the Tariff Act provided no relief to innocent owners or lienholders. Thus over time district attorneys increasingly relied upon customs and internal revenue laws as a legal foundation for prosecuting liquor traffickers. In doing this, the government hoped to curb the recidivous smuggling made possible by the National Prohibition Act's protection of innocent owners.[10]

Florida courts felt the full force of this constitutional stress and statutory tension. In fact the state's geographic location, coupled with its long indented coastline, fostered the emergence of a lucrative trade in smuggled liquor once national prohibition became law. This condition heightened the legal ambiguity that shrouded prohibition enforcement by spawning jurisdictional discord between state, federal, and international law. Yet when litigation arose, issues that appeared problematic in the abstract became clear, for in the vast majority of forfeiture proceedings Florida courts sided with property owners and thus championed economic liberty against legislative interference.[11]

Before the enactment of state and national prohibition, many forfeiture proceedings heard on appeal in the state's supreme court stemmed from violations of the local option law. These cases invariably turned on the question of whether a dry county had legal authority to confiscate liquor that originated beyond its jurisdiction. In November 1915, for example, Dade County Sheriff Dan Hardie, an avid prohibitionist, seized forty-one cases of liquor from a common carrier in dry Miami. He then placed the shipment in a government building for safekeeping. About four months later, in Dade County Circuit Court, Hardie filed a sworn testimony describing the quantity and kind of spirits seized and claiming that the liquor in question "was intended for sale in violation of law and not for the private use only of the consignee."[12]

Prior to this case, Hardie had established a reputation as a zealot due to his effective enforcement of the liquor laws. After assuming office in 1908, Hardie pledged to close down "every blind tiger in the county." Delivering on the promise, he arrested bootleggers, saloon-keepers, and many others who failed to obey the anti-liquor laws of the county. As a result of his campaign against vice, many blind tigers and brothels moved beyond the sheriff's jurisdiction and established a settlement called "Hardieville." Recalling his tenure as sheriff, Hardie said he showed gamblers and other criminals "the way out of town at the end of a revolver."[13]

At any rate, when Hardie seized the liquor cases (worth $450), they belonged to Gabe Lippman, a wholesale liquor dealer who had operated out of wet Duval County. Lippman held federal, state, county, and municipal liquor licenses. Complying with Florida law, he had plainly and conspicuously marked on the outside of each package the name and address of the consignee, as well as the kind, quality, and quantity of the liquor contained. He had printed the words "Intended only for the private use of _____ and family" on each case and had inserted the name of the consignee in the blank space. To Lippman, each twelve-quart case represented a reasonable quantity of liquor intended for lawful use.[14]

Nonetheless, on June 6, 1916, the circuit court, under Judge H. Pierre Branning, found the accused guilty and decreed that "all the liquor contained in the forty-one cases be forfeited and destroyed." Lippman appealed the decision, citing seven procedural errors. These included Hardie's failure to file his seizure of the liquor with the circuit court within the twenty-four hours specified by law and his failure to properly notify either Lippman or the consignees that he had seized the shipment.[15]

Lippman and his clients had not received any notice regarding court proceedings and probably would not have known of these matters if their attorney, Bart I. Riley, had not been present in the courtroom when Branning ordered the liquor forfeited. Responding immediately to the judgment, Riley gained Branning's attention. Stressing that neither Lippman nor any of the consignees had received notice, Riley complained that "the law had not been complied with in that the information required by [the controlling statute] had not been filed."[16]

With the court's concern then focused on the Lippman case, Judge Branning (trying to prevent a mistrial) directed Hardie to file the written accusations at once and issue the proper service in compliance with the law. The sheriff responded that "if his failure to file the informations within twenty-four hours would invalidate the seizure he would make a tender of the liquors back to Mr. Riley and seize them again." Hardie then turned to Riley and announced before the court: "I tender you back the liquor and I seize the liquor again."[17]

When the sheriff made his statement, the liquor remained locked and sealed in a stone building some two hundred feet from the courtroom. Unabashed, Riley ignored Hardie's dubious actions and concluded his remarks to Branning. The court then set Lippman's trial date for May 31, 1916, and ordered the sheriff to comply with the law governing the filing and serving of charges. Hardie took the affidavits he had signed on March 24 and changed the date to read May 26. He filed those with the circuit court and mailed copies to all parties involved.[18]

Eventually, the Lippman case reached the Florida Supreme Court, which took exception to Hardie's courtroom antics. In a unanimous opinion it reversed the decree ordering the destruction of the forty-one cases of liquor because Hardie had committed a signal error in failing to comply with the law. In ruling so, the court formalistically protected property rights and subsequently guaranteed the right to contract. But in this case the court grounded its protection of economic liberty on procedural error rather than constitutional safeguards. Questions remained unsettled.[19]

Yet before the high court could rule more definitively, Florida lawmakers launched an all-out campaign against intoxicating spirits. In 1917, the state legislature passed, and Florida Attorney General Van C. Swearingen endorsed, a law that enjoined property rights of any kinds in liquors for commercial purposes. With this measure, legislators hoped to "promote temperance and suppress the evils of intemperance." Deeming vessels and receptacles used to contain or carry liquor subject to forfeiture, the act granted lower courts the power to condemn and destroy such contraband after conviction.[20]

Soon thereafter the legislature buttressed another perceived weakness in the local option law by prohibiting the shipment or receipt of intoxicants from wet to dry counties. It also banned property rights in liquor in counties that had voted dry in local elections. The so-called Wells Quart Law, as previously discussed, was ruled unconstitutional by the Florida Supreme Court. Speaking for the majority, Chief Justice R. Fenwick Taylor asserted that the legislature had overstepped its constitutional authority by restricting the private ownership or personal use of liquors. While conceding that the liquor traffic was subject to the police power, Taylor claimed that the property right was not.[21]

Again, this setback failed to stem the tide of liquor reform, for a main goal of the dry crusade was achieved in late 1918. As noted, in a joint resolution the legislature amended the state constitution to prohibit the manufacture, sale, barter, or exchange of all intoxicating liquors in the state. Effective January 1, 1919, the constitutional alteration, coupled with its enabling statute, made Florida a "bone dry" state.[22]

Although the first test of state prohibition did not bear directly on forfeiture law, the judicial debate over the power of the legislature to restrict property rights in liquor did establish parameters for future constitutional and judicial discourse. In *Marasso* v. *Van Pelt, Sheriff* (1919), a polarized court voted three to two and upheld the constitutional restriction on liquor as a proper exercise of the state's police power. According to Justice James B. Whitfield, the police power of the state covered all matters that bore directly on individuals and the collective welfare of the people. It applied to every environment and all activities of human life including the family home, businesses, and public spaces. Whitfield concluded that the exercise of the police power could not be halted by the acquisition of property that is subject to such power.[23]

Chief Justice Jefferson B. Browne, who sanctified individual property rights, dissented. While conceding that life and property "may be forfeited by the state by due process," Browne retorted that the state could not confiscate property "by mere legislative enactment." Viewing Florida's prohibition law as an example of the proletariat using "its political supremacy to wrest by degrees all capital from the bourgeoisie," he feared a nonviolent but imminent Marxist revolution. "It is a short step," Browne reasoned, "from abolishing private property in intoxicating liquors to abolishing without compensation private property in lands, manufacturing, capital, railroads, or other public utilities." Perhaps caught up in the wave of hysteria that swept the nation during the Red

Scare of 1919–1920, Browne advised that the court "check further inroads upon the rights of property" before it became too late. If the courts failed to act, he warned, the American republic would suffer the combined destruction of its free institutions and constitutional guarantees.[24]

Although Whitfield's rhetoric in *Marasso* persuaded the majority of the court to broaden the scope of police powers, his reasoning failed to anticipate two future events. In the first place, numerous constitutional battles between property and prohibition lay ahead. Second, his judgment did not resolve the dispute between the two key contestants—Antonio Marasso and J. C. Van Pelt, Escambia County Sheriff. On January 28, 1919, Van Pelt discovered seven barrels of wine totaling about three hundred gallons in a Pensacola building that Marasso and several others had occupied. Van Pelt seized the wine and again charged Marasso with unlawful possession under Florida's prohibition law. In the ensuing litigation the circuit court found Marasso guilty as charged and ordered the seized liquors destroyed. Marasso appealed the decision to the state supreme court, thus raising several serious constitutional questions inherent in the enforcement of Florida's statewide liquor ban.[25]

The case that followed, *In re Seven Barrels of Wine* (1920), proved problematic. On the one hand, the Florida Supreme Court heard Marasso's appeal exactly two days before the Eighteenth Amendment to the federal Constitution effectively superseded the state law that the claimant allegedly violated. And on the other hand, unlike *Lippman*, which preceded national prohibition and involved a violation wholly within the state's jurisdiction, Marasso's appeal took place after the ratification of the Eighteenth Amendment and concerned not only state and federal regulations but also the laws of Italy. So the circumstances under which Marasso came into possession of the seven barrels of wine contributed still more to the legal and jurisdictional confusion that surrounded the case.[26]

The seven barrels of wine in Marasso's possession actually belonged to Phillipo Caffiero, master of the Italian steamer *Luchiano Manara*, a vessel engaged in foreign commerce between ports in the United States and the Kingdom of Italy. Caffiero had directed a subordinate to buy twenty-seven barrels of wine for the ship's store. At the time, Italian law stipulated that shipmasters furnish a certain quantity of wine daily to each crew member. Pursuant to Caffiero's instructions, the underling purchased the requested wine at New Orleans and shipped it to Pensacola where it arrived sometime in mid-October 1918. The *Luchiano Manara* then took on board twenty of the barrels, left the remaining seven with Marasso, and paid the purchase price of $79 for all twenty barrels. Before the ship returned for the seven other barrels of wine, however, the state prohibition law had gone into effect, and Van Pelt had seized the wine that Caffiero had left behind.[27]

Marasso and the other claimants did not belong to a smuggling operation. Instead, they had served as ship chandlers. To secure the business of a ship, chandlers customarily acted under the instructions and directions of a vessel's master to purchase and hold for the captain any items that the chandler did not carry in trade. Any article the chandler held (whether paid for or not) remained the ship's property until called for and taken up by the ship. The claimants were in a predicament. The sheriff had seized from them wine belonging to the ship, making it impossible for the claimants to deliver the property to its rightful owner. Since the master did not receive the remaining seven barrels of wine, he did not make further payment. Therefore, besides receiving allegations that they had violated the law, the claimants suffered a financial loss they could never recoup.[28] After reviewing the facts, the Florida Supreme Court agreed that the claimants had legally possessed the wine. This condition then brought into question whether Florida's statewide prohibition applied generally to intoxicants lawfully acquired and possessed in the state before its adoption. This question was especially relevant since the claimants lacked an opportunity to legally dispossess themselves of the wine before the seizure occurred.[29]

The court ruled that enforcement of this legislation could ultimately deprive persons of property in violation of the Fourteenth Amendment's due process clause. The provisions of the federal and state constitutions that secured property rights against invasion (here, destruction by state authority), the court insisted, limit the lawmaking power of the legislature, as well as the powers of the other departments of the state government. Although necessary to conserve individual rights and the public welfare, "the police power of the state is not absolute," the court claimed.[30]

The court then addressed other matters of constitutional law including the construction of statutes. In determining the legality and effect of a statutory regulation, the court directed judges to ascertain the legislative intent of the act, and if permissible, construct and effectuate the statute so as "to conform to rather than violate applicable provisions and principles of the state and federal constitutions." The court favored a "constitutional construction" because it assumed that the legislature intended the enactment to agree with the fundamental law. Ultimately, the court decided that the claimants did not have an opportunity to dispose of the wine in their possession before the constitutional revisions became operable. Since they had lawfully purchased the wine for use on a foreign vessel, and the evidence failed to show an intent to illegally sell or transport the wine, the Florida Supreme Court reversed the decree and ordered the seven barrels of wine returned.[31]

In forfeiture proceedings against automobiles used for transporting or concealing liquor, the court assumed a position on property rights more in tune with Browne than with Whitfield. In general, when the seized vehicle belonged to an innocent owner, high court judges curbed the police powers of the state. In *Spratt* v. *Gray* (1921), for example, Simon Spratt appealed a judgment by a Leon County court which stripped him of title to his automobile because the vehicle had unlawfully transported intoxicating spirits. Although he owned the car, the appellant did not participate directly or indirectly in the actual crime. And even though the circuit court had subpoenaed him to appear as a witness in the forfeiture proceedings, Spratt never received his summons. Therefore, he failed to appear in court. Additionally, the prosecution neglected to publish or post the condemnation and forfeiture proceedings at the courthouse door as mandated whenever an owner had not received notice of a confiscation.[32]

The Florida Supreme Court understood the statute to mean that the state could not confiscate an innocent owner's automobile even when used in the unlawful transportation of liquor. Moreover, if the owner had not received notice, any such proceeding would remain "ineffectual to divest." The court concluded that the prosecution failed to provide the appellant an adequate opportunity to defend his property rights. Because the condemnation and sale of Spratt's automobile occurred without lawful authority, the forfeiture proceeding became void. Thus the trial court had erred in directing a verdict for Gray and in overruling the motion for a new trial. In a unanimous decision the supreme court reversed the lower court's judgment.[33]

In similar fashion, in *Armstrong* v. *State* (1923), the appellant sought the return of his Ford truck—confiscated for liquor transportation—that the circuit court of Duval County had ordered forfeited. On the evening of May 11, 1922, Duval County deputy sheriffs seized the truck on a public highway because an informant had given the officers its license number and had told them that the vehicle transported moonshine whiskey on a regular basis. At the time of the seizure, C. F. Stokes and Claud Sweat had charge of the truck with its cargo of 120 gallons of moonshine whiskey, a large part of which the suspects had discharged from the vehicle during their attempted escape. The officers arrested both men for illegally transporting liquor.[34]

Caught red-handed, Stokes testified sheepishly that he had obtained the moonshine from a man who claimed to be a federal marshal. The pretender had stopped Stokes on the road and asked him to "haul it." Although Stokes did not say where or for what reason the alleged marshal requested him to transport the liquor, he did testify that his employer and uncle, S. B. Armstrong, owned the Ford truck and that Armstrong had never authorized him to use the vehicle for unlawful purposes. Stokes, in short, had used the truck on this occasion without his uncle's consent or knowledge. Armstrong's testimony verified his nephew's account. In addition, Armstrong insisted that he had not learned that Stokes had illegally used his truck until after the authorities had officially notified him. Pleading total innocence, he refused to assume responsibility for his nephew's actions and demanded that the state return his property.[35]

Convinced of Armstrong's innocence, the court claimed the evidence failed to show beyond a reasonable doubt that Armstrong knew beforehand that his nephew would use the truck to violate prohibition. The statute in question required proof that the accused had acted either as a principal in the first or second degree or as an accessory, before the state could legally confiscate a person's property. Since the state failed to prove Armstrong's culpability, the court unanimously reversed the judgment against him and ordered Duval County to return the Ford truck to its rightful owner.[36]

The court's rulings in the two preceding cases suggest that Florida's highest tribunal had not yet adopted the "family purpose" doctrine that had developed in many courts throughout the South and West (but not the more conservative East) during the 1920s. This doctrine, according to Morton Keller, "held that the purpose . . . of a family's car was pleasure; thus, when a family member drove it, he was acting as the agent of the car's owner. In this way the father-owner could be held liable for his agent-son's tort."[37] By failing to hold the father-owner liable, the Florida Supreme Court had strengthened "the bulwarks of vested rights."[38]

On May 20, 1930, to clarify some ambiguity concerning forfeiture proceedings, Florida Attorney General Fred H. Davis provided a guideline for state prosecutors. According to Davis, state law expressly and unequivocally enjoined property rights in alcoholic beverages or distilling apparatus. By implication, the specific statute authorized "the seizing officer to destroy intoxicating liquors taken into his custody without an order of the Court permitting such destruction . . . regardless of the adjudication of forfeiture." Of course, Davis realized that the officer "did this at his own risk, and his only absolute protection [was] to follow the procedure outlined by law so as to cut off any possible lawful claim, such as might be asserted under those rare instances which permit lawful possession of liquor." Davis added that Florida's forfeiture proceedings covered primarily "those things which are not contraband per se, for example, automobiles and the like."[39]

It turned out that Florida judges seldom ordered the confiscation of non-contraband. In the few exceptions in which the Florida Supreme Court did order forfeitures, the property owner had served as an accessory to the crime. In *State* v. *One Hudson Roadster* (1932), for example, the court, perhaps with Davis's construction in mind, upheld the state's appeal from the circuit court for Jackson County. In the original case the circuit court had convicted Ben C. Hughes for transporting a gallon of moonshine on a public highway in Jackson County and had seized the automobile used in the crime. One week later Mrs. Ben C. Hughes intervened by filing an affidavit that claimed she owned the seized automobile. After due consideration Judge Amos Lewis dismissed her claim and decreed "that Ben C. Hughes pay all the costs accrued in this cause" and then, somewhat unexpectedly, ordered the sheriff to return the automobile to Hughes.[40]

Chief Justice Rivers Buford, however, claimed that since the circuit judge had determined that Ben C. Hughes owned and used the automobile for the illicit transportation of booze, it followed that "the automobile must be declared forfeited to the State of Florida" and that Lewis's order constituted error. In a unanimous decision the court reversed the decree and remanded the case.[41]

The Florida Supreme Court rulings on forfeiture clearly underscored how significant property rights were within the context of prohibition enforcement. Though a divergence had become manifest during prohibition between what the Florida Supreme Court found as good law and what the lower trial courts did, this deviation does not suggest that the high court judges were necessarily more sensitive to property rights than their lower court counterparts. The lower courts were apparently more willing to sanction forfeiture than the state's highest court because the original trial concerned matters of criminal law and questions of culpability. Once that court found the defendant guilty of violating the liquor law, judges merely confiscated the property in compliance with existing statutes. Put simply, during the initial litigation the property issue remained unchallenged.

By appealing a lower court's forfeiture ruling to the state's supreme court, however, the accused had changed the nature of the legal contest. That is, the case became a civil dispute in which property rights emerged as the principal point of contention. Thus even though the Florida Supreme Court invariably overturned the forfeiture orders of the lower courts, the two judicial levels had not become locked in disagreement over property rights. Instead, the high court and lower courts had merely reached dissimilar decisions based on disparate legal questions that stemmed directly from the appeal process. A similar pattern of forfeiture litigation unfolded in Florida's federal courts.

The first major test of property forfeiture in the Southern District of Florida, *United States* v. *One Haynes Automobile* (1920), involved the seizure of nine automobiles, one gas screw vessel, and one seagoing yacht.[42] The government filed forfeiture proceedings under a section of the revenue law adopted to aid in the collection of the federal liquor tax. To that end, the act authorized forfeitures of property (regardless of the owner's innocence) used to remove, deposit, or conceal distilled spirits (owing a tax) to a place other than one permitted by law.[43] The defendants collectively challenged the libel in each instance on the ground that the Volstead Act had effectively repealed the section of the revenue law described above. Since each violation occurred after January 17, 1920, they claimed that the federal prohibition law, which protected an innocent owner's property, became the operative statute.[44]

Upon hearing the dispute, Judge Rhydon Call noted that the courts remained divided over this question. While some district courts had found the sections of the revised statutes relating to the collection of federal revenues derived from the taxes on distilled spirits still in force, others had ruled that the Eighteenth Amendment coupled with the Volstead Act had repealed those statutes. Unquestionably, government policy had changed completely on the liquor question. "Ordinarily, under the well-known canons of statutory construction," Call wrote, "the last act would repeal the former acts bearing upon the same subject matter." Still, according to Call, "Congress passed [this] section and many other[s] . . . to aid in the collection of the liquor tax." To illustrate his point, Call cited the section of the Volstead Act that reads: "All provisions of law that are inconsistent with this act are repealed only to the extent of such inconsistency, and the regulations herein provided for the manufacture or traffic in intoxicating liquor shall be construed as an addition to the existing law. No liquor revenue stamps or tax receipts for any illegal manufacture or sale shall be issued in advance, but upon evidence of such illegal manufacture or sale a tax shall be assessed against and collected from the person responsible for such illegal manufacture or sale in double the amount provided by law, with an additional penalty of $500 on retail dealers and $1,000 on manufacturers."[45]

Call then cited the section of the same act that apparently covered every illegal transportation of liquor, including the forfeiture proceedings for vehicles used in unlawful transportation. Having contemplated the meaning of these particular sections, Call argued that, despite the revenue law's previous judicial constructions, "it [was] immaterial that the owner of the vehicle did not participate in the illegal transportation." If an owner consented to the use of his vehicle by a party violating the law, that vehicle became subject to forfeiture no matter what the circumstances.[46]

Even so, Call said Congress did not intend for the section of the Volstead Act to continue in force the similar section of the revenue law. This struck Call as inconsistent. It seemed to him that some other principle had repealed the section of the revenue statute. "The proceeding for forfeiture provided in the latter act," he added, proved "much less stringent than that provided by section 3450 [of the revenue law] as construed by the courts." Call concluded that the government had failed to allege facts sufficient to sustain a forfeiture according to the Volstead Act. He then sustained the objections and dismissed the charges.[47]

Likewise, in *The Coldwater* (1922), the court dismissed a libel suit filed by the U.S. district attorney for the Southern District. The government alleged that an American steamship, the *Coldwater*, had imported and transported intoxicating liquors within the United States. While the ship was lying docked in port at Jacksonville, crew members sold part of its illegal cargo contrary to the Volstead Act. If the evidence demonstrated the allegations, the prosecution intended subsequently to divest the *Coldwater*'s owners of their title.[48]

While the facts revealed that the Carolina Shipping Company (a private corporation) had chartered the vessel, they also proved that the federal government held title to the *Coldwater*. Under an act of June 5, 1920, Congress had transferred certain vessels—including the *Coldwater*—to the U.S. Shipping Board to promote and maintain the American merchant marine. Given these conditions, if the United States prosecuted this case to a successful conclusion, the anomalous but inevitable result required that the government forfeit its own property to itself. "Such absurdity," declared District Judge Clayton, "cannot happen," because Congress in March of 1920 enacted a statute that explicitly prohibited the seizure under judicial process of a vessel owned by the United States.[49]

Besides that, Clayton doubted seriously whether any boat like a steamship even where privately owned was subject to seizure under the national prohibition laws. Clayton referred to an earlier case, *The Saxon* (1920), in which a court's ruling had exempted large iron steamships of ten thousand tons engaged in general commerce from forfeiture proceedings precipitated by the unlawful actions of crew members. In citing *The Saxon*, Clayton attempted to differentiate between those vessels engaged in legitimate commerce in which crew members used such trade to cover their smuggling operations, and smaller craft where bootlegging served as the boat's principal activity and in which both the captain and the crew openly defied the law. Accordingly, Clayton dismissed the government's case against the *Coldwater*.[50]

Still, legal incongruity persisted, and the forfeiture doctrine reached a higher level of uncertainty following the passage of the Tariff Act of 1922. This law complemented the Volstead Act by defining the terms that warranted forfeiture and providing for the imposition of other sanctions on violators of the customs or revenue law. Similar to the Volstead Act, the law exempted vessels and vehicles engaged as common carriers from confiscation proceedings. Nonetheless, ambiguity arose when the government sought forfeiture grounded on violations of both laws.[51]

In one such case, *United States* v. *One Packard Sedan* (1926), the government sought a forfeiture on two counts: a violation of the Tariff Act and a violation of the Volstead Act. To simplify its litigation, the prosecution abandoned the second ground and proceeded under the section of customs law that provided for the seizure and forfeiture of vessels used in conveying illegally imported merchandise. The claimant, the Packard Palm Beach Company, testified that they had sold the car to a man named "Maripou under a retained title contract in good faith and had no knowledge of any illegal use." Due to its claimed innocence, the company demanded its property returned.[52]

Judge Call responded that if a section of the customs law was in force, the good faith of the claimant could not prevent a forfeiture. Of course that was provided the government had sustained its lawsuit with adequate proof. In other words, the burden of proof as usual fell upon the prosecution. The government then proceeded to prove its case and produced "a customs inspector who testified that he found the car parked on a street, and in a valise found a bottle partly full . . . labeled Black and White Whiskey." He claimed that he recognized the label as one commonly found on Scotch whiskey but could not swear that the bottle contained imported whiskey. In addition, the witness stated that, before seizing the car, he had seen bags, which he suspected to contain whiskey, unloaded from a boat and placed in the car for transportation to some destination.[53]

The government then introduced as evidence, over the claimant's stern objection, receipts for liquor found at Maripou's home. Although the bills apparently came from a liquor dealer in the Bahamas, the dealer had not made them out to Maripou. Call found the bills inadmissible to prove unlawful importation. Furthermore, he did not think a bottle of whiskey found in a suitcase in a parked car sufficient to prove the crime of smuggling. "Surely something more than a suspicion, however well grounded in the mind of the customs inspector from his investigations," Call asserted, "must appear in evidence before the court can by decree deprive the citizen of his property." Finding nothing else relevant, Call dismissed the case.[54]

The burden of proof continued to weigh on the prosecution. In *United States* v. *Packard Sedan* (1928), customs agents had seized an automobile on a state highway in Pasco County at a point between Brooksville and Tampa. At the time of the seizure the disputed vehicle contained three hundred bottles of Canadian Club whiskey. The government alleged that the car's drivers had used the automobile to violate the Tariff Act. It consequently became subject to forfeiture under customs law.[55]

The Independent Indemnity Company filed a petition of intervention in this suit asserting that they held title to the automobile pending payment of $1,958 balance due on the loan for the car. Since they had become innocent bystanders in the government's war on liquor, and to prevent a total financial loss, the company wanted the seized automobile delivered to them.[56]

To sustain its case, the government introduced five customs officers and one prohibition agent as witnesses. While their testimonies corroborated the facts, each officer admitted that he did not know where the liquor came from or at what point bootleggers loaded the contraband into the vehicle. Customs Inspector G. W. Shaw stated that the car's driver, Joe Fresno, told him that smugglers had loaded the liquor from a boat near Bayport the night before the seizure. From there they removed the contraband to a place in the woods for safekeeping until Fresno came and loaded the whiskey into his car. The government then submitted as evidence "a signed statement made by Fresno to this effect."[57]

The counsels for the Independent Indemnity Company, H. S. Phillips and Cyrus W. Fields, objected, claiming Fresno's account was hearsay and did not show that their client had imported liquor. The witness had to testify in person. Otherwise, the prosecution could follow a line of questioning that would become immaterial, irrelevant, and illegal. In effect, the defense charged that the government's procedure had denied the defendants the right to confront their accusers in court.[58]

Undeterred, the government produced an expert witness to strengthen its claim that the liquor had entered the country illegally. Prohibition investigator Joseph Treglia testified that he had worked previously for a major liquor distributor. While employed by that company, Treglia had purchased large quantities of Canadian Club liquor at Halifax, Bermuda, and Nassau. Due to this "enormous responsibility," he claimed that he could not afford to take counterfeit whiskey. So to secure his job, Treglia learned how to distinguish the genuine article by taste. At the hearing, Treglia examined some seized liquor, tasted it, and testified that the whiskey came from Canada.[59]

In cross-examination, Fields attempted to discredit Treglia's expertise:

> Q. What is it about [Canadian Club] to make it taste so peculiar to you?
>
> A. It is the only brand with that taste.

Q. Do you know how any particular brand of liquor is produced?

A. No, sir.

Q. What is the distinguishing taste between rye and corn whiskey?

A. I never dealt in corn whiskey and would not know it if I saw it, except I would know it would not be either Scotch or rye.

Q. In other words, you cannot put into words the difference?

A. Canadian Club tastes different from any other whiskey in the world.

Q. Well, describe that difference in taste in words. If I say, "You look different from this man over here," that is stating a fact without stating the difference. Now, I want you to tell the difference in the taste.

A. The only difference that I can tell is that Canadian Club is rye whiskey made in Canada, and it has always been known as a hard whiskey to imitate.[60]

Under further questioning, Treglia proved unable to locate the province or municipality where the Canadian Club distillery operated. When asked if Canadian Club was distilled outside Canada, Treglia responded in the negative.

Q. Isn't it a fact that liquor is made in the United States in Ybor City, Florida, and branded and labeled Canadian Club?

A. I never run across any of it.

Q. Have you ever been to the plant where they manufacture Canadian Club whiskey?

A. I have not.

Q. You do not know anything about the manufacturer of the labels?

A. No, sir.

Q. You never have known of them shipping their labels to this country?

A. No, sir.

Q. Have you ever run across any loose labels [for other brands of liquor]?

A. Yes sir.[61]

The claimant's counsel followed the above line of questioning to show that the government had insufficient evidence to prove a violation of the Tariff Act. If the government, in pursuing a property forfeiture, proceeded under either the revenue law or customs law, instead of proceeding under the Volstead Act, counsel reasoned that not only should the court strictly construe the sections of the laws that governed property forfeitures, but it should also "hold the government to the highest degree of proof before declaring the forfeiture of the property of an innocent owner."[62]

Noting that the Tariff Act did not provide for the forfeiture of automobiles, Judge Lake Jones stated that the revenue and customs laws on which the government based its claims, when constructed together, provided "for the search of vehicles by authorized officers, where the officers suspect[ed] there [was] merchandise . . . subject to duty, or [that would] have been introduced into the United States in any manner contrary to law." Any such vehicle carrying merchandise as described above, Jones insisted, warranted forfeiture.[63]

Based on his reading of the revenue and customs statutes, Jones concluded that to effect the forfeiture of this vehicle "the goods found therein must have been subject to duty" or "unlawfully introduced into the United States." The facts, according to Jones, demonstrated that government agents had seized a vehicle containing liquor on a public highway without any evidence to illustrate its point of departure. The only evidence that the government offered as proof of smuggling consisted of the labels that suggested the liquor originated in Canada. Jones asked rhetorically: "Does this evidence justify the conclusion that this liquor was unlawfully brought into the United States?" If not, any such forfeiture, he concluded, could not stand.[64]

Jones noted that under the Tariff Act, the burden of proof fell upon the claimant, if the government first demonstrated probable cause. Jones claimed, "This must be by competent evidence and not by hearsay, suspicion, or guesses." Because the Canadian Club label appeared on the liquor found in the car did not give probable cause to institute a forfeiture of the vehicle, he ordered the car returned to its owner.[65]

Yet the problem of whether the government, when seeking the forfeiture of an automobile or truck in such cases, must proceed under the Volstead Act, which preserved the property rights of innocent owners/lienors, or prosecute under the customs laws, which took no notice of innocence, remained unresolved. *United States* v. *One Buick Coupe* (1931) provided the most pragmatic resolution offered up to that time. Invoking the appropriate sections of the customs laws, the federal government sought the forfeiture of a Buick coupe. The Tennant Finance Company then intervened as claimant.[66]

The matter came up for final hearing and the court found the following facts pertinent. On October 1, 1928, customs patrol inspectors had stopped James Provenza who was driving a Buick coupe over a highway bridge that connected the city of St. Augustine with Anastasia Island in St. Johns County. The officers immediately searched the automobile and discovered inside a large quantity of untaxed smuggled whiskey. They arrested Provenza for unlawful transportation contrary to the National Prohibition Act and concealment of unlawfully imported liquor in violation of the Tariff Act. The officers then seized the vehicle and delivered it to the Collector of Customs.[67]

As it turned out, the claimant held a conditional sales contract that reserved the automobile's title to a finance company in case Provenza defaulted on the note. Since he did, the claimant became legally entitled to the car and demanded that the court return the property to the company. The fate of the automobile, however, remained contingent upon what course of law the prosecution decided to pursue. The court had a wide but divided body of law to rely upon. Judge Louie Willard Strum handed down the court's decision. Born in Valdosta, Georgia, and raised in Florida, Strum received his legal education at Stetson Law School. Admitted to the Florida Bar in 1912, Strum practiced law in Jacksonville until 1925, when he began his tenure on the Florida Supreme Court. He remained there for six years and served as Chief Justice from January to March in 1931. He was then appointed to the U.S. District Court for the Southern District of Florida and served in this capacity until 1950. An Episcopalian and a Democrat, Strum capped his career as a Circuit Judge for the United States Court of Appeals for the Fifth Circuit.[68]

Strum managed to ferret out four principles governing the forfeiture of land vehicles. First, according to Strum: "There is an effective and distinct field of operation for each of the forfeiture provisions of the customs laws, the revenue laws, and the National Prohibition Act." Section 26 of the Volstead Act repealed neither the revenue nor the customs laws. But the prohibition law, Strum wrote, "is in the nature of specific legislation which operates where it applies, by way of exception to the general customs and revenue laws just mentioned." In other words, the courts had to follow the mandatory provisions of the National Prohibition Act when and where they applied.[69]

Second, "the dominant character of the enterprise in which the vehicle [was] engaged when captured," Strum reasoned, became "the controlling test in determining the appropriate procedural statute." Referring to *Richbourg Motor Co.* (1930), which the claimants had relied upon, Strum noted that "few cases of illegal transportation could occur which did not involve the concealment of non tax-paid liquor." On the other hand, Strum could imagine no case of smuggling where "the element of transportation would not have been at some time present."[70]

Third, if the vehicle's primary objective when seized was to relocate liquor from one place to another, then Strum deduced, "the dominant character of the enterprise [was] transportation." Therefore, it became the government's mandatory duty to proceed under the Volstead Act. Its forfeiture section furnished the exclusive remedy for property confiscation. The rule became controlling even when the liquor in question had "antecedent history as duty or tax unpaid liquor imported or manufactured contrary to the customs or revenue laws." To bolster his position, Strum cited *Commercial Credit Co.* v. *United States* (1927). In this earlier case a federal circuit court ruled that the prosecution must proceed under the Volstead Act even if "the liquors were clearly of foreign origin and unlawfully imported." The court reached this verdict because importation of the booze "had been fully accomplished and pure transportation undertaken prior to capture."[71]

Fourth, and in contrast, Strum noted that when smuggling or unlawful importation became the distinguishing characteristic of an enterprise in which the seized automobile served to facilitate those activities, libel proceedings came under the appropriate sections of customs law. To prevail under this body of law, however, the government had to "bring its case wholly and fairly within those statutes." Strum further emphasized that the same principles applied in forfeiture proceedings brought under the revenue laws "where the dominant character of the enterprise [was] the removal, deposit, or concealment of liquors with intent to deprive the United States of the tax thereof imposed by the revenue laws."[72]

Using these four principles as a guideline, Strum returned to the immediate case. While conceding that the liquors in question came from foreign sources, Strum noted that the facts did not show what length of time the liquor had been in this country. Strum found nothing to connect the vehicle with importation or with subsequent concealment. The bare fact that prior to its seizure the vehicle had been traveling on a public highway about three or four miles from the coast, with imported liquors aboard, proved insufficient, according to Strum, to connect the automobile with importation.[73]

Although someone had probably unlawfully imported the intoxicants and evaded the tax on those spirits, Strum concluded that "the dominant character of the enterprise, when the vehicle was captured, was not concealment, but was pure transportation, to which concealment was merely incidental." Clearly, the agents caught the culprit in the act of transporting liquor against the federal prohibition law. Since that statute saved the property rights of innocent lienors, Strum dismissed the case and awarded the Buick coupe to the claimant.[74]

On May 27, 1930, Congress approved the Prohibition Reorganization Act. This measure authorized the attorney general to claim title to any vehicles forfeited under the Volstead Act and deliver them to the Department of Justice. There, the Division of Investigation had the option of using the forfeited vehicles in the enforcement of the federal liquor laws.[75]

The revised statute, in part, reflected some underlying forces that began to influence prohibition enforcement. Toward the end of the 1920s, the repeal movement had gained momentum as groups such as the Association Against the Prohibition Amendment and the Women's Organization for National Prohibition Reform broadened their support. Both groups couched their arguments for repeal in law and order terminology. And each believed that the Eighteenth Amendment and its enabling legislation gave too much power to the central government and that it cost too much "in terms of tax revenues, enforcement expenses, police corruption, and threats to civil liberties."[76]

What is more, May of 1930 marked the sixth month of recession that followed the stock market crash of October 1929. America's future remained foreboding as no recovery appeared in sight. As the economy of the nation collapsed, federal revenues declined. Under these conditions, government agencies like the Bureau of Prohibition became hard pressed for funding.

Therefore, as a matter of departmental survival, federal bureaucrats developed new austerity programs that they could sell to both Congress and the American public.

The National Prohibition Reorganization Act, then, perhaps represented a compromise between Congress and the Justice Department. In other words, Congress approved a law that broadened the scope of the bureau's authority but did so without spending limited or non-existent dollars. To survive, the bureau had to be semi–self-supporting. In a way this allowed members of Congress the luxury of pleasing both their wet and dry constituents. The broader police power appealed to drys, while at the same time wets favored the notion that the agency's survival depended more on its independent actions.[77]

As it played out in Florida, the Reorganization Act had little impact on either prohibition enforcement or property forfeiture. In the exception that proved the rule, Judge Alexander Akerman, in *United States* v. *Philip Puglisi* (1933), ordered federal marshals to take charge of the defendant's Chevrolet and deliver it to the Department of Justice.[78] In the majority of forfeiture proceedings, however, the courts protected property rights against such legislation and ordered the seized vehicles returned, usually to an innocent lienor or owner.[79]

To illustrate, during the waning months of the Noble Experiment, District Judge William B. Sheppard, in *United States* v. *One Ford Automobile* (1933), ordered the return of a seized automobile to the car's innocent lienor, M. W. Miller. Customs Patrol Inspectors had seized the roadster on March 1, 1933, near Madison, Florida. The officers testified that they had received reliable information that a Tallahassee man named Troy Perry had hauled moonshine regularly from Madison to Tallahassee and to several Georgia towns. The informer had provided the officers with descriptions of Perry, his car, and the automobile's license number. After seeing the defendant pass through Madison shortly after five o'clock in the evening, the inspectors parked their cars and waited for Perry to return. An hour later Perry passed the officers again, this time heading toward Monticello.[80]

The agents followed Perry across the Jefferson County line where they stopped him. They then asked Perry, "What do you have back here?" (meaning in the back of his car). Perry replied, "Just a little 'shine'; the boys told me that you fellows were okay, that you did not bother with 'shine'." Although Perry told the inspectors that he bought the twenty gallons of whiskey from the Taylor Brothers, he later changed his statement claiming he "did not say that he bought the whiskey from [the] Taylor Brothers but that [he] had bought it from the boys." Also, Perry stated originally that he paid $17 per five-gallon jug, but, when questioned further, he lowered the price to $7 a jug. After being warned of his constitutional rights, Perry said he had used someone else's money to purchase the moonshine but assumed full responsibility for the twenty gallons of whiskey.[81]

Since Perry confessed and did not challenge the legality of the unwarranted search and seizure, the court needed only to divest Perry of his property rights in the Ford. After that the district court, following the reorganization act of 1930, could order Perry's car delivered to the Department of Justice. Yet, as it turned out, Perry did not have clear title to the automobile. He had defaulted on his loan. M. W. Miller had retained title and had petitioned the court to restore the vehicle to his possession. Judge Sheppard, convinced that Miller was an innocent lienor and entitled to his property, ordered the automobile delivered to Miller upon his payment "of all costs of seizure and storage to the date of delivery of said car."[82]

In Murchison's analysis of the Supreme Court's response to property forfeitures during the Noble Experiment, he cautioned against a reductionist, monocausal theory. Noting the complexity of the Court's role in effecting statutory reform, Murchison argued that the Supreme Court "was more likely to expand protections for the individual in situations that might involve otherwise law-abiding citizens and in situations that could be expected to disappear when prohibition was finally repealed." Viewing the judicial process as an imperfect mirror, he concluded that statutory "meaning is more likely to reflect the political and intellectual consensus existing at the time a judicial decision is rendered than the consensus existing when the statute was originally enacted."[83]

The history of prohibition enforcement in Florida suggests a different story. During the twelve years of forfeiture proceedings stemming from prohibition enforcement in Florida, the courts steadfastly championed property rights against legislative meddling. The three phases of judicial response to property forfeiture that Murchison found in Supreme Court rulings did not become manifest in Florida's federal courts or state supreme court decisions. Although the case law examined represents only a small sample of the property litigation that burdened judicial dockets, these cases provide a telling analysis. The Florida Supreme Court, for example, overturned 83 percent of lower court decisions that decreed property forfeited. The federal district courts in Florida dismissed an equally impressive 80 percent of forfeitures in favor of the owners. Moreover, when the confiscated property belonged to an innocent owner or lienor, both judiciaries ordered the property returned in 100 percent of the cases examined. Put another way, in all sample cases where the courts sustained a forfeiture, the courts had found the property owner either guilty of, or an accessory to, the alleged liquor violation. These simple statistics reveal a singular pattern for judicial decisions and suggest that the courts based their protections of property on firmly held principles as old as the republic itself.

Thus Murchison's thesis that Supreme Court decisions harmonized with contemporary social values seems overdrawn. Inasmuch as a consensus on prohibition never materialized, judges more likely based their rulings on precedent and citation of authority, the traditional methods of conducting court business, instead of some external stimuli. Furthermore, Murchison's mirror metaphor—that the Supreme Court simply reflected the legal demands of the citizenry—overlooks the important role that the lower courts play in shaping the law. For the most part, the lower courts serve as the initial testing ground for legislation. At this level of litigation, lawyers and judges begin to work out a law's meaning so that when the Supreme Court addresses the matter, it can draw upon several alternative interpretations. Still, even after the Supreme Court decides a case, its opinion remains subject to interpretation by the lower courts. A "house of mirrors" perhaps offers a more appropriate metaphor because jurisprudential ideas are a product of multiple reflections and interpretations within the judicial and legal system.

Finally, while it is correct that Murchison failed to fully appreciate the judiciary's consistent and traditional concern for property, his suggestion that certain prohibition enforcement techniques such as forfeiture played a large part in changing the general public's attitude toward prohibition is clear. As noted, by 1928 a state and national movement calling for the repeal of the Eighteenth Amendment began to form around the ideas that national prohibition had not only proved impracticable but had also affronted basic constitutional safeguards, perhaps none so important as the fundamental rights to privacy and property.

NOTES

1. Roy W. McDonald, "Automobile Forfeitures and the Eighteenth Amendment," *Texas Law Review* 10 (1931), 140–162. McDonald notes that, besides the Hebrews, the Babylonians, Greeks, Romans, Anglo-Saxons, and Normans had developed legal concepts of forfeiture.

2. *Parker Harris Co.* v. *Tate*, 135 Tenn. 509, 514 (1916).

3. McDonald, "Automobile Forfeitures and the Eighteenth Amendment," 142.

4. For property rights and the constitutional safeguards, see Leonard W. Levy, *A License to Steal: The Forfeiture of Property* (Chapel Hill and London: University of North Carolina Press, 1996); James W. Ely, Jr., *The Guardian of Every Right: A Constitutional History of Property Rights* (New York: Oxford University Press, 1992); Jennifer Nedelsky, *Private Property and the Limits of American Constitutionalism: The Madisonian Framework and Its Legacy* (Chicago: University of Chicago Press, 1990); Morton Keller, *Regulating a New Economy: Public Policy and Economic Change in America, 1900–1933* (Cambridge, Mass., and London: Harvard University Press, 1990); Melvin I. Urofsky, "State Courts and Protective Legislation During the Progressive Era: A Reevaluation," *Journal of American History* 72 (June 1985), 63–91.

5. For the most significant treatment of this aspect of prohibition enforcement, see Kenneth M. Murchison, *Federal Criminal Law Doctrines: The Forgotten Influence of National Prohibition* (Durham, N.C., and London: Duke University Press, 1994), 20, 22, 126–153, 177–182, 186; Idem, "Property Forfeiture in the Era of National Prohibition: A Study of Judicial Response to Legislative Reform," *Buffalo Law Review* 32 (1983), 417–463.

6. See "Forfeiture of Property of Innocent Owners Used in Transporting Liquor," *University of Pennsylvania Law Review* 74 (1925), 170; McDonald, "Automobile Forfeitures and the Eighteenth Amendment," 142.

7. Wilbur R. Miller, *Revenuers & Moonshiners: Enforcing Federal Liquor Law in the Mountain South, 1865–1900* (Chapel Hill: University of North Carolina Press, 1991), 6.

8. *Van Oster* v. *Kansas*, 272 U.S. 465 (1926).

9. McDonald, "Automobile Forfeitures and the Eighteenth Amendment," 153. See *Payne* v. *United States*, 279 Fed. 112 (C.C.A. 5th, 1922); *United States* v. *One Haynes Automobile*, 274 Fed. 926 (C.C.A. 5th, 1921).

10. See U.S. Department of Justice, Division of Taxation, Prohibition, and Prisons, *Report of the Attorney General* (Washington, D.C.: GPO, 1925), 46–47.

11. Ely, *The Guardian of Every Right*, iv.

12. *Lippman, Claimant* v. *State*, 72 Fla. 428, 431, 434 (1916); Ch. 7283, sec. 17, *Florida Acts*, 1917

13. Paul S. George, "Bootleggers, Prohibitionists and Police: The Temperance Movement in Miami, 1896–1920," *Tequesta* 39 (1979), 3–41, 36; Arthur E. Chapman, "History of South Florida," in Thomas S. Boswell, ed., *South Florida: The Winds of Change* (Miami: Association of American Geographers, 1991), 31–42; *The DeLand Sun News* [Florida], October 18, 1933.

14. *Lippman, Claimant* v. *State*, 436.

15. Ibid., 446–447. The Florida Legislature revised the law in 1924 so that "the sheriff, upon seizing any liquors or other things taken in connection therewith, shall deliver such articles into the custody of the Clerk of the Circuit Court of the county. The clerk is thereupon required to perform certain acts in connection with the reception and custody of the same." Attorney General of the State of Florida, *Biennial Report*, 1929.

16. *Lippman, Claimant* v. *State*, 441.

17. Ibid., 442.

18. Ibid., 443.

19. Ibid., 448.

20. Ch. 7283, sec. 17, *Florida Acts*, 1917; Attorney General of the State of Florida, *Biennial Report*, 1918.

21. *Florida Constitution* Article XIX; Ch. 7284, *Florida Acts* 1917; Ch. 7736, *Florida Acts*, 1918; *Ex parte Francis*, 76 Fla. 304, 314–316.

22. *Florida Constitution*, Article XIX (1918); Ch 7736, *Florida Acts* 1918; Ch. 7733, *Florida Acts*, 1918.

23. *Marasso* v. *Van Pelt, Sheriff*, 81 So. 529 (Fla. 1919).

24. Ibid., 534, 539.

25. *In re Seven Barrels of Wine*, 83 So. 627 (Fla. 1920).

26. Ibid., 630–631.

27. Ibid.

28. Ibid.

29. Ibid. See Ch. 7736, *Florida Acts*, 1918.

30. *In re Seven Barrels of Wine*, 631–632.

31. Ibid., 632, 634; *The Tampa Tribune*, January 16, 1920.

32. *Spratt* v. *Gray*, 87 So. 760 (Fla. 1921). See Ch. 7736, sec. 15, *Florida Acts*, 1918.

33. *Spratt* v. *Gray*, 762.

34. *Armstrong* v. *State*, 85 Fla. 452 (1923).

35. Ibid., 455.

36. Ibid.

37. Keller, *Regulating a New Economy*, 73–74. See also Walter E. Treanor, "The Family Automobile and the Family Purpose Doctrine," *Indiana Law Journal* 1 (1925), 89–95; "The Development of the Family Purpose Doctrine," *United States Law Review* 65 (1931), 645–651.

38. Harry N. Scheiber, "Property Law, Expropriation, and Resource Allocation by Government, 1789–1910," *The Journal of Economic History* 33 (March 1973), 232–251, 233.

39. Attorney General of the State of Florida, *Biennial Report*, 1930.

40. *State* v. *One Hudson Roadster Automobile*, 104 Fla. 301, 304 (1932).

41. Ibid.

42. *United States* v. *One Haynes Automobile and Eight Other Automobiles*, Case File Nos. 1135, 1136, 1148, 1149, 1151, 1157, 1158, 1162, 1167, 1176, and 1177, Box No. 59, U.S. District Court, Southern District of Florida, Jacksonville, December term 1920, Federal Records Center, East Point, Ga. (hereinafter FRC).

43. See *Revised Statutes*, sec. 3450.

44. See National Prohibition Act, *Statutes at Large*, 41 (1920).

45. Ibid.

46. Ibid. Section 26, title 2, provides that "The court, upon conviction of the person so arrested shall order the liquor destroyed, and unless good cause to the contrary is shown by the owner, shall order a sale by public auction of the property seized . . . and the proceeds after deducting the expenses and costs shall be paid into the treasury of the United States as miscellaneous receipts." *United States* v. *One Haynes Automobile*.

47. Ibid.

48. *The Coldwater*, 283 Fed. 146 (1922).

49. Ibid., 149. Merchant Marine Act, *Statutes at Large*, 41, 988 (1919).

50. *The Coldwater*, 149. See also *The Saxon*, 269 Fed. 639 (1920).

51. Tariff Act, *Statutes at Large*, 44. Ch. 356, sec. 5936 (1922), provided that if anyone fraudulently imported any merchandise into the United States or received, concealed, bought, sold, or facilitated such activities, they faced legal sanctions in the form of fine, imprisonment, or both. Section 594 of the act provided "that whenever a vessel or vehicle, or the owner or master, conductor, driver, or other person in charge thereof, has become subject to a penalty for the violation of the customs revenue laws, such vessel or vehicle shall be held for the payment summarily by libel to recover the same." See *United States* v. *One Packard Sedan*, 14 F.2d 874 (1926).

52. Ibid., 874–875.

53. Ibid. To resolve the inherent paradox the claimant attempted to convince the court that section 594 of the Tariff Act had repealed section 3062.

54. *United States* v. *One Packard Sedan*, 875–876.

55. *United States* v. *Packard Sedan, Motor Number 71005–A*, Case File No. 1440–T, Box No. 73, U.S. District Court, Southern District of Florida, Jacksonville, January term 1928, FRC.

56. Ibid.

57. Ibid.

58. Ibid.

59. Ibid.

60. Ibid.

61. Ibid.

62. Ibid.

63. Ibid.

64. Ibid.

65. Ibid.

66. See *United States* v. *One Buick Coupe*, 54 F.2d 800 (1931). For the controlling provisions of each law cited, see National Prohibition Act, sec. 26, title 2; Collection of Duties Act, secs. 3061, 3062; Tariff Act, secs. 482, 483; Revenue Law, sec. 3450.

67. *United States* v. *One Buick Coupe*, 801. The disposition of the first count did not appear in the court's "agreed statement of facts."

68. Harold Chase et al., *Biographical Dictionary of the Federal Judiciary* (Detroit: Gale Research Co., 1976), 265.

69. *United States* v. *One Buick Coupe*, 801.

70. Ibid., 802. Strum, supporting this point, cited *United States* v. *One Ford Coupe Automobile*, 272 U.S. 321 (1926) and *Two Ford Coupes* v. *United States* (C.C.A. 5), 53 F.2d 187 (1930). See also *Richbourg Motor Co.* v. *United States* 20 F.2d 519 (1927).

71. *United States* v. *One Buick Coupe*, 802. See *Commercial Credit Co.* v. *United States* (C.C.A. 5), 53 F.2d 977 (1930). Strum added that if the government had convicted the person in possession of the vehicle of unlawful transportation under the National Prohibition Act, "title 2, section 26 of that act . . . [mandated] that the forfeiture proceed under that section, precluding a resort to the forfeiture provisions of either the customs laws or the revenue laws."

72. *United States* v. *One Buick Coupe*, 802.

73. Ibid., 803.

74. Ibid.

75. Section 9 of the Prohibition Reorganization Act of 1930 amended section 2 of the Act of March 3, 1925.

76. David E. Kyvig, "Sober Thoughts: Myths and Realities of National Prohibition after Fifty Years," in David E. Kyvig, ed., *Law, Alcohol, and Order: Perspectives on National Prohibition* (Westport, Conn.: Greenwood Press, 1985), 15.

77. In a sense, several sides of the debate could claim a symbolic victory. As Joseph Gusfield has suggested, whether the law "actually prevailed among all members of the community" proved "less important to middle-class reformers than community endorsement for a value that middle-class people viewed as respectable." As quoted in Jack S. Blocker, *American Temperance Movements: Cycles of Reform* (Boston: Twayne Publishers, 1989), 54.

78. *United States* v. *Phillip Puglisi*, Case File No. 3809, Box No. 78, U.S. District Court, Southern District of Florida, Tampa, November term 1933, FRC.

79. See also *United States* v. *Stephens*, 1 F.Supp. 33 (1932).

80. *United States* v. *One Ford Automobile*, Case File No. 3, Box No. 43, U.S. District Court, Northern District of Florida, Tallahassee, April term 1933, FRC.

81. Ibid.

82. Ibid.

83. Murchison, "Property Forfeiture in the Era of National Prohibition," 461–462; Idem, *Federal Criminal Law Doctrines*, 143–153.

CHAPTER FIVE

National Prohibition to Local Option, 1928–1935

In 1928, the U.S. Senate introduced a bill calling for the addition of a third judge to the Southern District of Florida. According to Senator Duncan U. Fletcher, the bill's chief sponsor, Florida's overloaded dockets required federal judges from other jurisdictions to venture south to help clear the judicial backlog. Since 2,809 cases remained pending for the Southern District as of August 4, 1927, judges and other officials backed Fletcher's idea. The Department of Justice supported the proposal, and Chief Justice William H. Taft, who originally opposed the plan, gave his endorsement on March 23, 1928. Noting that the Southern District extended a distance of 520 miles from Florida's northern boundary to Key West, the chief justice realized that the expansive coastline provided "convenient hiding and landing places for smugglers and rumrunners."[1]

The judicial backlog underscores two important points. For one, many Floridians violated national prohibition. For another, the swollen court dockets provided empirical evidence for wets to argue that prohibition had failed utterly. These factors helped launch the repeal movement in Florida. Indeed, the path from national prohibition to local option in Florida unfolded in three separate, but often overlapping, stages. Between 1928 and 1933, during the first and longest phase of the state's wet crusade, a constituency consisting of judges, newspaper editors, lawyers, brewers, retailers, workers, hoteliers, state legislators, and many ordinary Floridians, coalesced around the idea of repeal. Disillusioned with the federal liquor law, this group began agitating for change. In the political debate that ensued, advocates for repeal generally couched their arguments in terms of either state sovereignty or economic principles. Besides encroaching upon state and local jurisdictions, wets said that the federal government had grown too expansive and posed a serious threat to liberty. Additionally, they claimed that prohibition caused economic hardship for both the public and the private sectors. As wets viewed it, repeal would assure profits for businesses, incomes for households, and tax revenue for government.

Over time, such rhetoric gradually began undermining the intellectual and constitutional foundations of prohibition. The crusade for repeal was advancing on several fronts. In 1932, wets provided crucial support that enabled Democratic candidates to gain control of both the Congress and the White House. Soon after taking office, the winning candidates rewarded the wets by making good on a major campaign pledge. In April 1933, Congress revised the Volstead Act and near beer became legal under federal law. This measure helped launch stage two of the repeal movement in Florida. During this phase, Florida wets and their dry opponents clashed over a proposed legislative package that would ultimately legalize near beer and light wine throughout the state. As it turned out, the wets prevailed. On May 8, 1933, Governor David Sholtz signed the bills into law.

Following this victory, Florida wets joined in the national campaign to repeal the Eighteenth Amendment. In December 1933, Utah became the thirty-sixth (and requisite) state to ratify the Twenty-First Amendment. This wet milestone returned the liquor issue to state and local governments for resolution. Because Florida's constitutional ban on booze remained intact, wet reformers confronted a seemingly major obstacle to their cause. But less than a year later, in November 1934, Florida's "bone dry" prohibition amendment went down in defeat at the polls, and phase two of the repeal movement in Florida came to an end.

Phase three of the movement began with the restoration of local option. By disassociating national and state prohibition, wets had sparked new debates about old liquor laws. For the most part, the discourse centered on the extent of governmental power over personal property. This final phase of the wet crusade would work itself out in the courts and come to an end in 1935.

The amount of business transacted by the federal courts in Florida during the 1920s warranted Taft's change of opinion noted above.[2] National prohibition, coupled with the state's rapid population increase, had spawned a massive amount of litigation that overwhelmed both federal judicial districts in Florida. In 1921, for example, the courts of the Southern District settled 551 criminal prosecutions, including 463 federal liquor violations. The Northern District closed 164 criminal prosecutions, including 121 liquor cases. In 1928, the southern courts decided 1,319 criminal prosecutions, 85 percent of these concerned federal liquor laws. Figures for the Northern District in the same year had increased to 210 and 191, respectively.[3]

Due in part to the massive amount of federal litigation, the presidential campaign of 1928 became a major battle in the war on "demon rum." The Anti-Saloon League, at the pinnacle of its national power, "mustered all its resources to elect the dry Republican, Herbert Hoover, over the wet Democrat [and Roman Catholic], Al Smith." The same contest reached Florida. There the WCTU, joined by the Anti-Saloon League, organized a conference of the state's leading prohibitionists to discuss a strategy for the forthcoming election. Under Bishop James Cannon's prompting, the conference quit the Democratic Party and endorsed Herbert Hoover for president.[4]

Meanwhile, on October 11, 1928, Florida Chief Justice William Ellis embroiled himself in the political controversy. Speaking before a Miami audience, he asked Florida and other southern Democrats "to rally to the support of Governor Alfred E. Smith for president." Claiming that prohibition was not an issue, Ellis assured his listeners that Smith would "enforce [it] as well as other parts of the Constitution." He asked rhetorically: "[I]s Mr. Hoover a prohibitionist?" He answered: "Not so anyone could notice." In comparing the two candidates, Florida's chief justice had created a distinction without illustrating any differences. Skirting prohibition, Ellis redirected the election's focus to other issues by appealing to the emotions of his audience. Waving the bloody shirt of the Civil War and pandering to sectional politics, Ellis thundered: "Our political hereditary enemy is before us again. For fifty years, he has tried in vain to overturn the traditional South [and] to destroy its political integrity."[5]

Ellis's effort to drum up support for Smith by attempting to exploit sectionalism proved no match for militant prohibitionism and its concomitant anti-Catholicism. Protestant fears that Smith's candidacy represented a papist plot to seize the White House, coupled with white anxiety that a Democratic victory "would put liquor into the hands of the negro," prevailed. In the end, Hoover carried the state because most Floridians had voted against Smith, rather than for the Republican candidate.[6]

Since Hoover's dry victory in 1928 fell short of a public mandate on prohibition, the controversy continued to burn. Eventually empirical evidence against the drys mounted and public support for national prohibition waned. By 1929, for example, the concurrent power to enforce the law shared by the states and the federal government proved at best impracticable and at worst "a costly failure."[7] Aware of the changing political climate, drys began devising plans to shore up national prohibition. Florida's new chief justice Rivers Buford, for one, proposed what he considered the most practicable plan to make the Eighteenth Amendment more effective. First, Buford recommended that the states set the alcoholic content of intoxicating liquors. Then, those states that authorized the sale of liquor—containing between 1 percent and 5 percent alcohol by volume—could sell spirits only in containers filled and sealed under government supervision. Finally, he advised bestowing the enforcement responsibility on the Justice Department.[8]

Apparently, many state and local authorities had already bestowed the burden of prohibition enforcement on the federal government. While federal court dockets swelled during the waning years of the Noble Experiment, the number of prohibition cases heard in Florida's supreme court and lower courts declined. Several reasons help explain the drop in litigation in these tribunals. The onset of the "Great Depression" precipitated a fiscal crisis for all levels of government in Florida. This in turn prompted many state and local officials to pass responsibility for prohibition enforcement to their federal counterparts. As the debt of counties, cities, and other political districts expanded from $100 million in 1922 to $600 million in 1929, local authorities saw little justification to fund or duplicate services that federal agencies provided concurrently.[9]

By the early 1930s the state's financial pinch had become so bleak that Governor Doyle E. Carlton proposed an austerity program to save Florida's precious dollars "by reducing the number of circuit courts, using grand juries in fewer cases, [and by] reducing the number of county offices and the salaries associated with them."[10] Faced with budgetary problems of unprecedented proportions, prohibition enforcement thus became a luxury that most Florida communities could ill afford.

Not surprisingly, grand juries reduced the number of indictments issued for transgressions against the liquor laws. An even smaller number of cases ended in conviction. According to one study, between 1929 and 1933, the Hernando County Circuit Court failed to convict anyone for violating national prohibition. Evidently, the state and local criminal justice systems had diverted the flood of prohibition litigation to the federal courts.[11]

State and local budget deficits aside, other factors also contributed to the federal judicial logjam. Some writers have contended that the tepid support for prohibition by regional officials stemmed from political concerns rather than economics. According to a contemporary account, after 1929 county sheriffs throughout the state willingly yielded to federal agents the burden of prohibition enforcement in order to avoid local political animosities. Or as Florida historian Charlton Tebeau put it: "Local Authorities proved indifferent if not outright hostile to enforcement."[12]

Local indifference to prohibition enforcement seems odd, given the electoral successes of drys in Florida. In June 1930, every candidate for office who advocated repeal of the state and federal liquor laws lost in the primaries. Later that year, the WCTU warned the major political parties to nominate only drys. Drys then began planning "a militant reorganization" of their forces. With an eye on the 1932 campaign, Clarence True Wilson, of the Methodist Board of Temperance, announced that presidential candidates "must be dry to obtain the support of his organization." The following spring the *Pensacola Journal* reported that "Dixie's Baptists" would seek the defeat of all candidates, from president down, "who opposed the present prohibition laws."[13]

Even so, the actions by the drys indicated the growing popularity of the wet cause. By 1930 the state's former dry consensus had come undone. The electorate split almost evenly between those who favored repeal, or at least a modification of the existing prohibition laws, and those who wanted the law to remain in effect. According to a *Literary Digest* poll, out of 560 Tallahassee residents surveyed, 232 wanted the Eighteenth Amendment repealed, 172 supported modification, and 156 endorsed continued federal enforcement of prohibition. The *Digest* went on to relate that, out of twenty-three Florida towns surveyed that had a population of 5,000 or more, twelve voted wet and eleven dry. The poll suggests that posing the wet-dry conflict as a simple urban-rural dichotomy fails to capture the pluralistic nature of the liquor controversy.[14]

Prompted in part by the public's growing aversion to national prohibition (as illustrated in the *Literary Digest* poll and other social barometers), President Hoover appointed a task force to investigate the entire structure of the federal criminal justice system. He ordered the commission "to make such recommendations for reorganization of the administration of federal laws and court procedure as may be found desirable." On January 20, 1931, the National Commission on Law Observance and Enforcement, better known as the Wickersham Commission, published its findings. Though filled with facts and statistics, the report remained open to interpretation and ended in a "welter of ambivalence." Finding the existing enforcement less than satisfactory, the commission opposed repeal of the Eighteenth Amendment but offered no alternatives to implement a dry national policy. Perhaps even more significant, all eleven commissioners who had collectively opposed repeal issued individual statements that underscored the underlying weakness of the coalition. Nine members emphasized the public's failure to support the law; six demanded immediate change; while only one commissioner, Federal Judge William I. Grubb (a Democrat, and one of the itinerant judges who had occasionally sojourned to Florida to help alleviate the state's federal judicial backlog), unequivocally endorsed continued pursuit of prohibition "in the hope of achieving better enforcement and public support." The controversy shrouding the report thus "ended any hopes that the Wickersham Commission could resolve the national prohibition issue."[15]

The Wickersham Commission's findings on prohibition enforcement in Florida proved as ambiguous as the national report and, if not rife with errors, appeared somewhat misleading. According to Frank Buckley, an attorney with the Bureau of Prohibition who had filed the Florida survey, prohibition agents considered Alexander Akerman's court at Tampa a level playing field where fair trials proceeded smoothly.[16] Akerman's judicial record, however, suggests that he sometimes tipped the scales of justice to favor the prosecution. One time, for example, he warned a rumrunner convicted in Tampa, "if you're figuring on keeping in the racket, you'd better go to Chicago."[17]

In perhaps the clearest illustration of Akerman's unbalanced approach, a jury under his prodding convicted Fritz Boyett of production and possession of intoxicating liquor. For this crime, they sentenced him to serve two years in prison. During the original trial, Boyett testified that he had rented a building, where the agents had discovered a still, to a man named J. Q. Smith. But he also claimed "he had nothing to do with the still and did not know it was there." Following his testimony, the jury retired to deliberate. They returned an hour later, and the foreman requested additional instructions from Judge Akerman. The jury wanted to know whether they could convict the defendant, if he had known previously that a still had operated on his property, but exerted no effort to stop it. "If the defendant knew that the still was in his house, on his property and in operation there, and took no steps to stop it," Akerman told the jury, "he would be equally guilty with the person, or persons, so operating the distillery . . . [as a] principle and accessory." Again the jury retired, deliberated, returned, and reported that they could not reach a verdict.[18]

The foreman then asked the judge for further instructions. Akerman replied impatiently: "I am afraid there are some of you who do not want instructions, and are not willing to follow the instructions given by the Court. It does not seem to the Court that there should be any difficulty in arriving at a verdict in this case." He then ordered the marshal of the court to prepare supper for the jury and a place for them to spend the night. Following dinner, he told the marshal to allow "them to consider their verdict until bedtime, and then permit them to retire until morning and after they have breakfast, return them to their jury room for further consideration of their verdict." Akerman's threat to sequester struck a responsive chord with the jury. They retired again and within five minutes returned with a verdict of guilty as charged.[19]

One could give Akerman the benefit of the doubt and suggest that the judicial backlog instead of personal bias prompted his injudicious behavior. Hearing cases strikingly similar time and again, from Akerman's perspective, prohibition litigation had transformed his bench into a tribunal bearing more resemblance to a traffic court than a federal district court. By the early 1930s, to illustrate the point, a diverse group of prohibition violators was parading through his court in Tampa. "More women were arraigned than ever before, and there were aged men and boys, blind men and cripples, some who sold liquor to buy bread." One woman convicted of selling moonshine begged Akerman to have mercy on her, because she only sold the booze to support her child. In addition, she taught Bible classes on Sunday. For the sake of the child, Akerman "let her off with a $25 fine."[20] Beleaguered, with his patience worn thin by such repetitive and mundane cases, Akerman apparently attempted to hasten prohibition litigation to enable the court to turn to more pressing matters. In doing so, Akerman probably hoped to recapture the influence that the bench formerly wielded over public policy.[21]

Between 1926 and 1933, to further emphasize the judicial backlog, the total number of liquor prosecutions instituted in Florida's federal courts jumped from 595 in 1926, to 986 in 1927, peaked at 1,804 in 1929, and then leveled off during the early years of the Great Depression at 1,332 cases per year. Then, in 1933 as national prohibition's future became less certain and near beer became legal, the number of prosecutions initiated plummeted to 547. During the same period, conviction rates for each judicial district increased significantly. Prosecutors in the northern jurisdiction improved their rate from 69 percent in 1926 to a high of 89 percent in 1932. Their counterparts in the southern courts achieved comparable success. While the latter convicted only 33 percent of cases tried in 1926, six years later 81 percent of its prosecutions ended in convictions. Furthermore, in 1933 as uncertainty set in concerning the future of prohibition, the courts in Florida's northern and southern federal districts experienced a greater than 20-point drop in their conviction rates (Table 5.1).[22]

Table 5.1
Liquor Prosecutions in Florida's Federal Courts

	Prosecutions Terminated		*Conviction Rates*	
Year	North	South	North (%)	South (%)
1919	151	72	81	57
1920	157	302	61	66
1921	121	463	73	44
1922	167	421	63	39
1923	209	425	70	32
1924	247	240	72	65
1925	117	475	70	77
1926	194	689	69	33
1927	206	529	70	61
1928	191	1,125	65	70
1929	294	1,523	82	71
1930	248	1,376	84	68
1931	337	1,028	89	78
1932	NA	NA	89	81
1933	NA	NA	63	59
1934	NA	NA	77	83

Source: Office of the Attorney General, *Annual Reports* (Washington D.C.: GPO, 1919–1934).

Both districts managed to sustain the high conviction rates because defendants often pleaded guilty. In 1931, for example, defendants pleaded guilty in 80 percent of the liquor prosecutions tried in the Northern District's courts, while in the southern courts the accused pleaded guilty in 66 percent of the cases. The widespread use of plea bargaining in federal courts during prohibition, according to one scholar, was a consequence of professional standards applied to police methods, trial procedures, and legal training.[23]

But plea bargaining was also a result of selective enforcement. Many alleged liquor violators suffered personally due to the failed economy. Beaten, bedraggled, and perhaps fatalistic, this lot—like many other Americans who suffered in the 1930s—blamed themselves for their hardships. Small wonder that when they took to moonshining and got caught, the poor submitted with dignity and pleaded guilty to preserve what little self-esteem they had left.[24]

Moonshiners became less submissive, however, when repeal of prohibition became more certain. Their new-found confidence, coupled with a change in attitudes by judges, juries, and defendants, helps explain the marked drop in conviction rates for 1933. With repeal appearing imminent, neither judges nor juries felt much obligation to convict a person for violating a moribund law. Perhaps equally significant, defendants, anticipating the inevitable repeal of the Eighteenth Amendment, became less inclined to plead guilty.

Furthermore, the raising of the Volstead Act's standard of intoxicating to 3.2 percent alcohol provides a crucial reason for the diminished number of liquor cases initiated during 1933. Because the new standard permitted sales of near beer after April 1933, the pool of potential violators probably decreased. It is possible that erstwhile moonshiners may have switched from whiskey to beer production to capture a share of the newly established legal market. If so, prohibition officers would have found fewer suspects to arrest.

Such speculation aside, according to the reports of district attorneys, by 1930 "enforcement officers had filed stronger and better cases . . . and as a rule the courts [had] acted upon them accordingly."[25] This achievement occurred in part because the Prohibition Bureau began to select agents "more carefully, training them to a higher standard of legal knowledge." It also arose, however, from the bureau's objective "to bring to justice commercial violators" inasmuch as they could "be reached by the law directly, whereas the purely private violators have many constitutional and statutory protections."[26]

In using the phrase "commercial violators," the Bureau of Prohibition seemingly referred to large-scale operations such as those controlled by organized crime. But as it turned out in Florida, agents usually defined "commercial violator" so broadly that virtually any person who produced spirits for domestic consumption or sold moonshine in amounts as small as a pint became a likely candidate for federal apprehension. Yet to simplify their task, these same agents narrowed the field of investigation by excluding from the pool of suspects the sort of people who best understood constitutional safeguards, who lived in relative economic comfort, and/or those who had earned substantial profits from a rather extensive involvement in the liquor trade. Such tactics in Florida thus led prohibition officers to target suspects based on a high probability of securing a conviction. They generally went after small-time moonshiners who lived marginal lives, lacked strong community ties, or possessed limited knowledge of due process.

To elaborate, by the late 1920s the Bureau of Prohibition confronted a dilemma. With public support for national prohibition waning, the repeal of the Eighteenth Amendment seemed almost certain. Furthermore, agents knew that they had a vested interest in the Eighteenth Amendment and had much to lose by its repeal. To show the efficiency of the department and to demonstrate that lawlessness had reached epidemic proportions, agents picked up the tempo of arrests and brought in as many violators as possible. As the drama unfolded, federal agents preyed generally on easy targets, such as small-time moonshiners and destitute dealers who possessed little knowledge of the legal system and whose stills contributed a mere trickle to the river of liquor production in the state. In other words, federal agents proved adept at apprehending small-time moonshiners and logged an impressive number of arrests but failed "to carry out the sophisticated undercover work needed to dry up the source of supply."[27]

The typical prohibition case in Florida, more often than not, arose from a citizen's complaint and invariably ended in conviction. Of twenty-two cases examined, approximately 91 percent resulted from a local citizen's discontent. Moreover, only one case in the entire sample stemmed from an investigation initiated by prohibition agents.

Although a multitude of factors prompted Floridians to inform on moonshiners, a few dominated. For instance, an irate customer denied credit by a former supplier may have evened the score by reporting the bootlegger to the authorities. Some moonshiners turned in competitors either to divert suspicion from their own operation or to capture a larger share of the liquor market. Still others could have turned informant for highly personal reasons. A woman married to a man who consumed too much liquor may have felt compelled to eradicate the source of her family's woes by notifying the authorities of the source of her husband's whiskey.

In one case, a group of Florida women met at their church and decided to put an end to a local bootlegger's business. Following through on the plan, one of them sent a letter to a prohibition investigator and asked him "to search [the dealer's] house and be sure to search all of his property, for I understand that he has some buried." She mentioned also that the women of her church would "keep watch on his place." She refused to sign the letter, however, fearing "he will know who done it, for he has said that I would report him, as he sells [liquor] to my husband and boys and I do not approve of it."[28]

After receiving this letter and other reports from neighbors that John P. Finley (the alleged liquor trafficker and a sixty-year-old paraplegic) had "stated on different occasions that the court would not put him in jail [for] he was crippled," the officers considered him a community nuisance. Agents went to his grocery store and requested a bottle of beer. When Finley delivered the drink, they immediately arrested the merchant as he sat in his wheelchair. The church women, who had wanted Finley's speakeasy shut down, could thus rest assured for they had purged the community of a perceived moral threat.[29]

Some Florida women, however, saw nothing immoral about dealing in alcoholic spirits. Prohibition investigators found 832 bottles of beer at the Crawfordsville home of Mrs. Lena M. Severance. Following her arrest, the sixty-three-year-old housewife confessed to owning the beer found at her home. Evidently, she had been handling beer for about eighteen months due to the poor health of her husband. As she put it, "We would do nothing else to make a living." But Severance countered that she did not sell the beer. "I sold cheese and crackers," she claimed, "and gave the beer to drink with the sandwiches." Severance asserted, "I have never been arrested for violating prohibition."[30]

In light of the socioeconomic conditions that characterized the state in the early 1930s, Severance and Finley probably had difficulty finding paying customers for their illicit product. Starting in 1929, per capita accountable income began a precipitous decline in Florida. Dropping from $510 to $478 in 1930, it fell again in 1931 to $392.[31] Anecdotal evidence amplifies the human element associated with these numbers. In 1931 an attorney who filed a report on prohibition enforcement in Florida for the Wickersham Commission described the panhandle as "a countryside barren of anything but pine forests, a few large sawmills, and miserable unpainted neglected habitations." Concluding that life throughout the region proved "anything but gay," he implied that the area's abject poverty had led to many liquor transgressions that involved primarily the "manufacture and distribution of a cheap moonshine product in small quantities."[32]

As the Great Depression deepened, poverty in Florida worsened. During the first quarter of 1933, the number of Florida families on relief averaged around ninety thousand, or a little more than 20 percent of all households. By the end of the year the percentage of families receiving public assistance had increased to 26 percent of the population. Although the proportion varied from county to county, 33 percent of the recipients "lived in rural areas and [in] towns under 500 people."[33]

Pressed by mean circumstances, many hardscrabble farmers turned to moonshining to tide them through the hard times. Consequently, agents found such violators vulnerable game. A rough analysis of data gleaned from the case files of twenty-two moonshiners tried in the Northern District indicates that the average north Florida bootlegger plied his trade with one or two assistants and owned personal property valued at $878. Still, if the five wealthiest violators are excluded from the sample, average net worth per moonshiner falls to about $75. Although these estimates remain open to further investigation, they suggest that prohibition enforcement in Florida fell unfairly upon poor people largely because federal agents cast a discriminatory eye toward violators.

Furthermore, when judged by the swollen dockets and high conviction rates in Florida's federal courts, authorities had little difficulty arresting or convicting violators during most of the prohibition era. Meeting little more than token resistance from either the culprits or the local institutions, agents usually arrested small-time bootleggers whose product served a limited local market. In fact, at the time of the arrest, the typical Florida moonshiner possessed only 5.1 gallons of whiskey. This is not to say, however, that the government was any closer to winning the war on illegal liquor. Rather, it seems that prohibition enforcement fell disproportionately upon the poor.[34]

Several cases highlight the selective nature of prohibition enforcement in Florida. In 1932, for example, Agent Clyde V. Land paid $3 to Charlie J. Jacobs for a gallon of moonshine, put a twenty-five-cent deposit on the jug, and then arrested him for the sale and possession of liquor. Jacobs, a forty-five-year-old poverty-stricken white, had been living in the Tallahassee vicinity for about three weeks. In his statement to the arresting officer, the Georgia transplant claimed he had moved to Florida in search of work. Finding no job offers there, he began "selling whiskey to negroes for fifty cents per pint." Although he had considered escaping and returning to Georgia," Jacobs said he "changed his mind and decided to take his medicine." Owning no real or personal property, and uncertain about his future, a destitute Jacobs added, "The place I [rent] belongs to a negro woman who teaches school near Tallahassee. I do not know what her name is, she comes to the house and collects the rent—$3.75 per week."[35]

Likewise, two days later a still found by officers in a Taylor County swamp prompted the arrest of Josh McCall and Dave Padgett—two backwoods yeomen farmers and part-time moonshiners—on charges of manufacturing and possession. McCall, a middle-aged widower with eight children to support, owned eighty acres of land on which he kept fifty hogs and four cows. Although his real estate and livestock had a combined value of $300, the farm proved inadequate to sustain his family. McCall, who claimed he had "never been arrested for anything before," turned to moonshining to supplement his family's meager income. Yet the distillery that McCall admitted owning produced little extra cash. He stated, "Times are hard and there is not much sale for whiskey."[36]

Unlike McCall, Padgett insisted that he had nothing to do with the still. "I was not getting one penny from it. I had been in the woods looking after some hog trap pens that I had [put] there for the purpose of catching hogs to be marked." Federal authorities remained unconvinced of Padgett's innocence and recommended that the government prosecute him along with McCall for violating the Volstead Act.[37]

Due to the severe dearth of money in the region, the local economy often regressed to a barter system. Perhaps with that in mind, and realizing that the Volstead Act banned the sale of alcohol, moonshiner N. W. Padgett, contrived that he did not sell whiskey but instead claimed he used liquor as a commodity of exchange. Unswayed by this pseudolegal defense, in 1933 the federal court at Tallahassee convicted Padgett for possession and sentenced him to pay a fine of $100. Since Padgett had no money to pay the penalty, he spent thirty days in the Leon County Jail.[38]

The illusion that moonshining would deliver easy money enticed many impoverished but otherwise law-abiding citizens to enter the illicit trade. Such mistaken beliefs made these people not only ripe for exploitation by bootleggers but also easy targets for federal agents. For example, Levie Thomas, a tenant farmer arrested for operating a still, initially claimed that his patron, Ralph Casseaux, owned the distillery. Later, Thomas changed his story and claimed the still "belonged to me and no one else had an interest in [it]." Thomas said that he had operated it for about two months and had produced fifty gallons of whiskey since he began the business. If Thomas spoke the truth, his thirst for moonshine knew no reasonable limit. Thomas announced, "I drank most of the whiskey that was made in the still and gave the balance to my friends." The prohibition investigators failed to seriously consider Thomas's confession and recommended that the government prosecute him.[39]

In addition to underscoring the selective nature of federal prohibition enforcement, some cases reveal the ubiquitous tension that has characterized race relations in Florida. After uncovering a white man's stock of moonshine stored in a shack where a poor black named William I. Riley had lived, federal agents arrested the African American. Subsequently, a frightened Riley gave anxious and somewhat inconsistent testimony. "The whiskey that the officers got out of the house was mine. I rented the place from Mr. Davis and I pay him $1.00 per month for rent. I do not want to tell on the white folks, as they would kill me. I did not put the whiskey in the house. A white man brought it from Taylor County. He left it there until he could come and get it."[40]

Unlike Riley, however, some poor black bootleggers possessed considerable entrepreneurial talent, enabling them to set up their own operations and compete confidently with whites in the illicit liquor trade. These enterprising African Americans did not intimidate easily. When caught and prosecuted, they rarely cowered before the white-dominated criminal justice system, and they often pleaded innocent. For example, in 1931 prohibition officers arrested Samuel Kilpatrick, a twenty-five-year-old African American, on charges of manufacturing liquor. Before the arrest, the agents had discovered twelve fifty-gallon fermenters, three hundred gallons of rye, some cane sugar mash (but no still) in an open swamp in Wakulla County. After seizing and destroying the contraband, the officers followed a well-traveled path approximately three hundred yards from the place of operation and found the missing still in a ditch to the side of the trail. They continued along the path until they reached a shack that appeared vacant. Without warrants they entered the shack through the backdoor and found Kilpatrick asleep on a cot in a corner. On the floor next to his cot the officers noticed the cap of the still and promptly arrested Kilpatrick. When they asked him if the cap belonged to the still that they had just seized, Kilpatrick remained calm. He fitted the cap on the still, and denied "knowing that the distillery was back in the swamp." Subsequently, an assistant district attorney scheduled Kilpatrick's trial for April 3, 1933—almost two years after the initial arrest![41]

While Kilpatrick awaited his trial, the debate over the future of prohibition heated, and organizations such as the Voluntary Committee of Lawyers (VCL) began successfully agitating for repeal. An elitist national organization led by some of New York's finest legal minds, the VCL had associates in virtually every state. "The committee formed upon an impulse to overcome a constitutional amendment which offended the members' sense of a sane society." Their perspective of the political-legal order in the age of Hoover "was one of laissez-faire and of state responsibility, which national prohibition, enforced from Washington, violated." They sought repeal and contributed significantly to that achievement.[42]

At the state level, Florida's chapter of the VCL also played a large role in shaping both public and legal opinion. One member in particular, Robert H. Anderson, had labored many hours "for the restoration of states' rights in the management of the morals of the people."[43] By 1932, his investment in time began to pay some handsome dividends. In the process, Anderson had helped engender a puissant force to counter the well-organized opposition to repeal. A Florida State Bar Association poll, for example, revealed that members of the state's legal profession favored repeal by "nearly six to one." The attorneys assumed their anti-prohibition position because the Noble Experiment, they claimed, had resulted in smaller government revenues, spawned disrespect for law, facilitated the growth of syndicate crime, and nearly crippled the judicial system.[44]

However, the true measure of the VCL's influence became manifest in 1932's hectic congressional races. Indeed, pressure by the VCL, coupled with shock waves that emanated from the Great Depression, contributed to a fundamental shift that transformed Florida's political topography and turned a minority into a majority. Out of thirteen candidates who sought the four contested congressional seats, eleven advocated repeal or at least a prohibition referendum. Perhaps most surprising, the daughter of the late William Jennings Bryan, Ruth Bryan Owen, an incumbent up for renomination and erstwhile champion of prohibition, promised to vote for the resubmission of the liquor question to the states for a referendum. Denying that she had capitulated to the wets, Owen maintained that "she was upholding the principles of her father—the Great Commoner—who ardently supported the referendum right of the people."[45]

In April 1933, in a special session under Franklin D. Roosevelt's prodding, Congress passed a bill that increased the Volstead Act's existing "standard of intoxicating" to 3.2 percent alcohol.[46] With this measure, the legislature had inadvertently ushered in the second stage of the repeal movement in Florida and prompted the wet and dry camps to vie for the most advantageous positions from which to influence the state's liquor policy. With the onset of this phase, four Florida legislators from the lower house, R. K. Lewis, Ervin Bass, Frank J. Booth, and A. O. Kanner, combined forces to introduce an important taxation bill premised on the legalization of 3.2 percent beer. The measure proposed a $3.50 tax per barrel of beer and suggested charging $500 for brewery licenses, $100 for wholesale permits, and $15 for retail licenses. If passed, the bill's sponsors estimated that it would annually raise over $1 million in tax revenue.[47]

The next day, following a favorable report by the Committee on Prohibition, the house introduced a compromise beer-wine bill. Led by S. Pierre Robineau of Dade County, fourteen representatives launched the revised bill with a proposal that called for the repeal of the state's "bone dry" prohibition amendment and its substitution with local option. Governor David Sholtz endorsed the proposal in his biennial message to the legislature and requested its passage. To ease the bill's enactment, Sholtz recommended that all revenue generated by the tax on beer and wine should go to schools.[48]

Finding little merit in taxing sin to support public education, the WCTU of Tallahassee adamantly opposed the near beer bill. Anticipating the repeal of the Eighteenth Amendment as a major blow to their cause, the WCTU rallied to stop the legalization of near beer in Florida. To stem the wet tide, they pressed for an amendment to the state constitution that they considered requisite before the legislature could pass the beer measure. Realizing the inherent difficulty posed by constitutional reform, the WCTU probably wanted to buy time to muster additional dry opposition. Then, Florida's anti-liquor forces could exert sufficient influence to make certain that the new state constitution proved at least as restrictive of intoxicating spirits as the old. Apparently, the WCTU hoped that victories won in Florida would help offset the losses suffered by the drys nationally.[49]

The WCTU faced a formidable task. Besides countering the appealing notion that the tax on near beer would produce substantial revenue for the state's hard-pressed coffers, the WCTU had to confront economic reality in the shape of a national depression. Small wonder the proponents who favored revising the Volstead Act and ultimately repealing the Eighteenth Amendment "added to their arsenal of arguments, the number of jobs lost by prohibition, the amounts of grain which could be consumed after repeal, [and] the costs of enforcement, which might be used for public relief." For example, according to the Association Against the Prohibition Amendment (AAPA) prohibition eliminated roughly $900 million in state and federal excise taxes on spirits, wines, and beer. This sum, added to the $40 million spent on enforcement, nearly equaled the $1 billion in federal income tax collected by the government in 1929.[50]

These facts and arguments fell on receptive ears in Florida. Because the Great Depression had lingered far too long in the Sunshine State, Floridians found the employment opportunities that legalized beer promised to deliver a compelling reason to approve the near beer bill. A *Florida Times Union* report estimated that the opening of the Jacksonville Brewing Company alone would provide employment for seventy additional workers. The distribution and sale of near beer in Florida would create six thousand new jobs throughout the state. Even those people that the beer industry did not hire stood to gain. While the bill's passage remained pending, the Jacksonville Brewing Company had granted conditional contracts for improvements and supplies valued at $100,000.[51] Theoretically, once the bill passed, the increased investment's multiplied effect guaranteed to provide even more employment opportunity by trickling down to brewing-related businesses. For the eighty-five thousand Floridians seeking work in 1933, legalization of near beer made good economic sense.[52]

On May 8, 1933, Sholtz signed five bills that legalized near beer, light wine, and similar beverages. Together the bills also permitted the manufacture, distribution, sale, and advertising of the same. Hoping to capitalize on legislative reform, Florida newspapers leaped at the opportunity, and almost immediately readers throughout the state found "alluring beer advertisements staring at them from printed pages."[53]

Clearly the newspapers had a pecuniary interest in wet reform. Legalized beer and wine broadened a paper's advertising market by including businesses engaged in manufacturing, wholesaling, and retailing of alcoholic beverages. Because newspaper revenue depends largely on paid advertising, many Florida editors agitated for repeal from its inception.[54] During the state's ratifying convention for the Twenty-First Amendment in 1933, one delegate claimed that the convention owed a real debt to "those newspapers of the state and their editors, who long before repeal became popular, fought the good fight against the evils of prohibition." Persuasive editorials by "Mr. Lambright of the *Tampa Tribune* and Mr. Stoneman of the *Miami Herald*," he asserted, "helped to open the eyes of the people and crystallize the sentiment that gave repeal its tremendous majority in this state." With that in mind, he asked the convention to extend its thanks "to these newspapers for their efforts in this cause." Another delegate claimed: "I am unwilling to let this opportunity pass without paying a tribute to the *Jacksonville Journal* for its constant and consistent fight on behalf of repeal." The delegates then adopted a motion that extended the convention's warmest appreciation "to the newspapers of this state whose efforts have contributed so much to the success of the repeal movement in Florida."[55]

Meanwhile, rumors circulated that drys had planned to test the new law in the state's supreme court. The gossip proved unfounded. After a full day of legal beer, the drys had not yet filed a petition with the court contesting the beer measure.[56] And according to the interpretation of Attorney General Cary D. Landis, a dry county could "in no way" prevent individuals from partaking of near beer or light wine within its borders.[57]

Nonetheless, Florida wets could not rest assured. Neither the sales receipts nor the promised additional tax revenue materialized quickly from the start. Apparently, illicit brewers retained customer loyalty and initially managed to stave off the competition offered by licensed breweries. According to one wholesaler, thousands of people accustomed to making their own beer continued to do so for two reasons. "[T]hey said it [was] cheaper and that it [had] a bigger kick." Eventually, however, economies of scale set in, legitimate supplies increased, prices dropped, and major breweries garnered the larger portion of the beer trade. Since smaller illicit producers left the market, the tax revenue generated by beer sales began to grow. Five months after it first went into effect, state officials announced that if not for the beer tax, the public school fund "would have been $140,000 in arrears."[58]

Encouraged by the beer bill's success, Florida's anti-prohibitionists then joined in the national crusade to amend the federal constitution. Governor Sholtz summoned a special election to choose "sixty-seven delegates-at-large to a ratification convention" scheduled to meet in the fall of 1933. In October, Florida residents voted two to one for an all-wet delegation to represent them in the upcoming convention.[59] The next month, when the meeting convened in Tallahassee, orators clothed their speeches in republican garb. One delegate, "jealous of the blessings of local and personal liberty," exclaimed: "The tragic error we are engaged in correcting . . . came from a misconception of the very essence of the federal principle." Another representative compared the liquor laws to the Four Intolerable Acts that helped spawn the American Revolution. "It was not so much the practical enforcement and results of those Acts that made them odious to the point of exciting revolt, for they were . . . evaded as has been our famous Volstead Law; but it was the outrage of having them made and their enforcement attempted by a distant tyranny with no regard to colonial interests or wishes. Such, too has been the Eighteenth Amendment."[60]

Echoing the same republican ethos, Anderson of the VCL bellowed: "As the yoke of British tyranny was cast off [the colonies], so now we rid ourselves of the shackles of organized minorities, which have falsely claimed to represent public sentiment. . . . [Our] victory is a tribute . . . to the deep-rooted faith in the American ideals of our Fathers concerning the Constitutional Government of the United States. It is a declaration that the people of the United States disapprove of Federal transgression of state's rights and that it will oppose and resist that transgression."[61] With little opposition, all sixty-three delegates present voted for the repeal of the Eighteenth Amendment and Florida became the thirty-third state to ratify the Twenty-First. The prohibition amendment thus became the only addition to the Constitution to be repealed.[62]

In the early months of 1934, federal judges began issuing general orders to dispose of any pending cases that involved violations of national prohibition. For the most part, they agreed that the federal courts retained no power to impose judgment in prohibition cases.[63] Yet in the wake of repeal, one federal judge, A. V. Long, warned Florida bootleggers and moonshiners that they could expect harsh treatment in the district courts. Although he did not say why, Long considered liquor law transgressions under repeal more serious than those that had occurred under prohibition. Long then announced that he would treat any cases involving the failure to pay the liquor tax "more severely" than previous infractions against the Volstead Act. Scolding a man who had pleaded guilty to manufacturing moonshine shortly after repeal, Long stated, "there is no prohibition law any more and it is just as unfair for a man to operate a liquor still and not pay the tax as it is for a man to sell shoes in a licensed business on one side of the street while a man sells shoes across the street in an unlicensed business. . . . [Such] business must be stopped.[64]

Despite Long's bluster, repeal of the Eighteenth Amendment removed liquor from federal control and placed it mainly under the jurisdiction of state and local governments. Because of this, prohibition remained a significant political issue in Florida. Unless intended for medical, scientific, or mechanical purposes, the manufacture, sale, and/or transportation of liquor violated state law. As Attorney General Landis put it, "Repeal of the Eighteenth Amendment, had nothing to do with . . . Florida's bone dry amendment, still in effect."[65]

Perhaps accepting Landis's words as a challenge, Florida wets then began agitating for the proposed resolution that called for the repeal of the state's constitutional ban on booze. As drafted, the bill stipulated that the status of all territory in Florida concerning the sale of intoxicants would become the same as it was on December 31, 1918. If passed, this meant that the old local option laws would be revived, and the importation, transportation, or manufacturing of ardent spirits would then remain unlawful only in those erstwhile dry counties.[66]

On November 6, 1934, in a record turnout for an off-year election, Florida voters decided the fate of the state's constitutional ban on liquor. As it happened, the wets carried the election by a more than two to one margin. In doing so, they initiated the third phase of the wet crusade in Florida by passing the liquor issue back to the counties that had held local option referendums concurrent with the statewide repeal ballot. Out of Florida's sixty-seven counties, forty-two rejected local option, twenty-four went dry, and one remained undecided.[67]

When viewed through the lens of liquor litigation, it appears that Florida wets won a somewhat hollow victory in the battle for repeal. With the liquor issue returned to the state, wets soon discovered, perhaps to their dismay, that provincial government, coupled with diverse popular and strong institutional support, could still restrict alcohol in their jurisdictions. No longer having to contend with issues relating to federalism or similar constitutional concerns, Florida's state and local governments managed to ban liquor more effectively than the federal government had during national prohibition.[68]

For example, the day after Florida voters elected to repeal the state's prohibition ban, R. G. Blanc, the mayor of St. Petersburg, called upon Governor Sholtz to place the question concerning the handling of liquor in wet counties before the state supreme court for an advisory opinion. According to Blanc, conflicting ideas on the effect of repeal had hampered preparation of local measures. Sholtz, who favored executive instead of judicial liquor control, responded, "There are plenty of laws on the books to govern liquor handling." These included the Davis package law, the Wells package law, and others passed before statewide prohibition became effective and, Sholtz erroneously claimed, "were revived by the terms of the repeal amendment."[69]

Yet, much to Sholtz's chagrin, he provided merely the first rather than the last words on the liquor matter. The impact that repeal had on Florida's liquor statutes struck much deeper than the governor had imagined. In effect, the repeal of Florida's constitutional ban on liquor reopened many of the same legal issues that the court had addressed during the years 1885 to 1919.

In *Coleman, Sheriff* v. *State ex rel Race* (1935), for example, a Dade County court had charged R. C. Race on three counts of selling liquor without a valid permit. The defense insisted that no such license was needed for Florida's constitution had repealed all local liquor laws. Regardless, the county sheriff insisted that the local statute was in effect December 31, 1918 and became operable again after the legislature revised the constitution in 1934.[70]

"We must bear in mind," Judge Buford wrote, that "we are dealing with provisions of the Constitution and not with statutes." The state constitutional ban on alcohol, which went into effect January 1, 1919, did not repeal local statutes, according to Buford. It instead placed the measures in repose or at rest, "so long as the Constitution remained as it came to be on January 1, 1919." When the people changed the constitution again in November 1934, "those statutes enacted which found their basis only in those constitutional provisions existing . . . from 1919 to 1934, were likewise put in repose." Thus, the terms of the 1934 amendment revived those provisions valid on December 31, 1918, and by that, Buford concluded, reinstated the old policy.[71]

While the court concurred that the state's recent constitutional amendment had reinstated the old liquor policy, dissent arose when they tried to attach meaning to that policy. One week later, in *State ex rel Hoffman* v. *Powell* (1935), the court ruled that the emergency prohibition law enacted in 1918 was revived and effective under the provisions of the state constitution, as amended by the electorate in 1934. The emergency prohibition law specifically banned the commercial transportation of intoxicants into Florida's dry counties. This case arose after Lillian H. Hoffman purchased two cases of vermouth and one case of gin from a New York liquor dealer "to entertain many guests during her sojourn in Leon County." But when the shipment arrived in Tallahassee, the American Railway Company refused to deliver the order to Hoffman in dry Leon County. She, in turn, sought a court order compelling the railway company to deliver the merchandise. With that, she tested the constitutionality of the emergency prohibition law.[72]

After hearing each side argue constitutional law, Chief Justice James B. Whitfield noted that Congress had designed federal constitutional and statutory policy to protect dry states against the transportation by common carrier or others of liquor into their territories. "Likewise, it is the purpose of the state constitution and statutes," Whitfield contended, "to protect the dry counties of the state against the commercial transportation by common carriers and others of intoxicating liquors into dry counties." According to Whitfield, Governor Catts's emergency prohibition law became effective December 9, 1918, and remained in effect on December 31, 1918. It did not violate Florida's first state prohibition amendment, nor did the second amended article render it invalid. In short, Whitfield concluded that the constitutional ban's enabling statute made the emergency prohibition law unnecessary for enforcing statewide prohibition. So by repealing the state constitutional ban on booze, the people had revived and reinstated Catts's emergency prohibition law as of November 6, 1934.[73]

In a five-page dissent, Justice Ellis presented a brief historical summary of Florida's liquor laws. When Florida ratified its local option article, Ellis noted, the state maintained the status of wet territory. That is, Florida permitted the sale of intoxicating liquors, wines, or beer. "The adoption of the local option article," Ellis said, "did not change that status." It merely "stipulated that elections might be held in the different counties under the conditions named to decide whether the sale of such liquors should be prohibited." Furthermore, Ellis contended that the local option article neither repealed nor suspended any legislation designed to regulate liquor sales. Those laws remained in effect, Ellis claimed, until a majority vote at a properly called election approved a local option ordinance, which would then suspend any statutes relating to liquor sales.[74]

Nonetheless, Ellis added that in 1918 Florida eliminated local option by substituting an amendment to its constitution which forever prohibited the manufacture, sale, barter, or exchange of ardent spirits in the state. This measure, according to Ellis, effectively and completely repealed every law purporting to regulate liquor sales. The status of the state had changed from wet to dry territory. Then, when the state revised the constitution again in 1934, Ellis conceded that all laws relating to liquor effective on that date became reinstated unless changed by the legislature. But Ellis emphasized that the new amendment merely reinstated the state's old policy under the local option article to the 1885 constitution, which related only to liquor sales. Thus, even though Leon County had not held elections under the most recent amendment, it assumed its prior dry status. And since he found no state laws effective on December 31, 1918 that prohibited liquor shipments into dry counties, Ellis concluded that the American Railway Company could lawfully deliver the liquor to Hoffman. The court's majority, however, sided with Whitfield, and upheld the emergency prohibition law as a valid exercise of the police powers.[75]

By 1935 the Supreme Court of Florida had come full circle on the liquor issue. The dismantling of national prohibition's institutional framework, coupled with the restoration of local option, spawned new (but similar) judicial discourse over old law. As in the pre-prohibition debate, the scope of the police powers relative to individual property rights lay at the heart of the post-repeal controversy. Although the court's dissonance in the 1930s remained less striking than that of its predecessors in the 1910s, a philosophical division had begun taking shape. Justices Buford, Ellis, and Armstead Brown emerged as the court's strict constructionists, while Fred H. Davis, Glenn Terrell, and James B. Whitfield became the standard bearers of loose constructionism.

Yet, unlike the pre-prohibition court that saw its divisions grow sharper the more restrictive the liquor statute became in terms of property, the court in the 1930s (after fourteen years of national prohibition) had agreed tenuously that local governments could exert prohibitive control over intoxicating spirits. In other words (and at risk of over-simplification), following repeal the court's consensus became clearer the more local the liquor statute. Under such conditions, judges proved more willing to broaden the police powers: the smaller the jurisdiction, the greater the power.

The consensus began to fray around the edges, however, as county and municipal governments began exercising their near absolute local control over liquor. To check such usurpation, the strict constructionists invoked the due process clause of the Fourteenth Amendment. But promoting this clause as a bulwark against governmental encroachment on constitutional liberties proved less effective than advocating the inalienable right to property. It seems probable that the court's majority at the time realized that the due process clause contradicted its notion of state sovereignty—the idea that the national government was the agent of the state responsible for safeguarding the liberties of citizens.[76] To endorse the Fourteenth Amendment's due process clause was to surrender state autonomy over local matters. This not only went against the traditional concept of federalism but also would have reduced the court's status. So in a sense, the Florida Supreme Court resisted the due process clause on both constitutional principles and self-interest.

On the other hand, the rules that governed property had been traditionally the function of the state. Not surprisingly, state and local judges felt more secure in checking the police power with arguments grounded in property rights than by advancing the due process clause. In *Ex parte Francis* (1918), for example, the court, with Jefferson B. Browne in the vanguard, had voted three to two and ruled that "liquor is property that is the subject of private ownership . . . and the legislature has no authority to prohibit its ownership." James B. Whitfield, who championed the welfare of the people as the supreme law, dissented. "All property rights," he huffed, "are subject to lawful governmental regulations under the police power of the state."[77] Although Whitfield lost that constitutional battle, his reasoning prevailed in the end. Seventeen years later, the Florida Supreme Court ruled that local jurisdictions such as counties and municipalities could exercise prohibitive control over liquor without fear of judicial intervention. In *State ex rel Atlantic Ice & Co.* v. *Weems* (1935), to illustrate the point, the court validated a local community's power to ban alcohol absolutely. This case arose after Alachua County had denied the Atlantic Ice & Company a license to construct a brewery for making near beer. The controlling statute then in effect, as noted, permitted sales of near beer statewide, including counties that had voted dry. The legislature had essentially classified near beer as non-intoxicating. The law seemed clear: neither Alachua nor any other county in the state could prohibit such sales.[78]

Those conditions notwithstanding, the Florida Supreme Court voted five to one and upheld Alachua County's refusal to grant the firm a permit to build the brewery. Speaking for the court's majority, Justice Whitfield wrote: "There is no inherent right in anyone to manufacture alcoholic beverages." Since the Constitution did not prohibit or regulate the manufacture of booze, he insisted "it [was] within the power of the legislature to prohibit or to regulate such manufacture by general or by local laws."[79]

Justice Armstead Brown challenged Whitfield's position. "Why should the legislature prohibit the manufacture of a beverage which it definitely permits to be sold in dry counties," Brown asked, "on the manifest ground that it is non-intoxicating?" Or, for that matter, "Why should Jacksonville or Tampa or Miami brewers be permitted to sell 3.2 percent beer in Alachua County, and yet the citizens of Alachua County be prevented from brewing the same kind of beer in their own county?" Put simply: "Why allow the sale, but deny the manufacture of a non-intoxicating beverage in certain counties merely because they have prohibited the sale of intoxicating liquor therein?" To Brown, the sale of near beer to the consumer posed no greater threat to the public than its manufacture. "It would seem that the legislative classification," Brown wrote, "makes a distinction between counties based upon differences in their local laws relating to intoxicating liquors which, as regards 3.2 percent beer, is a distinction without a difference."[80]

Since the controlling statute treated near beer as a non-intoxicant legally marketable anywhere in the state, Brown found the act "arbitrary and unreasonable." It denied "equal protection of the laws to those citizens of the so-called dry counties who desire[d] to manufacture this presumably harmless and non-intoxicating beverage on the same terms which the statute grant[ed] to the citizens of the so-called wet counties which have no local prohibitory laws."[81] Noting a vast difference between regulation and prohibition, Brown apparently wanted to know where to draw the line of demarcation beyond which the courts could say constitutionally, "thus far shalt thou go and no further."[82] The answer to this question (originally raised in 1916) depended on where the court decided to draw that line, that is, "the police power [became] essentially what the courts declared it to be."[83]

Ironically, since many drys in Florida never grasped that repeal could actually benefit their cause, they continued to clamor for the good old days of prohibition. Indeed, in 1937 at the fifty-fourth annual meeting of the WCTU of Florida, delegate Dr. Ella A. Boole insisted that repeal had failed miserably. "Unemployment has not been eliminated. Many on relief spend their money for liquor while their families go without necessities." Additionally, she asserted that "our girls and women are serving as barmaids in saloons of disrepute." She therefore encouraged the WCTU to continue the good fight of temperance and to keep the public's eye focused on the needless toll on human lives caused by the consumption of alcohol. Reminding her audience that "wets did not keep still when prohibition was law," Boole implored her sisters to "buy dry, patronize those who sell dry, and if we have to buy where alcohol is sold, to stand by our principles."[84] Deaf to the inherent contradictions in her words, Boole's closing comment suggests that the WCTU would henceforth base its actions more on expediency than on principle.

NOTES

1. U.S. Congress, House Committee on the Judiciary, *Additional Judge in Florida*, 70th Cong., 1st sess., 24 May 1928 (Washington, D.C.: GPO, 1928), 1859.

2. For more on the impact of prohibition on the federal courts, see John F. Padgett, "Plea Bargaining and Prohibition in the Federal Courts, 1908–1934," *Law and Society Review* 24 (1990), 413–450; Kermit L. Hall and Eric W. Rise, *From Local Courts to National Tribunals: The Federal District Courts of Florida, 1821–1990* (Brooklyn, N.Y.: Carlson Publishing Inc., 1991), 62, 74–77.

3. Data compiled from Department of Justice, Division of Taxation, Prohibition, and Prisons, *Report of the Attorney General*, 1915–1934. Because the Southern District encompassed the state's fastest growing region and, as Taft noted, the area most conducive to smuggling, prohibition's impact on that district proved more profound than on the northern jurisdiction. Between 1920 and 1930, for example, the Northern District's population grew only 13 percent, from 291,243 to 329,260. The Southern District, during the same period, realized a 68 percent population increase, adding 461,724 people to the 677,227 counted in 1920. One should bear in mind, however, that the number of cases cited plus the percentage of criminal prosecutions that they represent are overstated. As Padgett has noted: "Before 1922, charges were classified by legal charge; after 1922, charges were aggregated according to administrative categories. In particular, Volstead Act liquor cases were included in 'Public Health and Safety' along with internal revenue liquor cases, narcotics cases, white slavery (i.e., prostitution) cases, peonage cases, and a few others." Padgett claims that prohibition cases consistently comprised roughly 90 percent of the category "Public Health and Safety." For the purposes of this study, "Public Health and Safety" crimes will serve as a safe approximation for liquor cases. See Padgett, "Plea Bargaining and Prohibition in the Federal Courts," 413–450.

4. Jack S. Blocker, *American Temperance Movements: Cycles of Reform* (Boston: Twayne Publishers, 1989), 125; Frank W. Alduino, "The 'Noble Experiment' in Tampa: A Study of Prohibition in Urban America" (Ph.D. diss., Florida State University, 1989), 205–208; Herbert J. Doherty, Jr., "Florida and the Presidential Election of 1928," *Florida Historical Quarterly* 26 (October 1947), 179–181; Edward M. Hughes, "Florida Preachers and the Election of 1928," *Florida Historical Quarterly* 67 (October 1988), 131–146; Ida DeGarmo, *Life Story of Minnie E. Neal: President of Florida Woman's Christian Temperance Union* (Jacksonville, Fla.: WCTU, 1936), 8.

5. *Miami Herald*, October 11, 1928.

6. Doherty, "Florida and the Presidential Election of 1928," 179–181.

7. Kermit L. Hall, *The Magic Mirror: Law in American History* (New York: Oxford University Press, 1989), 251.

8. Rivers Buford, "Let States Fix Alcoholic Content," in W. C. Durant, ed., *Law Observance: Shall the People of the United States Uphold the Constitution* (New York: Durant, 1929), 103–105.

9. See Charlton W. Tebeau, *A History of Florida* (Coral Gables, Fla.: University of Miami Press, 1971), 394–396.

10. Ibid.

11. Richard Cofer, "Bootleggers in The Backwoods: Prohibition in the Depression in Hernando County," *Tampa Bay History* 1 (Spring/Summer 1979), 17–23.

12. See Frank Buckley, "Prohibition Survey of Florida," in U.S. Senate, *National Commission on Law Observance and Enforcement*, 71st Cong., 3rd sess. (Washington, D.C.: GPO, 1931), 114–116; Tebeau, *A History of Florida*, 390.

13. See Ernest Hurst Cherrington, ed., *The Anti-Saloon League Yearbook, 1930* (Westerville, Ohio: Anti-Saloon League of America, 1930), 17; *Tampa Tribune*, November 19, 23, 1930; *Pensacola Journal*, May 17, 1931.

14. *Daily Democrat*, June 2, 1930; Alduino, "The 'Noble Experiment' in Tampa," 213; *Tampa Tribune*, June 1, 1930.

15. Quoted in Clement E. Vose, *Constitutional Change: Amendment Politics and Supreme Court Litigation Since 1900* (Lexington, Mass.: Lexington Books, 1972), 105–107; David E. Kyvig, *Repealing National Prohibition* (Chicago: University of Chicago Press, 1979), 113–115; Harold Chase et al., *Biographical Dictionary of the Federal Judiciary* (Detroit: Gale Research Company, 1976), 110.

16. Buckley, "Prohibition Survey of Florida," 114–115.

17. *Tampa Tribune*, November 26, 1930.

18. *Boyett* v. *United States*, 48 F.2d 482 (1931).

19. Ibid.

20. *Tampa Tribune*, November 4, 1930.

21. An important study of state supreme courts (SSC) from 1870–1970 concluded that SSC caseloads declined after peaking in the early twentieth century because the courts managed to gain better control over their workloads. This, in turn, enabled judges to concentrate on more important cases, write longer opinions, and become "more self-conscious about their role as policymakers." Akerman's behavior seems to fit that model. See Robert A. Kagan et al., "The Business of State Supreme Courts, 1870–1970," *Stanford Law Review* 30 (November 1977), 121–156.

22. Data compiled from Department of Justice, *Report of the Attorney General* (Washington, D.C.: GPO, 1919–1934).

23. See Padgett, "Plea Bargaining and Prohibition," 449.

24. The enactment of liquor statutes at the turn of the twentieth century expanded the criminal law and fostered the use of plea bargaining as a method of resolving criminal cases. See Albert W. Alschuler, "Plea Bargaining and Its History," *Columbia Law Review* 79 (January 1979), 1–43, 6.

25. Department of Justice, *Report of the Attorney General* (1930), 55.

26. Department of Justice, *Report of the Attorney General* (1932), 66.

27. Dorothy M. Brown, *Mabel Walker Willebrandt: A Study of Power, Loyalty, and Law* (Knoxville: University of Tennessee Press, 1984), 53. Brown suggests that Willebrandt had reformed the bureau, making it far more professional. The Florida record indicates that the problems that plagued the bureau in 1925 still existed as late as 1932.

28. *United States* v. *John P. Finley and Dan Moore*, Box 7, U.S. District Court, Northern District of Florida, Tallahassee, August term 1932, Federal Records Center, East Point, Ga. (hereinafter FRC).

29. Ibid.

30. *United States* v. *Mrs. Lena Severance*, Box 7, U.S. District Court, Northern District of Florida, Pensacola, September term 1933, FRC.

31. Tebeau, *A History of Florida*, 400–401.

32. Buckley, "Prohibition Survey of Florida," 108.

33. Tebeau, *A History of Florida*, 399–400.

34. For a probing analysis along similar lines, see William A. Link, *The Paradox of Southern Progressivism,1880–1930* (Chapel Hill and London: University of North Carolina Press, 1992).

35. *United States* v. *Charlie J. Jacobs*, Box No. 7, U.S. District Court, Northern District of Florida, Pensacola, March term 1932, FRC.

36. *United States* v. *Josh McCall*, Box No. 7, U.S. District Court, Northern District of Florida, Pensacola, March term 1932, FRC. In 1930 the average Florida farm comprised 85.2 acres and had an estimated value of $7,175.54 at $84.22 per acre. In contrast, the national average was 157 acres worth $48.52 per acre, or $7,617.64. Although the size of McCall's farm fell just below the state mean, its given value ($300) represented only 4.2 percent of the value of a typical Florida farm. If McCall correctly stated the value of his property, he must have owned swampland or some other marginal-quality real estate. For these and other agricultural statistics, see Bureau of the Census, *Fifteenth Census of the United States: Agriculture* (Washington: GPO, 1930), 60, 129, 455.

37. *United States* v. *Dave W. Padgett and Josh McCall*, Box 7, U.S. District Court, Northern District of Florida, Tallahassee, March term 1932, FRC. Two years earlier the Federal Court at Gainesville had convicted Padgett and fined him $50 after he pleaded guilty of possession of liquor. Past records notwithstanding, Padgett and other moonshiners who owned no land could rightly consider themselves farmers because parts of the Florida range remained open until 1949. Tebeau, *A History of Florida*, 382.

38. *United States* v. *N. W. Padgett*, U.S. District Court, Northern District of Florida, Tallahassee, January term 1933, FRC.

39. *United States* v. *Levie Thomas*, Box No. 7, U.S. District Court, Northern District of Florida, Tallahassee, July term 1932, FRC.

40. *United States* v. *Frank Kinsey, William M. Riley, Charlie R. Hancock, and Homer Faglie*, Box No. 7, U.S. District Court, Northern District of Florida, Tallahassee, October term 1932, FRC.

41. *United States* v. *Samuel Kilpatrick*, Box No. 46, U.S. District Court, Northern District of Florida, Tallahassee, January term 1932, FRC.

42. Vose, *Constitutional Change*, 133.

43. Everett Somerville Brown, ed., *Ratification of the Twenty-First Amendment to the Constitution of the United States: State Convention Records and Laws* (Ann Arbor: University of Michigan Press, 1938), 72.

44. Alduino, "The 'Noble Experiment' in Tampa," 214; *Tampa Tribune*, June 4, 1932; *Florida Times Union*, June 4, 1932; Vose, *Constitutional Change*, 119.

45. *Daily Democrat*, June 6, 7, 1932.

46. Blocker, *American Temperance Movements*, 119.

47. *Florida Times Union*, April 7, 1933.

48. Ibid, April 9, 1933. Unlike the house, the senate remained unreceptive to the bill. Some upper chamber members argued that the money raised from beer sales should go into a general revenue account instead of going directly to a school fund. See Alduino, "The 'Noble Experiment' in Tampa," 219.

49. *Florida Times Union*, April 7, 1933.

50. Robert James Maddox, "The War against Demon Rum," *American History Illustrated* (June 1979), 10–18, 17–18; David E. Kyvig, "Women Against Prohibition," *American Quarterly* 28 (Fall 1976), 465–482.

51. *Florida Times Union*, April 11, 1933.

52. See Wayne Flynt, *Duncan Upshaw Fletcher: Dixie's Reluctant Progressive* (Tallahassee: Florida State University Press, 1971), 184.

53. *Florida Times Union*, May 9, 1933.

54. In fairness, some editors remained firmly opposed to repeal. Lillian C. West of the *Panama City Pilot* equated whiskey with crime. "Overdoses of bad liquor," said she, served as the root cause of every homicide that had been committed in Panama City. As she put it, "the repeal movement sprang from aliens and anarchists." See Bernadette K. Loftin, "A Woman Liberated: Lillian C. West, Editor," *Florida Historical Quarterly* 52 (April 1974), 396–405.

55. Brown, *Ratification of the Twenty-First Amendment*, 93–94.

56. *Florida Times Union*, May 9, 1933; Attorney General of the State of Florida, *Biennial Report* (1933); Ch. 15884, *Florida Acts*, 1933.

57. Attorney General of the State of Florida, *Biennial Report* (1933); Ch. 15884, *Florida Acts*, 1933.

58. Alduino, "The 'Noble Experiment' in Tampa," 221, 222; *Tampa Tribune*, May 9, 10, 21, 1933; *DeLand Sun News*, October 4, 1933.

59. Alduino, "The 'Noble Experiment' in Tampa," 222, 224.

60. Brown, *Ratification of the Twenty-First Amendment*, 69–71.

61. Ibid.

62. Ibid.; Blocker, *American Temperance Movements*, 128.

63. *United States* v. *Samuel Kilpatrick, Livingston Jarvis, et al.*, found in *United States* v. *Leo G. Carraway*, Box No. 7, U.S. District Court, Northern District of Florida, Tallahassee, July term 1932, FRC.

64. *Tallahassee Democrat*, November 9, 1934.

65. Ibid., December 12, 1933.

66. Attorney General of the State of Florida, *Biennial Report* (1933), 313. See House Joint Resolution No. 83 (1933).

67. *Tallahassee Democrat*, November 6–9, 1934.

68. Along these lines of analysis, see Clyde Wilson, "The Statist Drug War," *The Free Market* 12 (February 1994), 1, 7; Harry G. LeVine and Craig Reinarman, "From Prohibition to Regulation: Lessons from Alcohol Policy," *Milbank Quarterly* 69 (1992), 461–492.

69. *Tallahassee Democrat*, November 9, 1934.

70. *Coleman, Sheriff* v. *State ex rel. Race*, 118 Fla. 201 (1935). Ch. 6861, *Florida Acts*, 1915, provided fines or imprisonment for any persons who sold liquor without first paying the requisite license fees.

71. *Coleman, Sheriff* v. *State ex rel. Race*, 206–207.

72. *State ex rel. Hoffman* v. *Powell*, 118 Fla. 296 (1935).

73. Ibid., 299–300. To simplify matters: Ch. 7733, *Florida Acts, Extra Session*, 1918, banned possession and shipments of liquors into dry counties; *Florida Constitution*, Article XIX, (1919) and its enabling act, Ch. 7736, *Florida Acts, Extra Session*, 1918, imposed statewide prohibition; Article XIX, adopted November 6, 1934, repealed Florida's original prohibition article.

74. *State ex rel. Hoffman* v. *Powell*, 302–307.

75. Ibid.

76. Hall, *The Magic Mirror*, 65.

77. *Ex parte Francis*, 79 So. 753 (Fla. 1918).

78. *State ex rel. Atlantic Ice & Co.* v. *Weems*, 106 So. 453 (Fla. 1935).

79. Ibid., 455. See Ch. 16774, *Florida Acts*, 1935, entitled "An Act Regulating and Taxing the Manufacture, Distribution, and Sale of Beverages Containing More Than One Per Centum of Alcohol, Creating and Providing for a State Beverage Department,

Providing Penalties for the Violation of this Act, and Repealing Existing Laws Concerning Said Beverages." For later liquor cases, see *State ex rel. Muldon* v. *McCarthy, Chief of Police*, 165 So. 700 (Fla. 1936) and *Langston* v. *Lundsford*, 165 So. 898 (Fla. 1936).

80. *State ex rel. Atlantic Ice & Co.* v. *Weems*, 455–456.

81. Ibid.

82. Ibid. Quote from William Ellis's dissenting opinion in *Ex parte Pricha*, 70 Fla. 265 (1915).

83. See Melvin I. Urofsky, "State Courts and Protective Legislation during the Progressive Era: A Reevaluation," *Journal of American History* 72 (June 1985), 63–91, 67.

84. *Fifty-Fourth Annual Meeting of the Woman's Christian Temperance Union of Florida* (Bartow, Fla.: WCTU, 1937), 14.

Epilogue

The implementation of the intoxicating liquor laws, and their subsequent enforcement in Florida between 1885 and 1935, set into motion a host of constitutional issues that have troubled political philosophers from Plato to James Madison to the present generation.[1] The fundamental constitutional problems raised by the liquor laws revolved around the inevitable tension that exists between individual rights, public interest, and government authority, or what James Madison referred to as "a question between power and liberty."[2]

Prohibition enforcement in Florida provoked Madison's question and placed the burden of reconciling the matter largely upon the courts. The judicial response to the state and federal liquor laws in Florida thus sheds light on the evolutionary course of the criminal justice system, while underscoring those persistent traditions that have guided that change. This continuity in American constitutionalism reaches back in time to the founding of the republic and extends forward to and beyond the Progressive Era. To be sure, the prohibitionist crusade fell within the broader pluralistic movement that began agitating for progressive legislation in the late nineteenth century. Yet in many ways, the anti-liquor statutes revealed a recrudescence of the pre-Revolutionary notion that the purpose of criminal law was to "enforce the morals and religion of the people."[3] This legal concept, according to one authority, remained intact until the American Revolutionary War fostered a transformation in the law. Crimes of morality dropped to the wayside while property assumed the more prominent position within the emerging nation's legal culture.[4]

Moreover, the framers of the U.S. government designed a federal system that entrusted the police powers to the states.[5] They also attached a bill of rights to the written Constitution to safeguard specific liberties, such as owning property, from governmental intrusions. By all means, they provided the groundwork for a deeply conflicting system of law and government. But in

Madison's view, federalism coupled with constitutionalism promised to serve as an effective check on tyranny for many generations to come.[6]

As another way to check power, Madison and the framers allocated governmental authority to three independent branches: the executive, the legislative, and the judicial. This separation of power has spawned much legal ambiguity since each branch can have input in shaping a law and determining its scope. In the process, the separate branches occasionally find themselves locked in disagreement over a given law's purpose or meaning. More often than not, it is the legislature and the courts that are at odds with one another. Indeed, in Anglo-American legal culture there exists a long tradition of friction between legislators and those who interpret the law. This seemingly inevitable conflict stems partially from the collective awareness of the legislature that judges can wield substantial discretionary power by exercising judicial review. In using this power, judges not only define the rights that limit legislative authority, but they also set the parameters beyond which government can not legitimately enter.[7]

Clearly the judicial response to the liquor laws in Florida occurred within a traditional framework founded upon the twin pillars of federalism and constitutionalism and sheathed in the tension that emanates between the courts and the legislative bodies. The movement toward national prohibition in Florida, in a sense, followed a course marked by a series of legislative thrusts and judicial parries. Each time the state legislature passed a liquor statute, the Florida Supreme Court usually couched its response in terms of individual rights versus the state's police powers. Initially the Florida Supreme Court threw its weight behind the mainstay of Florida's liquor laws—local option—because it fit the republican ideal of home rule. To protect and preserve the commonwealth, judges therefore expanded the scope of the police powers.

Even so, by the end of the 1910s this judicial consensus began fraying as Florida's liquor laws became more prohibitive in terms of property rights. Consequently, the bench became more polarized. On one side of the rift stood jurists of a republican persuasion who viewed the stringent liquor measures as a legitimate use of the police power. Against them stood those who had begun championing the cause of natural rights. These judges claimed an unbridled police power posed a serious threat to individual liberties, of which property stood central.

With the ratification of the Eighteenth Amendment the constitutional tension moved to higher ground, for the concurrent power clause necessarily engaged the federal courts in the discourse. Federalism and states' rights then emerged as secondary matters in the larger constitutional issues that prohibition enforcement aroused. In other words, the concurrent power clause raised the question of whether state and federal authorities assumed an equal obligation to enforce national prohibition. If so, then the Eighteenth Amendment clashed directly with the Fifth Amendment's safeguard against double jeopardy. That is, it increased the likelihood of trying an individual twice for the same crime—

once by the state and once by the federal government. According to Kenneth M. Murchison, to resolve this dilemma the Supreme Court ignored precedent and innovated by formulating the dual sovereignty exception to double jeopardy. But Murchison too has ignored a wide body of law. Interstate commerce and diversity jurisdiction, for example, had dealt with the inherent problems of concurrent power long before the ratification of the Eighteenth Amendment. Taft's ruling in *Lanza* (1922), therefore, did not create a new doctrine. The Chief Justice merely reaffirmed a constitutional tradition that has helped guide state and federal relations since the founding of the republic.

Murchison has correctly suggested, however, that the overloaded state and federal dockets presented more prohibition cases than either judiciary could prosecute efficiently. Accordingly, the dual prosecution issue proved short-lived because neither jurisdiction wanted to waste time and resources trying a violator a second time. They knew that the weight of the Constitution would fall on the side of the defense, making second prosecutions exercises in futility. Small wonder pleas of double jeopardy vanished from court dockets after 1922.[8]

By the middle of the 1920s, other constitutional problems stemming from prohibition enforcement became more pressing. The crux of prohibition litigation then turned mainly on enforcement techniques. Questions arose concerning privacy and property rights. Responding to these issues, the courts imposed a test of reasonableness. Such discretionary power enabled the judiciary to balance diverse social interests in the name of the public welfare, which in turn allowed judges to draw on their common law traditions. As it happened, the courts provided a generally consistent approach in litigation involving either privacy rights or property forfeitures. For the most part, judges checked governmental intrusion on individual rights. Sometimes, however, they spoke in a language that deemed both the property and the activities of individuals public nuisances. Under those circumstances, judges occasionally tolerated unwarranted searches and subsequently upheld the forfeiture of the property involved in the crime.

Yet, in contrast to Murchison's findings, judicial rulings in Florida courts neither reflected "changing public attitudes toward prohibition" nor issued from "some external stimuli." In the Sunshine State, judges continued to exercise their independence and to ground their rulings on precedent and citation of authority, the traditional ways of administering justice. Like Judge William B. Sheppard, they believed "in law enforcement regardless of changing public sentiment."[9]

By the end of the era the constitutional confusion in the courts stemming from prohibition had lessened to a degree (largely due to decisions external to the court, such as selective enforcement). The basic problem, nevertheless, remained essentially a conflict between individual rights and governmental authority. The repeal of the Eighteenth Amendment merely returned the liquor question, with all its constitutional trappings, to the states. This event gave new life to Florida's Supreme Court. After several quiet years of judicial slumber, a revived court found itself in the midst of the liquor controversy. Picking up on a discourse that the bench had last addressed in 1920, a divided court began shaping the state's alcohol policy within the context of constitutional limitations and judicial precedent. Like the pre-prohibition rulings, the high court attempted to strike a balance between property rights and the public's welfare. Perhaps thirteen years of national prohibition had reduced the Florida Supreme Court's reluctance to expand the police powers. Whatever the case, this time the judicial proponents of the (then local) liquor laws prevailed. Ultimately, the Florida Supreme Court marked its resurgence as an architect of public alcohol policy by broadening the scope of the police powers.

Of course, to say that the courts invariably endorsed or refuted the liquor laws overlooks the substantial differences in personalities and perspectives that sundered the bench. During the period studied, the Florida Supreme Court's composition included judges who—based on their rulings—fit ostensibly into either the "wet" or "dry" category. In 1927, to elaborate, Judge Thomas M. Shackleford, who had supported the liquor laws as legitimate restrictions on individual liberties, died. It seems highly probable that no rounds of drink were shared in memory of this former chief justice of the Florida Supreme Court. At his funeral a leading member of the Hillsborough County Anti-Saloon League, Don C. McMullen, served as an honorary pallbearer.[10] Ten years later, Shackleford's former associate and rival on the court, Jefferson B. Browne, suffered a heart attack and died in the spring of 1937. Before passing away, Browne had penned a last will and testament in which he stipulated that his "entire collections of wines, licquers [*sic*], cordials, etc.," be distributed to a list of fifteen beneficiaries, which included some of the most prominent lawyers in Florida. In bequeathing his booze, Browne was mindful that "the gift to each one will be small." Nonetheless, he wished "for them sometime to pour out a draft," hold it up and say: "Here's to Jeff Browne."[11]

While the foregoing discussion might lead one to label Shackleford a dry and Browne a wet, to do so is a risky generalization. Browne, for example, had unsuccessfully campaigned for governor as an advocate of statewide prohibition in 1908. Later, after his appointment to the bench, he initially was sympathetic to the liquor laws. In fact, it was not until he became experienced with the full dimensions of the liquor laws in operation that Browne began opposing them. So to group judges together and categorize them as either wet or dry is to deny the complexity of the liquor issue and to ignore the contradictions that beset many rulings. It is better to recognize the judges who presided in the courts in Florida as strong-willed individuals who possessed diverse opinions and attitudes on a wide range of topics from individual rights and the commonweal to morality and liquor.

Although the diversity of ideas and personalities that comprised the courts produced a degree of ambiguous adjudication, such was the price of justice. As John T. Noonan, Jr., has argued, the legitimacy of law relies not upon the promotion of justice but on the prevention of injustice. Said differently—if you want certainty, the cost you pay for this is some injustice.[12] It seems then that the courts' response to the liquor laws in Florida underscored the durability of justice. If theirs was an uncertain legacy, it was mainly because the courts struck a balance between individual liberty and the police power of the state.

NOTES

1. See John Patrick Diggins, "Republicanism and Progressivism," *American Quarterly* 37 (Fall 1985), 572–598.

2. As quoted in James Morton Smith, "Liberty and Learning," *William and Mary Law Review* 29 (Fall 1987), 53–56, 54.

3. See James H. Timberlake, *Prohibition and the Progressive Movement, 1900–1920* (Cambridge, Mass.: Harvard University Press, 1963). The nature and origins of Progressivism have ignited much heated debate among historians. To get a sense of this controversy, see David P. Thelen, "Social Tensions and the Origins of Progressivism," *Journal of American History* 56 (September 1969), 323–341; Peter G. Filene, "An Obituary for The Progressive Movement," *American Quarterly* 22 (1970), 20–34; Richard L. McCormick, "The Discovery That Business Corrupts Politics: A Reappraisal of the Origins of Progressivism," *American Historical Review* 86 (April 1981), 247–274; Daniel T. Rogers, "In Search of Progressivism," *Reviews in American History* 10 (December 1982), 113–132.

4. William E. Nelson, "Emerging Notions of Criminal Law in the Revolutionary Era: An Historical Perspective," *New York University Law Review* 42 (1967), 450–482, and Idem, *Americanization of the Common Law: The Impact of Legal Change on Massachusetts Society, 1760–1830* (Cambridge, Mass.: Harvard University Press, 1975), 117–118.

5. Kermit L. Hall, ed., *Police, Prison, and Punishment: Major Historical Interpretations* (New York: Garland Publishing, Inc., 1987), xi.

6. The scholarship on the creation of the American republic and the ratification of the Bill of Rights is voluminous. For a sample of the important works, see Gordon S. Wood, *The Creation of the American Republic, 1776–1787* (Chapel Hill: University of North Carolina Press, 1969); Forrest McDonald, *Novus Ordo Seclorum: The Intellectual Origins of the Constitution* (Lawrence: University Press of Kansas, 1985); Drew R. McCoy, *The Last of the Fathers: James Madison and the Republican Legacy* (New York: Cambridge University Press, 1989); and John P. Diggins, *The Lost Soul of American Politics: Virtue, Self-Interest, and the Foundations of Liberalism* (New York: Basic Books, 1984).

7. See Jennifer Nedelsky, *Private Property and the Limits of American Constitutionalism: The Madisonian Framework and Its Legacy* (Chicago: University of Chicago Press, 1990), 188.

8. For Murchison's position see Kenneth M. Murchison, "Prohibition and the Fourth Amendment: A New Look at Some Old Cases," *Journal of Criminal Law and Criminology* 73 (Summer 1982), 471–532; Idem, "The Dual Sovereignty Exception to Double Jeopardy," *New York University Review of Law and Social Change* 14 (Spring 1986), 383–435; and Idem, "Property Forfeiture in the Era of National Prohibition: A Study of Judicial Response to Legislative Reform," *Buffalo Law Review* 32 (1983), 417–463.

9. *The Pensacola Journal*, April 22, 1934.

10. *Tampa Daily Times*, September 22, 1927.

11. J. Allison DeFoor II, "Here's to Jeff Browne," *Florida Supreme Court Historical Society Review* 2 (1986), 1–4.

12. See John T. Noonan, Jr., *Persons and Masks of the Law: Cardozo, Holmes, Jefferson, and Wythe as Makers of the Masks* (New York: Farrar and Strauss, 1976).

Selected Bibliography

PRIMARY SOURCES

Case Files, Record Group 21, Federal Records Center, East Point, Georgia

Alphonse Capone v. *Sheriffs of Florida*. Box No. 186, U.S. District Court, Southern District of Florida, Miami. March 1930.

Ex parte Ramsey. Case File No. 1094, Box No. 12, U.S. District Court, Southern District of Florida, Jacksonville. July term 1920.

United States v. *B. Miler*. Box No. 46, U.S. District Court, Northern District of Florida, Tallahassee. April term 1935.

United States v. *Charlie J. Jacobs*. Box No. 7, U.S. District Court, Northern District of Florida, Pensacola. March term 1932.

United States v. *Frank Kinsey, William Riley, Charlie R. Hancock, and Homer Faglie*. Box No. 7, U.S. District Court, Northern District of Florida, Tallahassee. October term 1932.

United States v. *George Adams*. Case File No. 550, Box No. 5, U.S. District Court, Southern District of Florida, Tampa. March term 1921.

United States v. *George W. Moore*. Box No. 72, U.S. District Court, Southern District of Florida, Miami. July term 1930.

United States v. *John P. Finley and Dan Moore*. Box No. 7, U.S. District Court, Northern District of Florida, Tallahassee. August term 1932.

United States v. *Josh McCall*. Box No. 7, U.S. District Court, Northern District of Florida, Pensacola. March term 1932.

United States v. *Leo Day*. Case File No. 539, Box No. 5, U.S. District Court, Southern District of Florida, Tampa. March term 1921.

United States v. *Levie Thomas*. Box No. 7, U.S. District Court, Northern District of Florida, Tallahassee. July term 1932.

United States v. *Mrs. Angelicio Diego, Joe Rubin, and Manuel Rubin*. Case File No. 555, Box No. 110, U.S. District Court, Southern District of Florida, Tampa. March term 1929.

United States v. *One Ford Automobile*. Case File No. 3, Box No. 43, U.S. District Court, Northern District of Florida, Tallahassee. April term 1933.

United States v. *One Haynes Automobile and Eight Other Automobiles*. Case File Nos. 1135, 1136, 1148, 1149, 1151, 1157, 1158, 1162, 1167, 1176, and 1177, Box No. 59, U.S. District Court, Southern District of Florida, Jacksonville. December term 1920.

United States v. *112 Cases of Hunter Rye*. Case File No. 1144, Box No. 58, U.S. District Court, Southern District of Florida, Tampa. September term 1920.

United States v. *Packard Sedan, Motor Number 71005-A*. Case File No. 1440, Box No. 73, U.S. District Court, Southern District of Florida, Jacksonville. January term 1928.

United States v. *Phillip Puglisi*. Case File No. 3809, Box No. 78, U.S. District Court, Southern District of Florida, Tampa. November term 1933.

United States v. *Pirl Todd, Leo Day, and T. M. Chevis*. Case File No. 2593, Box No. 36, U.S. District Court, Southern District of Florida, Tampa. July term 1930.

United States v. *Robert Burns*. Case File No. 934, Box No. 8, U.S. District Court, Southern District of Florida, Tampa. March term 1925.

United States v. *Rome Pressley*. Case File No. 320, Box No. 8, U.S. District Court, Northern District of Florida, Pensacola. November term 1922.

United States v. *Samuel Kilpatrick*. Box No. 46, U.S. District Court, Northern District of Florida, Tallahassee. January term 1932.

United States v. *Samuel Kilpatrick, Livingston Jarvis, et al.*, found in *United States* v. *Leo G. Carraway*. Box No. 7, U.S. District Court, Northern District of Florida, Tallahassee. July term 1932.

United States v. *Sutton*. Case File No. 269, Box No. 7, U.S. District Court, Northern District of Florida, Pensacola. November term 1922.

United States v. *Tom Allen*. Case File No. 1735, Box No. 18, U.S. District Court, Southern District of Florida, Tampa. December term 1926.

United States v. *William G. Shotwell and Sidney C. Shotwell*. Box No. 78, U.S. District Court, Southern District of Florida, Tampa. May term 1935.

Published Court Reports

Agnello v. *United States*, 269 U.S. 20 (1926).

Alderman v. *United States*, 279 Fed. 259 (1922).

Alderman v. *United States*, 31 F.2d 499 (1929).

Alford v. *State*, 6 So. 857 (Fla. 1889).

Anderson v. *State*, 32 Fla. 242 (1893).

Armstrong v. *State*, 96 So. 399 (Fla. 1923).

Bailey v. *Poitier*, 86 Fla. 160 (1923).

Balbontin v. *State*, 66 So. 421 (Fla. 1914).

Barbour v. *State*, 146 Ga. 667 (1911).

Barnhill v. *State*, 48 So. 251 (Fla. 1908).

Beer Co. v. *Mass.*, 97 U.S. 25 (1878).

Boyett v. *United States*, 48 F.2d 482 (1931).

Buchanan v. *State*, 95 Fla. 301 (1928).

Buchanan v. *State*, 97 Fla. 1059 (1929).

Bueno v. *State*, 40 Fla. 160 (1898).

Burns v. *United States*, 296 Fed. 468 (1925).

Burrows v. *Moran, Sheriff*, 89 So. 111 (Fla. 1921).

Butler and Chapman v. *State*, 25 Fla. 347 (1889).

Caldwell v. *State*, 43 Fla. 545 (1901).

Carroll v. *United States*, 267 U.S. 132 (1925).
Chandler v. *State*, 113 So. 91 (Fla. 1927).
Clark Distilling Co. v. *Western Maryland Railway Co.*, 242 U.S. 311 (1917).
The Coldwater, 283 Fed. 146 (1922).
Coleman, Sheriff v. *State ex rel. Race*, 118 Fla. 201 (1935).
Combs v. *Lake City*, 112 So. 51 (Fla. 1927).
Commercial Credit Co. v. *United States*, 53 F.2d 977 (1930).
Cooper v. *State*, 143 So. 217 (Fla. 1932).
Correlis v. *State*, 82 So. 601 (Fla. 1919).
Crane v. *Campbell*, 245 U.S. 304 (1917).
Dexter v. *United States*, 12 F.2d 777 (1926).
Dillon v. *Gloss*, 256 U.S. 376 (1921).
Donacker v. *State*, 42 Fla. 348 (1900).
Ellis v. *State*, 6 So. 768 (Fla. 1889).
Ex parte Francis, 76 Fla. 304 (1918).
Ex parte Huston, 282 Fed. 723 (1922).
Ex parte Lewinsky, 66 Fla. 324 (1913).
Ex parte Peacock, 6 So. 473 (Fla. 1899).
Ex parte Pricha, 70 Fla. 265 (1915).
Ex parte Sirmans, 94 Fla. 832 (1927).
Ex parte Westbrook, 250 Fed. 636 (1918).
Fine v. *Moran, Sheriff*, 77 So. 533 (Fla. 1917).
Frese v. *State*, 23 Fla. 267 (1887).
Galloway, Sheriff v. *Strauss*, 67 Fla. 426 (1914).
Gildrie v. *State*, 113 So. 704 (Fla. 1927).
Goldsmith v. *United States*, 254 U.S. 505 (1921).
Grosfield v. *United States*, 276 U.S. 494 (1922).
Haile v. *Gardner*, 91 So. 376 (Fla. 1923).
Hall v. *Moran, Sheriff*, 81 Fla. 706 (1921).
Hawke v. *Smith*, 253 U.S. 221 (1920).
Heitman v. *United States*, 5 F.2d 887 (1926).
Hester v. *United States*, 265 U.S. 57 (1924).
Hiers v. *State*, 52 Fla. 25 (1906).
Hilliard v. *City of Gainesville*, 213 So. 2d 689 (Fla. 1968).
Hilt v. *United States*, 12 F.2d 1504 (1926).
Housh v. *Anderson*, 128 Fla. 713 (1937).
In re Seven Barrels of Wine, 83 So. 627 (Fla. 1920).
In re Weeks, 83 Fed. 729 (1914).
Jackson v. *State*, 87 Fla. 262 (1924).
Johnson v. *State*, 89 So. 114 (Fla. 1921).
Katie L, 106 So. 414 (Fla. 1925).
Lachman v. *Walker*, 52 Fla. 297 (1906).
Langston v. *Lundsford*, 165 So. 898 (Fla. 1936).
Leisy v. *Hardin*, 135 U.S. 100 (1890).
Leser v. *Garnett*, 258 U.S. 130 (1922).
License Cases, 46 U.S. 504 (1847).
Lippman, Claimant v. *State*, 72 Fla. 428 (1916).
Long v. *Southern Express Co.*, 201 Fed. 441 (1912).

Marasso v. *Van Pelt, Sheriff*, 81 So. 529 (Fla. 1919).
Matthews, Chief of Police v. *Holloway*, 90 So. 924 (Fla. 1922).
McGriff v. *State*, 66 Fla. 332 (1913).
Moore v. *United States*, 57 F.2d 840 (1932).
National Prohibition Cases, 253 U.S. 350 (1920).
Neisel v. *Moran, Sheriff*, 85 So. 346 (Fla. 1919).
Noble State Bank v. *Haskell*, 219 U.S. 104 (1911).
Norwood v. *State*, 86 So. 506 (Fla. 1920).
Nussbaumer v. *State*, 54 Fla. 87 (1907).
Olmstead v. *United States*, 279 U.S. 849 (1925).
Osborne v. *State*, 14 So. 588 (Fla. 1894).
Palko v. *Connecticut*, 302 U.S. 319 (1937).
Parker Harris Co. v. *Tate*, 135 Tenn. 509 (1916).
Payne v. *United States*, 279 Fed. 112 (1922).
Polk Co. v. *Johnson & Co.*, 21 Fla. 578 (1885).
Pressley v. *United States*, 289 Fed. 476 (1923).
Purcell v. *State*, 61 Fla. 43 (1911).
Richbourg Motor C. v. *United States*, 281 U.S. 528 (1930).
Roberson v. *State*, 43 Fla. 156 (1901).
Ruppert v. *Caffey*, 251 U.S. 264 (1920).
The Saxon, 269 Fed. 639 (1920).
Slaughterhouse Cases, 16 Wall. 36 (1873).
Sligh v. *Kirkwood, Sheriff*, 65 Fla. 123 (1913).
Sloan v. *Hutchingson*, 120 Fla. 747 (1935).
Southern Express Co. v. *Long*, 202 Fed. 463 (1913).
Spooner v. *Curtis*, 96 So. 836 (Fla. 1923).
Spratt v. *Gray*, 87 So. 760 (Fla. 1921).
State v. *Atlantic Coastline Railroad Co.*, 47 So. 879 (Fla. 1908).
State v. *One Hudson Roadster Automobile*, 104 Fla. 301 (1932).
State v. *Smith Tax Collector*, 7 So. 848 (Fla. 1890).
State v. *Weems*, 106 So. 453 (Fla. 1935).
State ex rel. v. *Brown*, 19 Fla. 563 (1883).
State ex rel. v. *Jefferson County*, 20 Fla. 425 (1884).
State ex rel. Catts v. *Crawford*, 72 Fla. 253 (1916).
State ex rel. Catts v. *Mason*, 72 Fla. 251 (1916).
State ex rel. Davis v. *Rose*, 97 Fla. 710 (1925).
State ex rel. Hoffman v. *Powell*, 159 So. 508 (Fla. 1935).
State ex rel. Knott v. *Crawford*, 72 Fla. 232 (1916).
State ex rel. Knott v. *Haskell*, 72 Fla. 244 (1916).
State ex rel. Muldon v. *McCarthy, Chief of Police*, 165 So. 700 (Fla. 1936).
Strobhar v. *State*, 55 Fla. 167 (1908).
Sutton v. *United States*, 289 Fed. 488 (1923).
Tennessee v. *Davis*, 100 U.S. 257 (1880).
Theisen v. *McDavid*, 34 Fla. 440 (1894).
Tillman v. *State*, 81 Fla. 558 (1921).
Tittsworth, Chief of Police v. *Akin*, 159 So. 779 (Fla. 1935).
Todd v. *United States*, 48 F.2d 530 (1931).
United States v. *Alexander*, 278 Fed. 308 (Fla. 1922).

United States v. *Armstrong*, 275 Fed. 506 (1921).
United States v. *Bengochea*, 279 Fed. 539 (1922).
United States v. *Brown*, 31 F.2d 307 (1929).
United States v. *Burns*, 4 F.2d 131 (1925).
United States v. *Dowling*, 278 Fed. 630 (1922).
United States v. *Everson*, 280 Fed. 127 (1922).
United States v. *Ford Coupe Automobile*, 43 F.2d (1930).
United States v. *Jin Fuey Moy*, 241 U.S. 394 (1917).
United States v. *Lanza*, 260 U.S. 377 (1922).
United States v. *Marron*, 275 U.S. 192 (1922).
United States v. *Mitchell*, 274 Fed. 128 (1921).
United States v. *One Buick Coupe*, 54 F.2d 800 (1931).
United States v. *One Ford Coupe Automobile*, 272 U.S. 321 (1926).
United States v. *One Haynes Automobile*, 274 Fed. 926 (1921).
United States v. *One Packard Sedan*, 14 F.2d 874 (1926).
United States v. *Quantity of Extracts*, 54 F.2d 643 (1931).
United States v. *Smith*, 16 F.2d 788 (1927).
United States v. *Stephens*, 1 F. Supp. 33 (1932).
United States v. *Sutton*, 289 Fed. 488 (1922).
Van Pelt, Sheriff v. *Hilliard*, 78 So. 693 (Fla. 1918).
Waller v. *Florida*, 397 U.S. 387 (1970).
Waller v. *State*, 213 So. 2d 623 (Fla. 1968).
Wise v. *State*, 67 So. 871 (Fla. 1915).
Wood v. *Whitaker*, 89 So. 118 (Fla. 1921).
Wright v. *Worth, Municipal Judge*, 91 So. 87 (Fla. 1922).

Federal Statutes
Espionage Act. *Statutes At Large*. Vol. 40 (1917).
Liquor Taxing Act. *Statutes at Large*. Vol. 56 (1934).
Merchant Marine Act. *Statutes at Large*. Vol. 41 (1919).
National Prohibition Act. *Statutes at Large*. Vol. 41 (1919).
Post Office Appropriation Act. *Statutes at Large*. Vol. 39 (1917).
Supplement to National Prohibition Act. *Statutes at Large*. Vol. 43 (1921).
Tariff Act. *Statutes at Large*. Vol. 44 (1922).
Webb-Kenyon Act. *Statutes at Large*. Vol. 34 (1913).

Florida Statutes
Ch. 3413. *Florida Acts*. (1885).
Ch. 3416. *Florida Acts*. (1885).
Ch. 3700. *Florida Acts*. (1887).
Ch. 4832. *Florida Acts*. (1901).
Ch. 4932. *Florida Acts*. (1901).
Ch. 5190. *Florida Acts*. (1903).
Ch. 5443. *Florida Acts*. (1905).
Ch. 5689. *Florida Acts*. (1907).
Ch. 6236. *Florida Acts*. (1911).
Ch. 6513. *Florida Acts*. (1913).
Ch. 6516. *Florida Acts*. (1913).
Ch. 6860. *Florida Acts*. (1915).
Ch. 6861. *Florida Acts*. (1915).
Ch. 7283. *Florida Acts*. (1917).
Ch. 7284. *Florida Acts*. (1917).
Ch. 7287. *Florida Acts*. (1917).
Ch. 7733. *Florida Acts*. (1918).
Ch. 7735. *Florida Acts*. (1918).
Ch. 7736. *Florida Acts*. (1918).
Ch. 7890. *Florida Acts*. (1918).
Ch. 9321. *Florida Acts*. (1923).
Ch. 16774. *Florida Acts*. (1935).

Published Government Documents

Attorney General of the State of Florida. *Biennial Reports*, 1900–1935.

Commissioner of Internal Revenue. *Annual Reports*, 1885–1905.

Department of Justice. Division of Taxation, Prohibition and Prisons. *Report of the Attorney General*. Washington, D.C.: GPO, 1925.

Department of Justice. Office of the Attorney General. *Annual Reports*, 1915–1935.

Department of Treasury. *State Cooperation and State Responsibility Under Concurrent Power*. Washington, D.C.: GPO, 1930.

U.S. Congress. House. Committee on the Judiciary. *Additional Judge in Florida*. 70th Cong., 1st sess. 24 May 1928.

U.S. Congress. House. *Congressman Clark of Florida Speaking against the Humphrey Bill*. 59th Cong., 1st sess. 22 February 1906.

U.S. Congress. Senate. Committee on Law Observance and Enforcement. *Official Records of the National Commission on Law Observance and Enforcement*. 71st Cong., 3rd sess. Washington, D.C.: GPO, 1931.

Speeches, Pamphlets, and Letters

Browne, Jefferson B. "The Super Constitution." University of Florida College of Law, 16 March 1920. Special Collections, P. K. Yonge Library of Florida History, University of Florida, Gainesville.

Bryan, Nathan P. "Labor Day Speech." St. Augustine, Florida, September 1917(?). Bryan Papers 1906–1935, Manuscript Collection, Box 19, P. K. Yonge Library of Florida History, University of Florida, Gainesville.

Carter, Francis B. "A Powerful Argument and Plea for Prohibition." Escambia County Prohibition League, 16 September 1907. Manuscript Collection, Box 58, P. K. Yonge Library of Florida History, University of Florida, Gainesville.

DeGarmo, Ida. *"Life Story of Minnie E. Neal: President of Florida Woman's Christian Temperance Union."* (1936) Manuscript Collection, Box 54, P. K. Yonge Library of Florida History, University of Florida, Gainesville.

McMullen, Don C. "To Albert Roberts." Don C. McMullen to Albert Roberts, 18 November 1910. Manuscript Collection, Box 60, P. K. Yonge Library of Florida History, University of Florida, Gainesville.

Newspapers

The DeLand Sun News
Florida Times Union (Jacksonville)
Gainesville Sun
Jacksonville Journal
Miami Herald
New York Times
Pensacola Journal
Public Record (Pensacola)
Tallahassee Democrat
Tampa Tribune

SECONDARY SOURCES

Articles

Alduino, Frank. "Prohibition in Tampa." *Tampa Bay History* 9 (Spring/Summer 1987): 17–28.

Alschuler, Albert W. "Plea Bargaining and Its History." *Columbia Law Review* 79 (January 1979): 1–43.

Appleton, Thomas H., Jr. "Prohibition and Politics in Kentucky: The Gubernatorial Campaign and Election of 1915." *The Register of the Kentucky Historical Society* 75 (January 1977): 28–54.

Bailey, Josiah William. "The Political Treatment of the Drink Evil." *South Atlantic Quarterly* 6 (April 1907): 109–124.

Barker, Earl M., Jr., and Donald J. Hall. "Multiple Prosecution: Federalism vs. Individual Rights." *University of Florida Law Review* 20 (1968): 355–368.

Browne, Jefferson B. "The Super-Constitution." *The American Law Review* 54 (May 1920): 321–350.

———. "The American Law Institute, Its Organization and Purpose." *Proceedings of the Florida State Bar Association* (1923): 85–102.

Buchanan, Patricia. "Miami's Bootleg Boom." *Tequesta* 30 (1970): 13–31.

Buckley, Frank. "Forfeiture of Vehicles for Unlawful Movement of Liquor." *Boston University Law Review* 4 (1924): 183.

Burnham, John C. "New Perspectives on the Prohibition 'Experiment' of the 1920's." *Journal of Social History* 2 (Fall 1968): 51–68.

Carroll, John D. "The Search and Seizure Provisions of the Federal and State Constitutions." *Virginia Law Review* 10 (1923): 124–146.

Carson, James M. "Historical Background of Florida Law." *Miami Law Quarterly* 3 (1949): 254–268.

Cofer, Richard. "Bootleggers in the Backwoods: Prohibition in the Depression in Hernando County." *Tampa Bay History* 1 (Spring/Summer 1979): 17–23.

Cuddihy, William, and B. Carmon Hardy. "A Man's House Was Not His Castle: Origins of the Fourth Amendment to the United States Constitution." *William and Mary Quarterly* 3rd Series. 37 (1980): 371–400.

Dannenbaum, Jedd. "Crusade Against Drink." *Reviews in American History* 9 (December 1981): 498–500.

Daur, Manning J., and William C. Havard. "The Florida Constitution of 1885—A Critique." *University of Florida Law Review* 8 (Spring 1955): 1–92.

Davis, Jack E. "The Spirits of St. Petersburg: The Struggle for Local Prohibition, 1892–1919." *Tampa Bay History* 10 (Spring 1988): 19–33.

Decker, E. H. "Double Jeopardy in Cases Coming under Both the Eighteenth Amendment and State Prohibition Laws." *Oregon Law Review* (1923): 124–128.

"The Development of the Family Purpose Doctrine." *United States Law Review* 65 (1931): 645–651.

Doherty, Herbert J., Jr. "Florida and the Presidential Election of 1928." *Florida Historical Quarterly* 26 (October 1947): 174–181.

Dripps, Donald A. "Precommitment, Prohibition, and the Problem of Dissent." *Journal of Legal Studies* 22 (June 1993): 255–263.

Eagles, Charles W. "Congressional Voting in the 1920s: A Test of Urban-Rural Conflict." *Journal of American History* (September 1989): 528–534.

Elazar, Daniel J. "Federal-State Collaboration in the Nineteenth-Century United States." *Political Science Quarterly* 79 (June 1964): 248–281.

Ely, James W., Jr. "That Due Satisfaction May Be Made: The Fifth Amendment and the Origins of the Compensation Principle." *American Journal of Legal History* 36 (January 1992): 1–18.

Ely, James W., Jr., and David J. Bodenhamer. "Regionalism and American Legal History: The Southern Experience." *Vanderbilt Law Review* 39 (1986): 539–567.

"Enforcing Prohibition under Federal Rule on Unreasonable Searches." *Yale Law Journal* 36 (1927): 988.

Eslinger, Ellen. "Antebellum Liquor Reform in Lexington Virginia: The Story of a Small Southern Town." *The Virginia Magazine of History and Biography* 99 (April 1991): 163–186.

Fahey, David M. "The Good Templars and the African American Temperance Movement: W. M. Artrell of Florida." *Social History of Alcohol Review* 28–29 (Spring 1994): 28–30.

Finkelman, Paul. "Exploring Southern Legal History." *North Carolina Law Review* 64 (1985): 77–86.

Flynt, J. Wayne. "William V. Knott and the Gubernatorial Campaign of 1916." *Florida Historical Quarterly* 51 (April 1973): 423–444.

"Forfeiture of Offending Vehicles under Revenue and Prohibition Laws—A Conflict in Statutes." *Columbia Law Review* 130 (1930): 1039–1045.

"Forfeiture of Property of Innocent Owners Used in Transporting Liquor." *University of Pennsylvania Law Review* 74 (1925): 170.

Foxcroft, Frank. "Prohibition in the South." *Atlantic Monthly* 101 (May 1908): 627–634.

Frazier, Paul. "Profitable Trickle: The Diversion of Industrial Alcohol in Prohibition Philadelphia." *Prologue: Quarterly of the National Archives* 26 (Winter 1994): 224–233.

Friendly, Henry J. "The Historic Basis of Diversity Jurisdiction." *Harvard Law Review* (1934): 483–510.

George, Paul S. "Bootleggers, Prohibitionists, and Police: The Temperance Movement in Miami, 1896–1920." *Tequesta* 39 (1979): 3–41.

Gewirtz, Jerry M. "Pre-empting State Action Pursuant to the Twenty-First Amendment." *Temple Law Quarterly* 53 (Winter 1980): 590–612.

Graebner, William. "Federalism in the Progressive Era: A Structural Interpretation of Reform." *Journal of American History* 64 (1977): 331–357.

Grant, J.A.C. "The Lanza Rule of Successive Prosecutions." *Columbia Law Review* 32 (June 1932): 1309–1331.

———. "The Scope and Nature of Concurrent Power." *Columbia Law Review* 34 (June 1934): 995–1040.

Hall, Kermit L. "The Promises and Perils of Prosopography—Southern Style." *Vanderbilt Law Review* 32 (1979): 331–339.

Hamm, Richard Francis. "Southerners and the Shaping of the Eighteenth Amendment, 1914–1917." *Georgia Journal of Southern Legal History* 1 (Spring/Summer 1991): 81–107.

Harris, Carl V. "Reforms in Government Control of Negroes in Birmingham, Alabama, 1890–1920." *Journal of Southern History* 38 (November 1972): 567–600.

Hersch, Philip L., and Jeffrey M. Netter. "State Prohibition of Alcohol: An Application of Diffusion Analysis to Regulation." *Research in Law and Economics Annual* 12 (1989): 55–70.

Hohner, Robert H. "Prohibition and Virginia Politics: William Hodges Mann versus Henry St. George Tucker, 1909." *Virginia Magazine of History and Biography* 74 (January 1966): 88–107.

———. "Bishop Cannon's Apprenticeship in Temperance Politics, 1901–1918." *Journal of Southern History* 34 (February 1968): 33–49.

Holmes, William F. "Moonshining and Collective Violence: Georgia, 1889–1895." *Journal of American History* 67 (December 1980): 589–611.

———. "Moonshiners and Whitecaps in Alabama, 1893." *Alabama Review* 24 (January 1981): 31–49.

Horwitz, Morton J. "The Transformation in the Conception of Property in American Law, 1780–1860." *University of Chicago Law Review* 40 (1973): 248–290.

Hughes, Edward M. "Florida Preachers and the Election of 1928." *Florida Historical Quarterly* 67 (October 1988): 131–146.

Johnson, Paul. "Bottoms Up: Drinking, Temperance, and the Social Historians." *Reviews in American History* 13 (March 1985): 45–53.

Kabat, Ric A. "Everybody Votes for Gilchrist: The Florida Gubernatorial Campaign of 1908." *Florida Historical Quarterly* 67 (October 1988): 184–203.

Kagan, Robert A., Bliss Cartwright, Lawrence M. Friedman, and Stanton Wheeler. "The Business of State Supreme Courts, 1870–1970." *Stanford Law Review* 30 (November 1977): 121–156.

Kens, Paul. "The Source of a Myth: Police Powers of the States and Laissez Faire Constitutionalism, 1900–1937." *American Journal of Legal History* 35 (January 1991): 70–98.

Kersfelt, David S. "The Effect of the Twenty-First Amendment on State Authority to Control Intoxicating Liquors." *Columbia Law Review* 75 (1975): 1578–1610.

Kett, Joseph. "Temperance and Intemperance as Historical Problems." *Journal of American History* 67 (March 1981): 878–879.

Kyvig, David E. "Women Against Prohibition." *American Quarterly* 28 (Fall 1976): 465–482.

Levine, Harry G. "The Birth of American Alcohol Control: Prohibition, the Power Elite, and the Problem of Lawlessness." *Contemporary Drug Problems* (Spring 1985): 63–115.

Levine, Harry G., and Craig Reinarman. "From Prohibition to Regulation: Lessons from Alcohol Policy for Drug Policy." *Milbank Quarterly* 69 (1991): 44–94.

Mandel, Richard S. "Liquor Advertising: Resolving the Clash between the First and Twenty-First Amendments." *New York University Law Review* 59 (1983–1984): 157–186.

McDonald, Roy W. "Automobile Forfeitures and the Eighteenth Amendment." *Texas Law Review* 10 (1931): 140–162.

Miller, Wilbur R. "The Revenue: Federal Law Enforcement in the Mountain South, 1870–1900." *Journal of Southern History* 55 (May 1989): 195–216.

Miron, Jeffrey A., and Jeffrey Zwiebel. "Alcohol Consumption during Prohibition." *American Economic Review* 81 (May 1991): 242–248.

Moline, Brian J. "Prohibition and the Attorney General, 1880–1900." *The Journal of the Kansas Bar Association* 61 (June 1992): 31–39.

Murchison, Kenneth M. "Prohibition and the Fourth Amendment: A New Look at Some Old Cases." *Journal of Criminal Law and Criminology* 73 (Summer 1982): 471–532.

———. "Property Forfeiture in the Era of National Prohibition: A Study of Judicial Response to Legislative Reform." *Buffalo Law Review* 32 (1983): 417–463.

———. "The Dual Sovereignty Exception to Double Jeopardy." *New York University Review of Law and Social Change* 4 (Spring 1986): 383–435.

Neeley, Julia Whitfield, and Randolf Whitfield. "Our Father, James Bryan Whitfield." *Florida Supreme Court Historical Society Review* 3 (1987): 1–12.

Padgett, John F. "Plea Bargaining and Prohibition in the Federal Courts, 1908–1934." *Law and Society Review* 24 (1990): 413–450.

Pegram, Thomas R. "The Dry Machine: The Formation of The Anti-Saloon League of Illinois." *Illinois Historical Journal* 83 (Autumn 1990): 173–186.

———. "Temperance Politics and Regional Political Culture: The Anti-Saloon League in Maryland and the South, 1907–1915." *Journal of Southern History* 63 (February 1997): 57–90.

Pritchard, R. "The Failure of Prohibition in the South." *Harpers Weekly* 55 (18 March 1911): 12–13.

"The Right to Privacy in Nineteenth Century America." *Harvard Law Review* 94 (1981): 1892–1910.

Rogers, Daniel T. "In Search of Progressivism." *Reviews in American History* 10 (December 1982): 113–132.

Roizen, Ron. "Redefining Alcohol in Post-Repeal America: Lessons from the Short Life of Everett Colby's Council for Moderation, 1934–1936." *Contemporary Drug Problems* (Summer 1991): 237–272.

Scheiber, Harry N. "Property Law, Expropriation, and Resource Allocation by Government, 1789–1910." *Journal of Economic History* 33 (March 1973): 232–251.

———. "Instrumentalism and Property Rights: A Reconsideration of American Styles of Judicial Reasoning in the 19th Century." *Wisconsin Law Review* (1975): 1–18.

"Search and Seizure and the Fourth and Fifth Amendments." *Yale Law Journal* 31 (1931): 518–522.

"Search and Seizure Provisions of the Federal and State Constitutions." *Virginia Law Review* 10 (1923): 124.

Shofner, Jerrell H. "Custom, Law, and History: The Enduring Influence of Florida's 'Black Code.' " *Florida Historical Quarterly* 55 (January 1977): 277–298.

Sigler, Jay A. "A History of Double Jeopardy." *Journal of American Legal History* 7 (1963): 283–309.

Solomon, Rayman L. "The Politics of Appointment and The Federal Courts' Role in Regulating America: U.S. Courts of Appeals Judgeships from T.R. to F.D.R." *American Bar Foundation Research Journal* (1984): 285–343.

Treanor, Walter E. "The Family Automobile and the Family Purpose Doctrine." *Indiana Law Journal* 1 (1925): 89–95.

Tyrrell, Ian R. "Drink and Temperance in the Antebellum South: An Overview and Interpretation." *Journal of Southern History* 48 (November 1982): 485–510.

———. "Prohibition, American Cultural Expansion, and the New Hegemony in the 1920s: An Interpretation." *Histoire Sociale/Social History* 54 (November 1994): 423–446.

Urofsky, Melvin I. "State Courts and Protective Legislation during the Progressive Era: A Reevaluation." *Journal of American History* 72 (June 1985): 63–91.

Versfis, David S. "The Effect of the Twenty-First Amendment on State Authority to Control Intoxicating Liquors." *Columbia Law Review* 75 (1975): 1578–1610.

Washington, Booker T. "Prohibition and the Negro." *Outlook* 88 (14 March 1908): 587–589.

Wexler, Natalie. "The Prophet Stumbles: Brandeis, the Bill of Rights, and Prohibition." *Cardozo Law Review* 13 (December 1991): 1355–1368.

White, John E. "Prohibition: The New Task and Opportunity of the South." *South Atlantic Quarterly* 7 (April 1908): 130–142.

Wickersham, George W. "The Police Power: A Product of the Rule of Reason." *Harvard Law Review* 27 (February 1914): 297–316.

Wilson, Clyde. "The Statist Drug War." *The Free Market* 12 (February 1994): 1, 7.

Books

Appleby, Joyce O. *Capitalism and a New Social Order: The Republican Vision of the 1790s*. New York: New York University Press, 1984.

Ayers, Edward L. *Vengeance and Justice: Crime and Punishment in the 19th Century American South*. New York: Oxford University Press, 1984.

Bashful, Emmett. *The Florida Supreme Court: A Short History in Judicial Selection*. Tallahassee: Florida State University Press, 1958.

Blocker, Jack S. *Retreat from Reform: The Prohibition Movement in the United States, 1890–1913*. Westport, Conn.: Greenwood Press, 1971.

———. *American Temperance Movements: Cycles of Reform*. Boston: Twayne Publishers, 1989.

Blocker, Jack S., ed. *Alcohol Reform and Society: The Liquor Issue in Social Context*. Westport, Conn.: Greenwood Press, 1979.

Bodenhamer, David J. *Fair Trial: Rights of the Accused in American History*. Bicentennial Essays on the Bill of Rights. New York: Oxford University Press, 1992.

Bodenhamer, David J., and James W. Ely, Jr., eds. *Ambivalent Legacy: A Legal History of the South*. Jackson: University of Mississippi Press, 1984.

Boder, Robert Smith. *Prohibition in Kansas: A History*. Lawrence: University of Kansas Press, 1986.

Boles, John B., and Evelyn Thomas Nolen, eds. *Interpreting Southern History: Historiographical Essays in Honor of Sanford W. Higginbotham*. Baton Rouge and London: Louisiana State University Press, 1987.

Bordin, Ruth. *Frances Willard*. Chapel Hill: University of North Carolina Press, 1986.

Brown, Dorothy M. *Mabel Walker Willebrandt: A Study of Power, Loyalty, and Law*. Knoxville: University of Tennessee Press, 1984.

Brown, Everett Somerville, ed. *Ratification of the Twenty-First Amendment to the Constitution of the United States: State Convention Records and Laws*. Ann Arbor: University of Michigan Press, 1938.

Brown, Richard Maxwell. *No Duty to Retreat: Violence and Values in American History and Society*. New York: Oxford University Press, 1992.

Browne, Jefferson B. *Key West: The Old and the New*, reprint. Gainesville: University of Florida Press, 1973.

Burnham, John C., and Robert M. Crunden. *Progressivism*. Cambridge, Mass.: Harvard University Press, 1977.

Carter, Paul A. *Another Part of the Twenties*. New York: Columbia University Press, 1977.

Chase, Harold, Samuel Krislov, Keith O. Boyum, and Jerry N. Clark. *Biographical Dictionary of the Federal Judiciary*. Detroit: Gale Research Co., 1976.

Cherrington, Ernest Hurst, ed. *The Evolution of Prohibition in the United States of America*. Westerville, Ohio: American Issue Press, 1920.

Clark, Norman H. *Deliver Us from Evil: An Interpretation of American Prohibition*. New York and London: W. W. Norton & Company, 1976.

Coffey, Thomas. *The Long Thirst: Prohibition in America, 1920–1933*. New York and London: W. W. Norton & Company, 1975.

Colburn, David R., and George E. Pozzetta. *Reform and Reformers in the Progressive Age*. Westport, Conn.: Greenwood Press, 1983.

Colburn, David R., and Richard K. Scher. *Florida's Gubernatorial Politics in the 20th Century*. Tallahassee: Florida State University Press, 1980.

Corwin, Edward S. *The Commerce Power versus States' Rights*. Princeton, N.J.: Princeton University Press, 1936.

Cresswell, Stephen. *Mormons & Cowboys, Moonshiners & Klansmen: Federal Law Enforcement in the South and West, 1870–1893*. Tuscaloosa: University of Alabama Press, 1991.

Dannenbaum, Jed. *Drink and Disorder: Temperance Reform in Cincinnati from the Washington Revival to the WCTU*. Urbana: University of Illinois Press, 1984.

Dobyns, Fletcher. *The Amazing Story of Repeal: An Exposé of the Power of Propaganda*. Chicago: Willett Clark, 1940.

Duis, Perry R. *The Saloon: Public Drinking in Chicago and Boston, 1880–1920*. Urbana and Chicago: University of Illinois Press, 1983.

Durant, W. C., ed. *Law Observance: Shall the People of the United States Uphold the Constitution*. New York: Durant, Inc., 1929.

Eagles, Charles W. *Democracy Delayed: Congressional Reapportionment and Urban-Rural Conflict in the 1920s*. Athens: University of Georgia Press, 1990.

Elazar, Daniel J. *American Federalism: A View from the States*. 3rd ed. New York: Harper and Row, 1984.

Ely, James W., Jr. *The Guardian of Every Right: A Constitutional History of Property Rights*. New York: Oxford University Press, 1992.

Engelmann, Larry. *Intemperance: The Lost War Against Liquor*. New York: Macmillan Free Press, 1979.

Epstein, Barbara Leslie. *The Politics of Domesticity: Women, Evangelism, and Temperance in Nineteenth Century America*. Westport, Conn.: Greenwood Press, 1981.

Fehrenbacher, Don E. *Slavery, Law and Politics: The Dred Scott Case in Historical Perspective*. New York: Oxford University Press, 1981.

Finkelman, Paul, and Stephen E. Gottlieb, eds. *Toward a Usable Past: Liberty under State Constitutions*. Athens: University of Georgia Press, 1991.

Flynt, Wayne. *Duncan Upshaw Fletcher: Dixie's Reluctant Progressive*. Tallahassee: Florida State University Press, 1971.

———. *Cracker Messiah: Governor Sidney J. Catts of Florida*. Baton Rouge: Louisiana State University Press, 1977.

Foucault, Michel. *Discipline and Punishment: The Birth of the Prison*. New York: Vintage Books, 1979.

Franklin, Jimmie Lewis. *Born Sober: Prohibition in Oklahoma, 1907–1959*. Norman: University of Oklahoma Press, 1971.

Frazer, William, and John J. Guthrie, Jr. *The Florida Land Boom: Speculation, Money, and the Banks*. Westport, Conn., and London: Quorum Books, 1995.

Friedman, Lawrence M. *A History of American Law*. New York: Touchstone Books, 1973.

———. *Crime and Punishment in American History*. New York: Basic Books, 1993.

Geetz, Clifford. *The Interpretation of Cultures*. New York: Basic Books, 1973.

George, Paul S. *A Guide to the History of Florida*. Westport, Conn.: Greenwood Press, 1989.

Gould, Lewis L. *Progressives and Prohibitionists: Texas Democrats in the Wilson Era*. Austin: Texas State Historical Association, 1992.

Grantham, Dewey W. *Southern Progressivism: The Reconciliation of Progress and Tradition*. 2nd ed. Knoxville: University of Tennessee Press, 1987.

Gusfield, Joseph R. *Symbolic Crusade: Status Politics and the American Temperance Movement*. Urbana: University of Illinois Press, 1963.

Hall, Kermit L. *The Politics of Justice: Lower Federal Judicial Selection and the Second American Party System*. Lincoln: University of Nebraska Press, 1979.

———. *The Magic Mirror: Law in American History*. New York: Oxford University Press, 1989.

Hall, Kermit L., and Eric W. Rise. *From Local Courts to National Tribunes: The Federal District Courts of Florida, 1881–1990*. Brooklyn, N.Y.: Carlson Publishing Inc., 1991.

Hamm, Richard F. *Shaping the Eighteenth Amendment: Temperance Reform, Legal Culture, and the Polity, 1880–1920*. Chapel Hill and London: University of North Carolina Press, 1995.

Hendricks, Edwin. *Liquor and Anti-Liquor in Virginia, 1619–1919*. Durham, N.C.: Duke University Press, 1967.

Hofstadter, Richard. *The Age of Reform: From Bryan to FDR*. New York: Vintage Books, 1955.

Horwitz, Morton J. *The Transformation of American Law, 1870–1960: The Crisis of Legal Orthodoxy*. New York: Oxford University Press, 1992.

Isaac, Paul E. *Prohibition and Politics: Turbulent Decades in Tennessee, 1885–1920*. Knoxville: University of Tennessee Press, 1965.

Johnson, Paul. *A Shopkeeper's Millennium: Society and Revivals in Rochester, New York, 1815–1837*. New York: Hill and Wang, 1978.

Keller, Morton. *Affairs of State: Public Life in Late Nineteenth Century America*. Cambridge, Mass., and London: Harvard University Press, 1977.

———. *Regulating a New Economy: Public Policy and Economic Change in America, 1900–1933*. Cambridge, Mass., and London: Harvard University Press, 1990.

———. *Regulating a New Society: Public Policy and Social Change in America, 1900–1933*. Cambridge, Mass., and London: Harvard University Press, 1994.

Kerr, Austin. *Organized for Prohibition: A New History of the Anti-Saloon League*. New Haven, Conn.: Yale University Press, 1985.

Kyvig, David E. *Repealing National Prohibition*. Chicago: University of Chicago Press, 1979.

Kyvig, David E., ed. *Law, Alcohol, and Order: Perspectives on National Prohibition*. Westport, Conn.: Greenwood Press, 1985.

Landynski, Edward. *Search and Seizure and the Supreme Court*. Baltimore: Johns Hopkins University Press, 1966.

Lender, Mark E., and James Kirby Martin. *Drinking in America: A History*. New York: Free Press, 1982.

Levy, Leonard W. *A License to Steal: The Forfeiture of Property*. Chapel Hill and London: University of North Carolina Press, 1996.

Lewis, Merlin, Warren Bundy, and James L. Hague. *An Introduction to the Courts and Judicial Process*. Englewood Cliffs, N.J.: Prentice-Hall, 1976.

Link, William A. *The Paradox of Southern Progressivism, 1880–1930*. Chapel Hill and London: University of North Carolina Press, 1992.

Marks, Henry S. *Who Was Who in Florida*. Huntsville, Ala.: Strode, 1973.

McCoy, Drew R. *The Last of the Fathers: James Madison and the Republican Legacy*. New York: Cambridge University Press, 1989.

McCraw, Thomas K. *Prophets of Regulation: Francis Adams, Louis D. Brandeis, James M. Landis, Alfred E. Kahn*. Cambridge, Mass.: Belknap Press, 1984.

McDonald, Forrest. *Novus Ordo Seclorum: The Intellectual Origins of the Constitution*. Lawrence: University Press of Kansas, 1967.

McIver, Stuart B. *Murder in the Tropics: The Florida Chronicles*. Sarasota, Fla.: Pineapple Press, 1995.

Miller, Wilbur R. *Revenuers & Moonshiners: Enforcing Federal Liquor Law in the Mountain South, 1865–1900*. Chapel Hill: University of North Carolina Press, 1991.

Moore, Mark H., and Dean R. Gerstein, eds. *Alcohol and Public Policy: Beyond the Shadow of Prohibition*. Washington, D.C.: National Academy Press, 1981.

Mormino, Gary R., and George E. Pozzetta. *The Immigrant World of Ybor City*. Urbana and Chicago: University of Illinois Press, 1988.

Murchison, Kenneth M. *Federal Criminal Law Doctrines: The Forgotten Influence of National Prohibition*. Durham, N.C., and London: Duke University Press, 1994.

Nedelsky, Jennifer. *Private Property and the Limits of American Constitutionalism: The Madisonian Framework and Its Legacy*. Chicago: University of Chicago Press, 1990.

Nelson, William E. *Americanization of the Common Law: The Impact of Legal Change on Massachusetts Society, 1760–1830*. Cambridge, Mass.: Harvard University Press, 1975.

Noonan, John T., Jr. *Persons and Masks of the Law: Cardoza, Holmes, Jefferson, and Wythe as Makers of the Masks*. New York: Farrar and Strauss, 1976.

Odegard, Peter H. *Pressure Politics: The Story of the Anti-Saloon League*. New York: Columbia University Press, 1928.

Ownby, Ted. *Subduing Satan: Religion, Recreation, & Manhood in the Rural South, 1865–1920*. Chapel Hill: The University of North Carolina Press, 1990.

Paulson, Ross Evans. *Women's Suffrage and Prohibition: A Comparative Study of Equality and Social Control*. Glenview, Ill.: Scott, Foresman and Co., 1973.

Proctor, Samuel. *Napoleon Bonaparte Broward: Florida's Fighting Democrat*. Gainesville: University of Florida Press, 1950.

Rorabaugh, W. J. *The Alcoholic Republic*. New York: Oxford University Press, 1979.

Rumbarger, John J. *Profits, Power, and Prohibition*. New York: State University of New York Press, 1985.

Saffell, David C. *State and Local Government: Politics and Public Policy*. 4th ed. New York: McGraw Hill Publishing, 1990.

Schwartz, Bernard. *A History of the Supreme Court*. New York: Oxford University Press, 1993.

Sellers, James Benson. *The Prohibition Movement in Alabama, 1702–1943*. Chapel Hill: University of North Carolina Press, 1943.

Shattuck, John H. F. *The Rights of Privacy*. Skokie, Ill.: National Textbook Co., 1977.

Sinclair, Andrew. *Prohibition: The Era of Excess*. Boston: Harper and Row, 1962.

Sklar, Martin J. *The Corporate Reconstruction of American Capitalism: The Market, the Law, and Politics, 1890–1916*. New York: Cambridge University Press, 1988.

Skowronek, Stephen. *Building a New American State: The Expansion of National Administrative Capacities, 1877–1920*. New York: Cambridge University Press, 1982.

Tebeau, Charlton W. *A History of Florida*. Coral Gables, Fla.: University of Miami Press, 1971.

Thornton, Mark. *The Economics of Prohibition*. Salt Lake City: University of Utah Press, 1991.

Timberlake, James H. *Prohibition and the Progressive Movement, 1900–1920*. Cambridge, Mass.: Harvard University Press, 1963.

Tyrell, Ian R. *Sobering Up: From Temperance to Prohibition in Antebellum America, 1800–1860*. Westport, Conn.: Greenwood Press, 1979.

Urofsky, Melvin I. *A March of Liberty: A Constitutional History of the United States*. New York: Knopf, 1988.

Vose, Clement E. *Constitutional Change: Amendment Politics and Supreme Court Litigation Since 1900*. Lexington, Mass.: Lexington Books, 1972.

Walker, Samuel. *Popular Justice: A History of American Criminal Justice*. New York: Oxford University Press, 1980.

Waller, Altina L. *Feud: Hatfields, McCoys, and Social Change in Appalachia, 1860–1900*. Chapel Hill: University of North Carolina Press, 1988.

Whitener, Daniel J. *Prohibition in North Carolina, 1717–1945*. Chapel Hill: University of North Carolina Press, 1945.

Wiebe, Robert H. *The Search for Order, 1877–1920*. New York: Hill and Wang, 1967.

Williamson, Joel W., ed. *An Appalachian Symposium*. Boone, N.C.: Appalachian Consortium Press, 1977.

Woodward, C. Vann. *Origins of the New South, 1877–1913*. Baton Rouge: Louisiana State University Press, 1951.

———. *The Strange Career of Jim Crow*. 3rd ed. New York: Oxford University Press, 1974.

Wright, A. J. *Criminal Activity in the Deep South, 1700–1930: An Annotated Bibliography*. Westport, Conn.: Greenwood Press, 1989.

Wyatt-Brown, Bertram. *Southern Honor: Ethics and Behavior in the Old South*. New York: Oxford University Press, 1982.

Dissertations

Alduino, Frank. "The 'Noble Experiment' in Tampa: A Study of Prohibition in Urban America." Ph.D. diss., Florida State University, 1989.

George, Paul S. "Criminal Justice in Miami, 1896–1930." Ph.D. diss., Florida State University, 1975.

Index

About the Author

JOHN J. GUTHRIE, JR., is Associate Professor of History at Daytona Beach Community College. He holds a Ph.D. from the University of Florida and is the coauthor of *The Florida Land Boom: Speculation, Money, and the Banks* (Quorum, 1995).

www.ingramcontent.com/pod-product-compliance
Ingram Content Group UK Ltd.
Pitfield, Milton Keynes, MK11 3LW, UK
UKHW041636031026
15587UKWH00001B/322

9 780313 301902